Managing Information Systems

PEARSON
Education

We work with leading authors to develop the strongest
educational materials in management information systems,
bringing cutting-edge thinking and best learning practice
to a global market.

Under a range of well-known imprints, including
Financial Times Prentice Hall, we craft high quality print
and electronic publications which help readers to
understand and apply their content, whether studying or
at work.

To find out more about the complete range of our
publishing, please visit us on the World Wide Web at:
www.pearsoned.co.uk

Second Edition

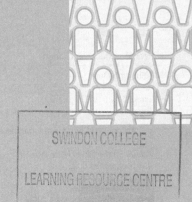

MANAGING INFORMATION SYSTEMS

An Organisational Perspective

David Boddy
University of Glasgow

Albert Boonstra
University of Groningen (The Netherlands)

Graham Kennedy
The Royal Bank of Scotland

FT Prentice Hall
FINANCIAL TIMES

An imprint of **Pearson Education**
Harlow, England • London • New York • Boston • San Francisco • Toronto
Sydney • Tokyo • Singapore • Hong Kong • Seoul • Taipei • New Delhi
Cape Town • Madrid • Mexico City • Amsterdam • Munich • Paris • Milan

10th September 2008

540 50000 301937

Pearson Education Limited

Edinburgh Gate
Harlow
Essex CM20 2JE
England

and Associated Companies throughout the world

Visit us on the World Wide Web at:
www.pearsoned.co.uk

First published 2002
Second edition published 2005

ISBN-10: 0-273-68635-6
ISBN-13: 978-0-273-68635-4

British Library Cataloguing-in-Publication Data
A catalogue record for this book is available from the British Library

Library of Congress Cataloging-in-Publication Data
Boddy, David.
   Managing information systems : an organisational perspective / David Boddy, Albert
Boonstra, Graham Kennedy.
     p. cm.
   Includes bibliographical references and index.
   ISBN 0-273-68635-6 (alk. paper)
   1. Management information systems. 2. Information resources management. 3. Business
enterprises—Computer networks—Management. I. Boonstra, Albert. II. Kennedy, Graham,
1961– III. Title.

HD30.213.B627 2004
658.4′038′011—dc22

                                              2004056729

10 9 8 7 6 5 4 3 2
09 08 07 06 05

Typeset in 10/12pt Century by 35
Printed and bound by Ashford Colour Press Ltd., Gosport

The publisher's policy is to use paper manufactured from sustainable forests.

CONTENTS

Chapter 10 Managing a programme of projects

Instructor resources

Visit www.pearsoned.co.uk/boddy to find valuable online resources

For instructors

- Complete, downloadable Instructor's Manual
- PowerPoint slides that can be downloaded and used as OHTs

For more information please contact your local Pearson Education sales representative or visit www.pearsoned.co.uk/boddy

---

PREFACE

Developments in technology continue to enable far-reaching changes in the access people have to information. To use this potential to improve long-term performance requires more than the latest technology. It requires managers to take a coherent approach to organisational as well as technical change. There is now a great deal of evidence showing how some managers have succeeded in this, and how others have failed. There are also many theoretical models derived from that and related research. This book uses that material to present a coherent organisational perspective on the management of computer-based information systems. The aim is to help managers sustain organisational performance in the information revolution. To do so they need to initiate thoughtful and coherent changes in both their organisation and in their information systems.

This book is intended for those who are studying towards a management qualification either at honours level on undergraduate courses or on MBA or similar postgraduate courses. We offer them the accumulating evidence of current practice, based on our own personal research and on published studies. The book includes many case studies drawn from these sources, which will enable readers to be more confident in handling similar situations.

The book will take a management perspective towards information systems (IS). It will identify the issues of organisation and strategy that managers face as they decide how to respond to technological opportunities. Managing successive IS projects as part of a coherent organisational process (rather than as isolated technological events) will produce an information system that enhances broader strategy.

The issues will be presented within a coherent theoretical framework. This is based on the interaction between computer-based projects and their context. The chapters deal with the components of the model in turn, so that readers can link to it at different points. The cases (from a wide range of sectors) illustrate aspects of the model.

This means we can draw from a broad range of technological applications – with a consistent focus on realising the business opportunities. It is not tied to a particular technological fashion. It offers a timeless framework which managers can use to consider new developments in the information revolution as they arise.

This new edition takes account of helpful comments from staff and students who used the first edition and the suggestions of six anonymous reviewers. The book retains all the contents of the first edition, but the structure of Part 1 is more logical and some other chapters have been repositioned. The distinctive theoretical perspective is now introduced in Chapter 1, while Chapter 2 outlines four major applications of information systems.

Three of the Chapter Cases are new: Siemens, Aalsmeer Flower Auction and the RBS/NatWest takeover. There are many new examples and illustrations, and over 50 new references. A new pedagogical feature has been added – 'Case Questions' – which links the Chapter Case more closely with the text – a suggestion made by the reviewers of the first edition.

▨ Objectives

When they have read the book, managers should be able to:

- ▨ Evaluate current IS provision in their organisation, in the light of emerging technical possibilities.
- ▨ Outline how IS could support their organisation's strategy, including developing new products, services and markets.
- ▨ Propose how IS can add value to a business process, and enable radical re-engineering of existing processes.
- ▨ Propose how human and structural changes should be made to gain more value from a computer-based IS.
- ▨ Evaluate how their IS function is organised, and propose alternatives.
- ▨ Manage organisational and IS changes to achieve complementarity between them.
- ▨ Avoid the common pitfalls that damage many IS projects.
- ▨ Evaluate and discuss their organisation's approach to these issues, and make well-grounded recommendations on actual or planned IS applications.
- ▨ Take a balanced view of how computer-based IS can benefit their organisation.

▨ Outline of the book

There are four parts in the book, dealing with foundations, strategy, organisation and implementation. Chapter 1 outlines the role of information in organisations and the components of an information system. This includes the fundamental point that information systems include people as well as technology. It also presents the central theoretical perspective of the book, that people interpret and interact with their context as they respond to an information system. These interactions shape the outcomes of a project – and identify whether these match the promoters' objectives.

Chapter 2 concentrates on recent developments in computer-based information technologies, such as in customer relationship management and enterprise resource planning. It illustrates the far-reaching possibilities these make possible, while indicating that the issues they raise are more to do with management than with technology.

Part Two deals with some strategic issues. Chapter 3 examines the interaction between strategy and information systems. It begins by using established models of the strategy development process to show how companies have used information systems to change the way they compete. It then considers the concept of strategic alignment, and concludes with an analysis of the practical complexities of forming an information system strategy.

Chapter 4 examines how companies have used computer-based systems to modify their business processes. Modern systems make it possible for people to link the horizontal processes of organisations more effectively, by eroding established functional boundaries. This depends on a good understanding of different approaches to business process redesign and the managerial and organisational interactions which such projects involve.

Chapter 5 considers an issue of concern to many senior managers: how to evaluate proposed IS investments. The dilemma which all managers face is that, while they can usually predict the costs of an information system, they are much less certain about the benefits. The chapter outlines briefly the principles, and the weaknesses, of conventional investment appraisal methods. It then introduces some alternative evaluation methods, such as the Balanced Scorecard, which take account of non-financial criteria.

Part Three of the book turns to organisational issues. Cultural, structural and political issues dominate Chapter 6. It is increasingly clear that the prevailing culture in an organisation affects how people react to information systems. It is equally clear that managers can use information systems to centralise or to decentralise decisions – which approach gives most coherence with wider strategy? A major issue for companies introducing an Internet venture is whether to integrate this with the existing structure or to create it as a separate business unit. And the chapter ends with a consideration of the links between power and information systems.

Chapter 7 considers one aspect of structural choice, namely the place of the information function itself within the organisation. It outlines the main options – centralised, decentralised, federal or outsourcing – and the benefits and costs of each. It also considers alternative approaches to charging for information services and the problem of balancing the conflicting expectations of user, IS and corporate constituencies.

Chapter 8 takes a human perspective. Theories of human motivation offer some guidance on how people will react to new systems – whether as users or customers. Staff tend to welcome those which complement valued skills and experience and reject those which do not. The chapter also considers research into distributed working arrangements – which indicates that they are more likely to bring worthwhile benefits if management creates a coherent context for the people concerned.

The two chapters in Part Four concentrate on implementation – Chapter 9 on projects and Chapter 10 on programmes. Chapter 9 presents a research-based framework for diagnosing the critical dimensions of information systems projects that enables managers to identify where to focus effort. It then compares four theoretical perspectives on change – life-cycle, emergent, participative and political – which can each contribute to the effective management of IS projects. In line with the interaction perspective of the book, it then outlines a method for identifying and influencing stakeholders and for creating project structures to support individual action.

The idea of project structures is developed more fully in Chapter 10, which deals with the management of programmes – a collection of related projects. Clearly there are interactions not only between contemporaneous IS projects, but also with other strategic or structural changes. Companies have developed various techniques for managing these interactions within a programme, and the chapter presents and illustrates these.

Pedagogical features

The book includes these pedagogical features:

- Learning objectives at the start of each chapter. These serve as a focus for the chapter and a reference point for learning.
- Cases at the start of each chapter. These are usually based on research done by the authors in companies introducing computer-based information systems. Later developments in the case, or additional perspectives, are usually brought in at

several points in the chapter. These have all been used by the authors in their teaching, and provide an excellent basis for group work before or during a class.

- Case Questions throughout the chapter that encourage students to make connections between the case and the theoretical perspectives of the chapter;
- Short boxed examples. Each chapter contains short examples which illuminate a point either from the authors' research or from secondary sources. These help to link theory and practice, and provide readers with points of comparison with their experience (as do the Chapter Cases).
- Activity boxes. Each chapter contains several Activity features that invite readers to make some connections between theory and practice. They invite them, for example, to comment on the Chapter Case, or to reflect on practice in their organisation or their wider experience.
- End-of-section summaries. Each section concludes by summarising the topic covered, which helps students to draw the material together.
- End-of-chapter questions. At the end of each chapter there are at least five questions, which readers can use to test their understanding of the topics or which teachers can use as a way of structuring class discussion.
- Further reading. As well as extensive references to (accessible) sources, each chapter contains an annotated guide to at least two books or articles that deal with issues in greater depth or from a different perspective.

Supplementary material

An Instructor's Manual is available at www.pearsoned.co.uk/boddy to adopters of the text. This offers:

- suggested responses to the Activity (where appropriate) and Chapter Questions;
- additional or more recent information about some of the Chapter Cases and other cases;
- some additional models or diagrams, to supplement those in the text;
- suggested tutorial and/or examination questions;
- a set of PowerPoint slides for each Chapter, including many of the figures.

ABOUT THE AUTHORS

David Boddy, BSc (Econ), MA (Organizational Psychology), is Research Fellow in the School of Business and Management at the University of Glasgow. He teaches courses for experienced managers on the management issues raised by computer-based information systems – which has been the main focus of his research. His books include *Management: An Introduction* (now in a 2nd edition) and *Managing Projects: Building and Leading the Team*, both with Financial Times/Prentice Hall, Harlow. He has recently had articles published in the *Journal of Information Technology*, the *Journal of General Management*, the *Journal of Management Studies* and *New Technology, Work and Employment*.

Albert Boonstra, Bec, MBA, PhD, is an associate professor at the Faculty of Management and Organisation, University of Groningen, The Netherlands. His research focuses on the human and organisational issues of implementing and using information and communication technologies. He teaches IT-management-related courses for students as well as for experienced managers. He also consults for profit and not-for-profit organisations on the management of information systems. He has recently had articles published in the *Journal of General Management*, the *European Journal of Information Systems* and *New Technology, Work and Employment*.

Graham Kennedy holds an MBA degree from the University of Glasgow and currently works in the internal consultancy division of The Royal Bank of Scotland. He has over eighteen years' experience as a manager of change initiatives in industries as varied as financial services and engineering. A common thread throughout his career has been the application of information systems to business areas, and this has provided him with many insights into the opportunities – and problems – which new technologies present to users.

More information is available from www.pearsoned.co.uk/boddy.

ACKNOWLEDGEMENTS

This book is the result of several years' cooperation between the authors in teaching an MBA elective on the topic. They have delivered this to managers taking the Executive MBA programme at the University of Glasgow, and also to managers on Executive MBA programmes from around the world who have attended the European Summer School for Advanced Management or the Asian Intensive School for Advanced Management as part of their MBA studies. The managers attending these Executive MBA programmes are too numerous to mention, but they have contributed beyond measure to the development of our thinking in this area.

We are also grateful to the following staff at The Royal Bank of Scotland: Graeme McArthur, John Murray and Charles Buchan (for material in Chapter 5); and Grahame Walker (for material in Chapter 10).

▓ Publisher's acknowledgements

We are grateful to the following for permission to reproduce copyright material:

Table 2.4 from Knowledge management and knowledge management system: conceptual foundations and research issues in *MIS Quarterly*, 25(1), 107–36, Table 3, p. 125 (Alavi, M. and Leidner, D.E. 2002) with permission from Management Information Systems Research Center (MISRC) of the University of Minnesota; Table 2.5 from *Case Studies in Knowledge Management*, p.11, Chartered Institute of Personnel and Development (Scarborough, H. and Swan, J. 1999) copyright Chartered Institute of Personnel and Development, London; Figure 3.1 from *The Strategy Process: Concepts, Contexts, Cases*, p.18, Financial Times/Prentice Hall (Mintzberg, H., Quinn, J.B., Ghoshal, S. 2003) copyright Pearson Education; Table 3.1 from Six IT decisions your IT people shouldn't make in *Harvard Business Review*, 80(11) 84–91, p.87 (Ross, J.W. and Weill, P. 2002) copyright Harvard Business Review; Figure 3.2 from *Competitive advantage: creating and Sustaining Superior Performance* (Porter, Michael E, 1985, 1998) with permission from The Free Press a Division of Simon and Schuster Adult Publishing Group; Figure 3.7 from Strategy and the Internet in *Harvard Business Review*, 79(2), 63–78, (Porter, M.E. 2001) copyright Harvard Business Review; Figure 3.8 The dynamics of alignment: insights from a punctuated equilibrium in *Organization Science* 12(2), 179–97 (Sabherwal, R., Hirschheim, R. and Goles, T. 2001) with permission from Institute for Operations Research and the Management Sciences (INFORMS); Figure 3.10 from *E-Business and E-Commerce Management*, Prentice Hall/Financial Times, (Chaffey, D. 2002) copyright Pearson Education; Table 4.1 and 4.2 from *Process Innovation: Reengineering Work through Information Technology*, p.88, Harvard Business School Press (Davenport, T.H. 1993) copyright Harvard Business Review; Table 4.3 from Preconditions for BPR-success in *Information Systems Management*, 11(2), 7–14, CRC Press, (Markus, M.J. 1994); Figure 5.1 from New approaches to IT investment in *MIT Sloan Management Review*, 43(2), 51–59 (Ross, J.W. and Beath, C.M. 2002) copyright Tribune Media Services; Figure 5.2 from An expanded instrument for evaluating information system success in *Information and Management*, 31, 103–18, p.106 (Saarinen, T. 1996) copyright Elsevier; Table 5.3 from The impact of inadequacies in the treatment of organisational issues on information systems development projects in *Information and Management*, 41, 49–62 (Doherty, N.F., King, M. and Al-Mushayt, O. 2003) copyright Elsevier; Figure 5.3 from The Balanced Scorecard: measures that drive performance in *Harvard Business Review*, 70(1), 71–9, (Kaplan, R.S. and Norton, D.P. 1992) copyright Harvard Business Review; Figure 6.1 from The inertial impact of culture on IT implementation in *Information and Management*, 27(1), 17–31 (Cooper, R. 1994) copyright Elsevier; Table 6.2 from Get the right mix for bricks and clicks in *Harvard Business Review*, 78(3), 107–14, p. 114 (Table: A roadmap . . . success) (Gulati, R. and Garino, J. 2000), copyright Harvard Business Review; Figure 6.3 from Real strategies for virtual organizing in *Sloan Management Review*, 40(1), 33–48, p. 34, figure 1, (Venkatraman, N. and Henderson, J.C. 1998) copyright Tribune Media Services; Table 7.2 from *Hybrid Managers: What Should You Do?*, British Computer Society (Skyrme, D.J. and Earl, M.J. 1990); Figure 7.5 from Information politics in *Sloan Management Review*, 34(1), 53–66. p.54 (Davenport, T.H., Eccles, R.G. and Prusak, L. 1992) copyright Tribune Media Services; Figure 8.1 from Perceived usefulness, perceived ease of use, and user acceptance of information technology in *MIS Quarterly*, 13(3), 319–40 (Davis, F.D. 1989) with permission from Management Information Systems Research Center (MISRC) of the University of Minnesota; Figure 8.2 from *Influencing within Organizations*, Prentice Hall (Huczynski, A.A. 1996) copyright Pearson Education; Table 8.2 from Sociotechnical principles for system design in *Applied Ergonomics*, 31(5), 463–47. table 1, (Clegg, C. W. 2000), copyright Elsevier; Figure 8.3 from *Work Redesign*, p.77, Addison-Wesley (Hackman, J.R. and Oldham, G.R. 1980) copyright Pearson Education Inc; Figure 8.5 from Distributed work arrangements: a research framework in *Information Society*, 14(2), 137–52, p.139 figure 1 (Belanger. F. and Collins, R.W. 1998) copyright Taylor and Francis Inc; Figure 8.6 from *Organizational Behaviour: An Introductory Text (5th edition)*, Financial Times/Prentice Hall (Huczynski, A.A. and Buchanan, D. 2004) copyright Pearson Education; Table 9.1 from *Steps to the Future: Fresh thinking on the management of IT-based Organizational Transformation*, p. 19, Jossey-Bass, San Francisco (Sauer, C. and Yetton, P.W. 1997) copyright John Wiley & Son Inc; Table 9.4 from Consequences of influence tactics used with subordinates, peers and the boss in *Journal of Applied Psychology*, vol. 77, pp.525–35, American Psychological Association (Yukl, G. and Tracey B. 1992) copyright American Psychological Association; Figure 9.5 from *Business Information Systems*, Financial Times/Prentice Hall (Chaffey D. (ed.) 2003) copyright Pearson Education.

Harvard Business Review for an extract adapted from *Make your dealers your partners* by D. Frites published in the *Harvard Business Review* March–April 1996 and *Putting the enterprise into the enterprise system* by T. Davenport published in the *Harvard Business Review* July–August 1998 © 1996 and 1998 Harvard Business School Publishing Corporation. All rights reserved; The Economist for extracts adapted from 'Flowering of feudalism' published in *The Economist* 27th February 1993 and 'Riding the Storm' published in *The Economist* 4th March 1995 © The Economist Newspaper Limited, London 1993 and 1995;

Taylor & Francis Ltd, Vassilis Serafeimidis PhD and Steve Smithson for an extract adapted from 'Information systems evaluation in practice: a case study of organizational change' by Serafeimidis and Smithson published in *Journal of Information Technology* vol 15, 2000 © www.tandf.co.uk/journals; Routledge for extracts from *Organizations in the Network Age* by Boddy and Gunson published by Routlege 1996; Niels Bjorn – Andersen and Jon A. Turner for an extract adapted from 'Creating the twenty – first century organization: the metamorphosis of Oticon' published in *Transforming Organisations with Information Technology* 1994; Tribune Media Services for an extract adapted from 'What makes a virtual organization work?' by M Marcus, B. Manville and C. Agres published in *MIT Sloan Management Review* 42 (1) 2000; ACM for an extract adapted from 'Power, politics and MIS Implementation' by M.L. Markus from *Communications of the ACM* 26(6) 1983; Carlson School of Minnesota for an extract adapted from 'Research of the Technology Acceptance Model' by F. D. Davis published in 'Perceived Usefulness, Perceived Ease of Use and User Acceptance of Information Technology' *MIS Quarterly* 13(3) 1989; Blackwell Publishing Ltd for extracts adapted from *New Technology, Work and Employment* volumes 13(2) 1998 and 19(2) 2004, and Blackwell Publishing Ltd and Dr R Rhodes for an extract adapted from *Implementing New Technologies* edited by R Rhodes and D Wield 1981; Pearson Education Limited for an extract adapted from *Managing Projects: Building and Leading the Team* by David Boddy; and The Royal Bank of Scotland plc for extracts about The Royal Bank of Scotland Group (RBS).

In some instances we have been unable to trace the owners of copyright material and we would appreciate any information that would enable us to do so.

PART 1

Foundations

In this part we set the scene by examining the links between information systems and organisations. Chapter 1 considers what we mean by 'information' and why it is essential to organisational performance. It also describes the components of an information system (IS) and introduces the central theme of this book: that information systems include people as well as technology. It presents the idea that the outcomes of an information system depend on the interaction between people, technology and the organisational context, which the rest of the book develops in more detail. The Chapter Case illustrates how managers introduce computer-based information systems to improve performance, but only achieve the outcomes they expect if they also change other aspects of the organisation at the same time. This makes the task of implementing major information systems a challenging management task.

Chapter 2 illustrates the growing power and reach of information systems, and classifies them in terms of their reach, roles and functions. It presents examples of major business applications of IS: enterprise systems, knowledge systems, customer relationship systems and systems which cross organisational boundaries.

CHAPTER 1

Information systems and organisations

Learning objectives

By the end of your work on this topic you should be able to:

- Outline the reasons for organisations' increased dependence on IS

- Explain the difference between data, information and knowledge

- List the elements of computer-based IS and compare them with human and paper systems

- Identify the elements in the organisational context of an IS

- Compare determinist, social choice and interaction models of IS and organisations

- Explain why the outcomes of IS projects are unpredictable and open to interpretation

- Use the interaction model to analyse an IS project in an organisation

Contracting Services

Contracting Services maintains and repairs refrigeration equipment for retailers throughout the UK. At the start of this IS project it had 22 service branches and 250 service engineers. Each branch employed a manager, a working supervisor, about 12 engineers and about 4 office staff. The branches operated independently, and senior management treated them as distinct profit-and-loss centres. The only advantage of being part of a larger company was that they had greater buying power – which reduced the cost of spare parts.

The established process was that someone from the shop telephoned the nearest branch to report a refrigeration fault. An operator took the call and used a pager to contact one of the engineers, who found a telephone and called the branch. The branch controller gave the details of the call and the engineer visited the retailer, typically a small grocery shop or a store belonging to a large chain. If the parts were in the van, he did the repair. If not, he returned to the branch, or visited a wholesaler, to collect the part. When the job was finished the engineer completed the paperwork and passed it to the branch (usually on his next visit) for processing. Invoices and performance monitoring data were prepared in the branch from this paperwork.

The problem

As well as high branch costs (about £1.4m a year excluding the cost of the engineers), supermarket chains found the service inconsistent between branches. Branch managers varied in the performance data they provided to customers. The pager system caused communication problems – so much so that some service engineers had bought mobile phones at their own expense.

After office hours, calls were passed to answering machines and then to an outside agency which contacted stand-by engineers. The inventory of parts was hard to locate. An independent survey showed that customers regarded the service as poor. Trading conditions were difficult as it was easy for small local firms to enter the market and offer a similar service.

Nevertheless the company won a facilities management (FM) contract with a major supermarket group for 44 of their stores (about one-fifth of the total). This involved Contracting Services staff dealing with all mechanical facilities in a store as well as refrigeration. This was attractive as small competitors were less likely to be able to offer such a comprehensive service. The company was keen for it to succeed.

The call centre solution – phase 1, design and piloting

The IS director had been hoping to introduce call centre technology for some time, whereby all calls would come to staff in one place who would then pass information directly to the engineers. This would reduce the cost of the physical branches. He gained some support from the board, though they were reluctant to make the investment. The FM contract had been running for about six months, using the branch network. That customer now wanted to be able to telephone one number for all services and favoured the call centre proposal. This convinced the board, who decided to set up a pilot call centre to deal with this contract. If the pilot was satisfactory, they would consider extending the system to the whole business.

Source: Personal communication from managers in the company, and Boddy (2000).

CASE QUESTIONS 1.1

Before reading further, make notes on these questions:

At this stage of the case study, what issues should the board of Contracting Services have on their agenda?

Which two of these should have priority?

Introduction

People in organisations can only do their work effectively if they receive accurate and timely information. Systems which provide such information help people to make internal processes more efficient, integrate business functions and link an organisation with suppliers and customers. Managers who are aware of this dependence work to ensure the quality of their information systems (IS). So while the design of information systems depends on the skills of IS experts, management rarely leaves the whole task to them. It is a management responsibility to ensure that IS staff develop systems that serve the needs of people and of the business.

This responsibility has become more widespread as computer-based information systems have moved from the background to the foreground of organisations. Technological developments mean that the power, and so potential value, of information systems is greater than ever before. This means that managers throughout the organisation can take an active role in shaping the information systems that will have such profound effects on their performance.

This chapter begins by outlining the development of computer-based information systems and the role of information in organisations. It also describes different kinds of system and their common components: hardware, software, networks, telecommunications and data. The aim of the chapter is to show why managers need information and how they can make the most of computer-based information systems.

1.1 A dependence on information

The Chapter Case described a company about to introduce a new information system to help staff manage the business more profitably. The chapter will give more information about events during this project, which illustrates common features of a business information system:

- the need to convince the board that the cost will be worthwhile;
- the possible effects of an IS on the way people work and on the structure of the organisation (especially the network of branches);
- the system will enable information to flow more smoothly between some people (customers, call centre staff, engineers), though perhaps it will disrupt some traditional communication practices;
- the possible effects of the modern information system on the performance of the organisation in terms of cost and quality.

People managing activities of all kinds depend on information. As you manage your work on an assignment you need information – such as what your teacher requires, the due date, advice from previous assignments, and which theories and evidence you should use. People in organisations need information which reflects the fact that organisations are open systems – that is, they interact with their environment. They draw resources from the external environment (inputs), transform

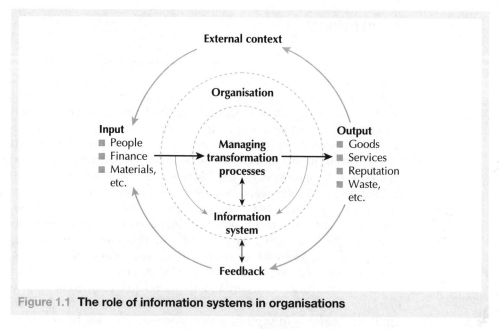

Figure 1.1 The role of information systems in organisations

them into outputs and pass them back to the environment. Figure 1.1 illustrates the flow, and shows that the value the organisation obtains for their outputs (money, reputation, goodwill, etc.) enables them (shown by the feedback arrow from output to input) to continue attracting resources. If the outputs fail to generate sufficient new resources, the enterprise cannot continue in business.

People at all levels of the organisation need to work in ways that add value to the resources they use; to do that they need information – about inputs, the transformation process and outputs. Information about inputs could include the cost and availability of materials, staff, equipment; information to help manage the transformation process could include delivery schedules, capacity utilisation, efficiency, quality, costs; output information could include prices, market share, customer satisfaction. Figure 1.1 shows how information systems support these fundamental organisational processes.

Activity 1.1 Collecting examples of IS

Arrange a short discussion with someone who works in an organisation (or use your experience of being in an organisation). Ask them to give examples of some information that is used regularly by

(a) a senior manager

(b) a departmental manager

(c) a professional specialist.

Also ask them how they receive that information and how it helps them in their work.

People depend more on computer-based information system for three main reasons: electronic coordination, globalisation, and information-intense firms.

■ Electronic coordination

Most firms still deliver products and services through physical activities – supplying a book ordered online still requires the production and delivery of a tangible item. Developments in IS mean that more of the input, transformation and output activities needed to produce that item can be linked electronically. Such systems can extend beyond the boundaries of a firm to include suppliers and customers, all linked together through electronic means.

Exchanging information by direct human contact – face-to-face meetings, telephone calls, letters and faxes – is often the most effective means of communication, especially when the issue is unusual or the solution unclear. But where the information is routine, modern information systems enable communication to be conducted almost entirely by electronic means. Early systems dealt with isolated aspects of the internal transformation process, such as a salary payment system or one for employee records – often with separate systems in different parts of the organisation. Gradually companies are bringing these together within single, company-wide systems. As an example, BP, the global energy company, maintains all human resource information on a single electronic database, which any authorised staff can access. They can check their records and company policies online, enabling everyone to work on the same, up-to-date information. They can deal with, say, overseas postings more efficiently than when they used manual systems or unconnected computer systems. Others companies use IS to link widely dispersed functions so that, for example, marketing, engineering, manufacturing and design units can exchange information electronically in designing new products.

Some companies extend such systems so that their internal transformation processes link electronically with suppliers' and customers' systems. Customer orders are automatically processed to work out the implications for raw materials or other inputs, and these orders are then automatically passed to relevant suppliers. They in turn send invoices and receive payment electronically. The computer industry itself is a leading player in using IS to link individual customer orders to manufacturing processes and back through the supply chain. The IBM case below is an example of this, in that all routine information – orders, invoices, payments – between the company and established suppliers is handled electronically.

■ Globalisation

There has been international trade since the earliest times, and by the nineteenth century many great trading businesses were operating across the world. What is new today is the much greater proportion of production that crosses national boundaries, organised by businesses operating on a global scale. They need to coordinate their input, transformation and output processes between widely dispersed locations. Distribution companies such as Federal Express or Frans Maas operate delivery services across the world and develop information systems accordingly. Oil companies such as Shell or mining companies such as Lonrho necessarily secure resources in some parts of the world and sell it in others. Many financial businesses such as ABN-Amro (a Dutch bank) or retailers such as Tesco or Carrefour have ambitions to operate on a global scale.

Information systems influence globalisation by enabling the efficient flow of data on which international operations depend. Complex supply, manufacturing and distribution networks depend on computer systems to track and monitor the flow of orders, components and payments. Without information systems of the kind now common, globalisation could not have grown to the present scale.

MIS in Practice   IBM becomes more globally integrated

IBM has long been a major player in the world electronics industry. Yet until quite recently the separate business units and manufacturing operations operated with a high degree of independence from each other. Each manufacturing unit made its supply arrangements independently of the others.

By 2000, management had centralised most business functions, including the responsibility for securing supplies of components and services to be used by IBM in meeting customer orders. Global Commodity Councils manage the supply of a group of parts (such as drives or monitors) for the whole company. Global Commodity Managers handle strategic relations with suppliers, regularly agreeing prices and forecast volumes for the following quarter, based on the requirements of all the company's divisions. The suppliers, most of whom are themselves global players, then deliver as required to any of the company's manufacturing facilities around the world. A customer order triggers a flow of components through the transport networks which links these sites – and the whole process is supported at each stage by IS. Orders are transmitted electronically to suppliers, as are the subsequent invoices from the supplier to the company. These automatically trigger electronic payments from IBM to the supplier in settlement of the account.

Source: Information provided by the company.

■ Information-intense firms

Many companies in developed economies provide their customers with information and knowledge rather than with physical manufactured products. Such 'information-intense' companies depend on being able to capture, create and distribute information and knowledge to their customers – who may themselves be widely dispersed around the world. Information-intense sectors include financial services, software, media, reservation services, commodity or stock trading and consultancy. Moreover, more companies now deliver products and services electronically – selling information, music or videos through a website, or encouraging customers to pay utility or credit card bills electronically. The box below illustrates an information-intense company which depends on distributing information in its knowledge base to the consultants.

Such businesses – a growing proportion of economic activity in advanced economies – depend on information systems to support the flow of data, information and knowledge. Ensuring that IS can support more electronic coordination, globalisation and information intensity is a significant management challenge. This book presents and analyses the issues involved in meeting that challenge.

■ Summary

■ People depend on information to manage the inputs of resources to the organisation, the transformation processes and the outputs of these activities.

> **MIS in Practice** **Sharing information in a global consultancy**
>
> The company is a leading management consultancy, whose 10,000 professional staff work around the world. The company traditionally operated as a collection of national or regional groups, further divided into functions. These worked in relative isolation from colleagues, especially those in other countries. The company realised that clients (especially global businesses) required it to handle bigger and more complex jobs. Staff would have to offer a wider range of experience – which was largely available in the collective but unorganised experience of the consultants. How could rapidly changing information be efficiently shared to help the business learn, so it could meet client needs more effectively?
>
> Senior managers decided to use information technology in the form of a groupware system that enables staff to share common information quickly across the world. They use their personal computers (PCs) to communicate with each other, to access standard practice information and to draw on the knowledge of other people either through databases or online bulletin boards. They can link to the network from wherever they are.
>
> *Source*: Information provided by the company.

> Computer-based information systems enable electronic coordination, globalisation and the growth of information-intense firms.

1.2 Information and information systems

Data, information and knowledge

We need to clarify the terms 'data', 'information' and 'knowledge'.

- Data refers to recorded descriptions of things, events, activities and transactions – their size, colour, cost, weight, date and so on. It may or may not convey information to a person.

- Information is a sub-set of data that means something to the person receiving it – which they judge to be useful, significant, urgent and so on. It comes from data that has been processed (by people or with the aid of technology) so that it has meaning and value for the recipient. This means that information is subjective since what one person sees as valuable information, another may see as data with no particular significance.

- 'Knowledge builds on information that is extracted from data' (Boisot, 1998, p. 12). While data is a property of things (size, price, etc.), knowledge is a property of people that predisposes them to act in a particular way. Knowledge embodies prior understanding, experience and learning, and is either confirmed or modified as people receive new information.

The significance of the distinction is that people use knowledge to economise on the use of resources. If people can draw on accurate knowledge, they will react differently to information and data than if they have no prior experience and learning to guide them. Someone with good knowledge of a market will use it when they

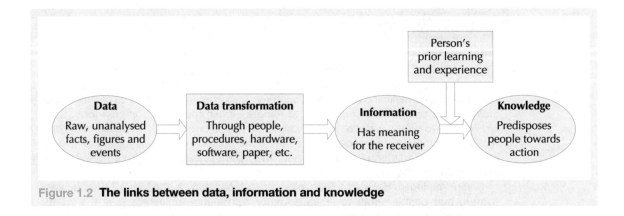

Figure 1.2 **The links between data, information and knowledge**

interpret some information about current sales. They will be able to identify significant patterns or trends and so attach a different meaning to the information than someone without that knowledge. Using relevant knowledge enables people to act in ways that add more value and so supports more effective organisational working.

Figure 1.2 shows this relation between data, information, knowledge and information systems. It should be clear from the figure that information systems are much better at producing information than knowledge.

Information systems

An information system is a set of people, procedures and resources that collects data which it transforms and disseminates. Human societies have developed successively more powerful ways of communicating with one another over space and time. The earliest humans communicated through sign language, painting and drawing, and speech. The development of writing and numeric symbols, and especially the development of printing technology, greatly extended the capacity of people to communicate information to people in distant places. People could now record data on paper, transform it into information and present it on paper. Computer-based systems, which transform other symbols into digital form, dramatically extend this historic process of lowering the cost of processing and disseminating information. For many tasks, people use electronic systems to record, transform, store and present information.

This does *not* mean that all communication becomes electronic. For all the power of this medium to handle internal and external data, organisations have infinite networks of informal communication. People use these to pass gossip, rumour and useful information to colleagues often with astonishing speed. These informal systems exist in parallel with the formal, computer-based information systems that are the subject of this book.

Figure 1.3 shows the elements of a computer-based information system. It shows that an information system does not consist only of hardware and software, but includes people and procedures. This system is part of a wider system which we call the organisational context. This is as important as technical factors to the outcomes of an IS project. The interactions between information systems and their organisational context are the distinctive focus of this book.

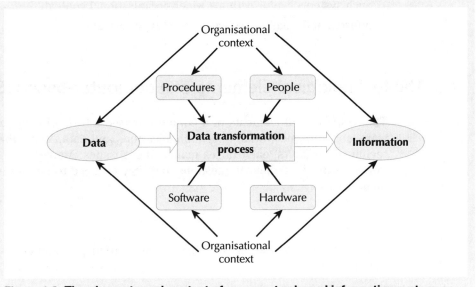

Figure 1.3 **The elements and context of a computer-based information system**

The example of a computer-based student record system illustrates each element in Figure 1.3. It requires people (course administrators) to enter data (name and other information about students and their results) following certain procedures – such as that one person reads from a list of grades while another keys the data into the right field on that student's record.

The hardware consists of the computers and peripherals such as printers, monitors and keyboards. This runs the student record system, using software to manipulate the data in a particular way and to print out the results for each student. Another procedure sends results to each student – which they see as information. Managers of the department might compare the pass rate of each course – so the record system is now part of the university's management information. Staff will use their knowledge (based on learning and experience) to interpret trends and evaluate the significance of any patterns.

'Information systems management' is a term used to describe the activities of planning, acquiring, developing and using information systems such as this. It involves dealing not just with technical matters, but also with how the technology relates to people, procedures and the organisational context.

Summary

- Raw data is transformed into information which has meaning.
- People use their knowledge (based on experience and learning) to interpret information.
- Human society has developed as people have increased their capacity to communicate.
- Formal information systems use people, procedures, software and hardware to convert data into information and disseminate it.

■ Such systems evolve within a wider organisational context.

■ Informal information systems coexist with formal ones.

1.3 The technological elements of a computer-based IS

The technological elements of a computer-based information system include hardware, software, networks, telecommunications and data. While these elements are technical products, each raises management issues. Managers do not need to be familiar with the technical questions, but they do need to be aware of the management ones.

■ Hardware

Hardware refers to the physical components within a computer system. These consist of:

■ **input devices** (such as keyboard, mouse, joystick, scanner, touch screen, camera, microphone, sensor);

■ **central processing unit** (manipulates data and controls the computer system);

■ **storage devices** (the primary (internal) storage, and secondary storage such as magnetic disk (e.g. floppy disk) or optical disk (e.g. CD-ROM, DVD));

■ **output devices** (such as printers, plotters, monitors, voice output); and

■ **communication devices** (to link the computer with computer networks).

Figure 1.4 shows the relationship between these hardware elements.

Mainframes are very large computers with massive memory and very rapid processing power, used in large businesses and government. Users work with

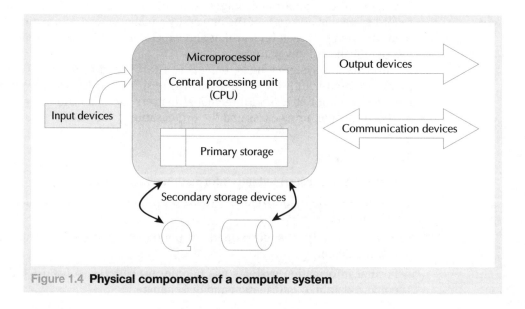

Figure 1.4 **Physical components of a computer system**

workstations to enter data and receive information from the mainframe. A **mini-computer** is a mid-range computer often used in factories and middle-sized companies. **Personal computers** (PCs) sit on a desktop or are carried around by the user (portable desktops, laptops, notebooks and palmtops). A network to link PCs enables users to share files, software, printers and other network resources. A network requires specifically designed **server computers** with large memory and disk storage capacity. Laudon and Laudon (2004) and Turban et al. (2001) examine these points in more detail.

Management issues with respect to hardware are:

- Whether to use the latest hardware. It is easy to be attracted by the promotional literature about a new technical development, but much harder to show that the benefits will justify the investment.

- Which applications will have the greatest effect on productivity or other competitive factors. For example, whether to develop new services such as loyalty programmes.

- Whether to provide all mobile staff with personal computers that enable them to remain connected to office and colleagues at all times.

- Whether to invest directly in computer systems, or to buy these services from other companies.

Software

Software is a set of instructions written in a specialised language that controls the operation of the computer. **System software** is a set of programs that manage the resources of the computer, such as the central processor, communication links and peripheral devices. Windows, Unix and Linux are examples of system software. **Application software** enables users to apply the computer to specific tasks, such as e-mail, word-processing or stock control.

Management issues with respect to software are:

- Whether to obtain software by buying an off-the-shelf package or investing in having it custom-made to suit specific requirements.

- How fully to involve users in such decisions.

- How much local variation of software to allow within the business. For example, can departments use software to suit their needs or should they use common packages which make it easier to share information with others?

Telecommunications

This is the communication of information by electronic means over distance. In the past this meant voice transmission over the telephone. Today a great deal of telecommunication is digital data transmission, using computers, software and devices such as modems and cables to transmit data from one location to another. There is a worldwide digital telecommunications network that enables businesses and private individuals to obtain and distribute information – sending e-mails or visiting a website.

A telecommunication system is a set of compatible hardware and software (computers, input/output devices, communication channels and communications software) that makes it possible to send and receive information. Communication networks are a linked group of computers. They can be local area networks (LANs), usually limited to a single building, or wide area networks (WANs) that cover greater distances. Chapter 2 discusses the use of a special WAN, the Internet.

Management issues with respect to telecommunications are:

- How they can use the falling costs and increasing speed of telecommunications to expand the business or to support the existing business more effectively.
- While it is technically possible to link many business units together, is it managerially wise to do so?
- Whether the company will face competition from unexpected quarters, as distance provides less protection.

Data

Technology makes it possible for people in organisations to use data much more effectively than when they could only analyse it with manual, paper-based systems. Many now put great effort into capturing data that is generated with each transaction and making portions of that data available to people who can use it in their work. They do so by creating databases – collections of data organised to service many applications at the same time, using the same integrated set of data. Distributed databases are stored and updated in more than one location, yet the data remains consistent. When a database is designed around major business subjects such as customers, vendors or activities, it may be called a 'data warehouse'. Using such data to discover trends, patterns or behaviours is called 'data mining'.

Management issues with respect to database technologies are:

- Whether to develop a fully integrated customer database to enable more effective marketing.
- How to balance the advantages of this with possible ethical issues of privacy and data protection.

Summary

- Continuing technological developments raise management issues over whether to use IS systems and over which applications will be worthwhile.
- A continuing issue is whether to use off-the-shelf or customised technologies.
- While IS systems enable companies to create new products and services, they also raise the challenge of substantial organisational and human change.

1.4 The social elements of a computer-based system

People

However sophisticated the technical elements of an IS, it will depend on people to make it work effectively. This includes staff and managers who enter data into the system and those who receive information from it and use the results. The latter includes staff in supplier or customer organisations who, as their systems become more closely linked, may be dealing directly with the main organisation's IS system. It may also include members of the public visiting the website or entering data and receiving information from the system. We discuss in Chapter 8 how all these users have unique needs and interests and will see the system from a different point of view from those who designed it.

Management issues with respect to people include:

- Ensuring that systems are designed in a way that encourages the motivation and commitment of staff to enter data accurately and to use it appropriately.
- Acknowledging that people interpret the information they receive and asking whether they understand it.
- Finding out what customers or members of the public expect of an information system (such as a website) and how well the IS meets their expectations.

Procedures

These are the rules or routines that people (staff or others) are expected to use when interacting with the IS. When staff enter data, they must follow certain procedures – which may be tightly specified in the system itself or left flexible. Implementing an IS can make procedures more rigid, with less opportunity for staff to use their initiative: this is not a force of nature, but a management choice. Another issue is whether the procedures require people to use the system or whether it is voluntary – systems used by professional staff are sometimes of the latter kind.

Management issues with respect to procedures could include:

- Whether the procedures around an IS mirror earlier procedures or differ from them.
- Whether staff see them as supporting their established ways of working.
- Whether the procedures should be flexible or inflexible.

Organisation

These procedures, and the actions of people using the system, are the immediate parts of the IS. They are set within the elements which make up the organisational context of an information system. The results of an IS depend on the interaction between people, system and context.

Figure 1.5 illustrates the organisational context of an information system – elements that represent the organisational environment of those working on an IS project. Table 1.1 gives an example of each element and shows the chapters in which we discuss them, thus giving an overview of the book.

The context represented by this model occurs at several levels of the organisation: operating, divisional and corporate. Acting to change an element at one level will have effects at this and other levels. Some will give consistent, supporting signals about the project, others will not. There is no certainty that events elsewhere in the business provide a coherent context to help the IS project.

Finally, the context has a history, which affects how people react to present proposals. Pettigrew et al. (1992) have stressed this aspect when they refered to

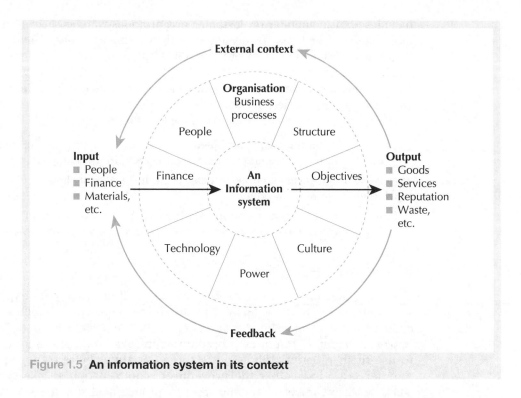

Figure 1.5 **An information system in its context**

Table 1.1 **An organisational perspective on the context of information systems**

Context element	Chapter	Example
Technology	1, 2	Type and location of physical facilities, machinery and information systems that people use to transform inputs into useful outputs.
Project objectives	3	How these relate to wider strategies and some desired future state of the organisation or project.
Business processes	4	The activities that people and technologies perform on materials and information to meet the objectives. They include designing products, receiving orders, making the product, delivering it and receiving payment. Information systems are an opportunity to redesign business processes to add more value to resources.
Financial resources	5	Assessing what financial resources to use on IS projects when organisational and external factors make the future so unpredictable.
Culture, structure and power	6	How cultural features (norms, beliefs, underlying values) influence the way people interact with information systems. Does the way tasks (including the IS function itself) are divided and coordinated in conjunction with information systems encourage productive human activity? How information systems interact with existing distribution and sources of power, and encourage or discourage innovation.
IS function	7	The choices managers face on how to organise the IS function.
People	8	Their knowledge, skills and interests, whether inside or outside the organisation. How to ensure that people develop information systems that are attractive to people and teams affected, and optimise their contribution.

Contracting Services: Changing the context

The IS staff developed the system, with little input from the service side of the business. The call centre manager (who reported to the IS director) recruited staff from within the business and arranged their training. Four members of staff took calls from the stores, and gathered as much information as they could using a detailed script. They recorded the replies on their computer screen and, when the call was complete, transferred the information electronically to the despatchers. These were experienced service staff who sent the engineers details of the store and the work required. A further group dealt with administration and invoicing.

The board was satisfied with the pilot and decided to extend the system to the whole company. The call centre developed rapidly and the company soon closed 17 of the 22 branches. At the same time they won a contract from the supermarket chain for another 45 FM stores and for 132 stores from another chain in a smaller facilities management deal.

However, after a few months the company changed policy and stopped closing branches.

There were several problems. The most alarming was that they quickly began to lose much of the traditional business to small competitors.

Introducing the call centre had a major effect on the management of the branches and the engineers. The supervisors became working engineers. The branch managers (now working from home) were expected to concentrate on generating new business. They felt insecure and no longer had a physical place of work. Most had never seen a computer – instead of encouraging the engineers and customers to overcome difficulties they were dismissive of the changes. They were responsible for the engineers but did not know where they were or what they were doing: staff in the central call centre had despatched them.

The branch managers who were being displaced by the new system had a very demotivating effect on staff and customers. (Chief accountant)

Source: Personal communication from managers in the company, and Boddy (2000).

CASE QUESTIONS 1.2

1 *Which aspects of the context had managers changed when introducing the call centre?*
2 *How may these changes have affected the outcomes observed, in terms of the cost and quality of service delivery?*

'temporal interconnectedness – the need to locate change in past, present and future time' (p. 269). Most analyses of organisational change now see this as an evolutionary process that takes place within the historical and contemporary context of the organisation. Managers implement an IS against a background of previous events. Past decisions shaped the business as it is today and affect how easy it is to change. The past affects whether people are willing and able to change.

The significance of these contextual elements is that managing an IS project is not a matter of managing a technical project but an organisational one. Promoters need to be able to change both the technology and the organisation – which require very different skills. They design an IS to meet what they understand to be the requirements of senior managers. They must also take account of the elements in the context. How other people (users, managers, etc.) react to the resulting system will be influenced by *their* view of the system entering the context. Will it increase or

Activity 1.2 The context of an IS

Think of an information systems change you have observed or about which you can collect some primary data from people who were involved. You may want to combine this work with Activity 1.3.

- *What was the new system intended to achieve?*
- *Consider each element of the context in Figure 1.5/Table 1.1 and make notes on whether, and how, each of these elements was changed during the project.*
- *Which, if any, elements of the internal context did they try to change as part of the project?*
- *How did other people see (interpret) and react to those changes?*
- *Did the project achieve what those promoting it intended?*

decrease their power? Is it consistent with the prevailing culture? Will they be better off in some way? These are the areas to which promoters and project managers need to give attention. As well as investing in the technology, they need to reconstruct other aspects of the organisational context in which people are working. The outcomes of the project (success, embarrassing failure or something in between) will depend on how they manage these contextual elements.

Summary

- An information system is part of a wider organisational context, made up of the elements in Figure 1.5/Table 1.1.
- This context has both hierarchical and historical dimensions.
- Those introducing a new information system may or may not change elements of the context to support the IS change.
- Since organisations are systemic in nature, any such changes are likely to have ripple effects on other elements.
- The outcomes of an IS project depend on whether changes made to the context encourage people to act in a way that supports the project.

1.5 IS and their context – alternative perspectives

Few IS projects produce the results that their promoters expect (for examples see Lucas, 1975; Sauer, 1993; Drummond, 1996; or Currie, 1997). The probable explanation is that changing an information system will almost always involve changing contextual as well as technical elements. To expect hardware or software alone, however sophisticated, to solve a business problem or improve performance is a delusion. Those responsible for implementing an IS project will usually be dealing with a much broader, linked and therefore unpredictable set of changes. The breadth of the change means that managers cannot be certain where it will lead. 'Implementing a new information system is best seen as a *process* with indeterminate outcomes' (McLoughlin, 1999, p. 73).

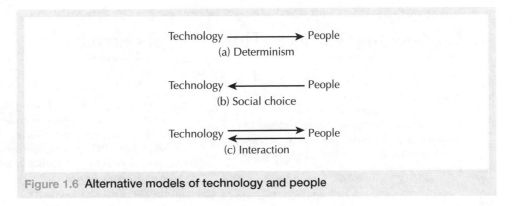

Figure 1.6 **Alternative models of technology and people**

Anyone managing an IS project bases their work on a theory of how change occurs in organisations. They use this theory (even if subconciously) to decide how to develop and implement their plans. This section sets out three alternative models of IS change: determinism, social choice and interaction.

Determinism

The determinist view is that people have no influence on the course of events and that technology itself will produce the results required. Technology is available, people will have no choice but to use it, and doing so will produce the expected results. Those who take this 'technological determinism' view treat technology as the dominant influence. They range from some of the earliest observers of the management implications of computers (Leavitt and Whisler, 1958) to those recently making predictions about the Internet (Cairncross, 2001). Technology is the independent variable that has predetermined 'impacts'. People have little influence over its direction or consequences. Organisations have to use the latest technologies to survive. People expect banks to have cash machines and to offer Internet banking. Banks have little choice but to use these technologies if they wish to remain in business. Figure 1.6(a) represents this position.

Social choice

An alternative view is that people have free will and can influence the course of events. People shape what science develops and choose how to use it. Managers have minds of their own and choose which technologies to develop, promote and install to further their interests. So do the people who work for them. Users have some choice over which aspects of a system to reject, ignore, adapt or welcome, considering their interests and situation. Some people ignore e-mail systems and insist that a secretary prints any messages. Other staff ignore software that is on their system, or use it in unintended ways (Kimble and McLoughlin, 1995). In this model, technology is a dependent variable, reflecting a succession of human choices. Figure 1.6(b) shows this position.

Interaction

The interaction model (Figure 1.6(c)) expresses the idea that change happens when people are able and willing to change the context in which they and others work.

CHAPTER CASE: PART 3

Contracting Services: The rising phone bill

The phone bill rose rapidly. The engineers now used their mobiles to talk to each other between jobs. Part of this was to exchange information about the work. Managers also believed a substantial amount was social chat which previously took place when they met at the branch:

Now that they are isolated they use the mobile to keep in touch with each other and that proved very expensive.

A manager in the company acknowledged that:

We went too fast in trying to close the branches without first getting the management in place to control the mobile workforce without a physical branch. We did not define the job and we lost control of our engineers in terms of where they were and what they were spending their time on.

Source: Personal communication from managers in the company, and Boddy (2000), p. 34.

They interpret the existing context and act to change it to promote personal, local or organisational objectives – for example by advocating the purchase of an IS application (technology) or changing reporting relationships (structure). Others interpret this proposal in the light of *their* interpretation of personal, local or organisational objectives. All the players use their power (also an element of the context) as best they can to influence decisions about the plans and how to implement them. The evolving outcomes from these interactions may or may not support the interests of the players, but will affect the context – which is now the historical background to future action.

Figure 1.7 illustrates these interactions. The existing context contains the elements in Figure 1.5 and new technological developments open up the possibility, if adopted, of changing that context (a). People who see those possibilities (b) and interpret them as an opportunity to advance personal, local or business needs (c) promote a project. This involves planning how to incorporate the general technological possibility into the specific context (technology). They also consider which other elements of the context to change (business processes, structure, etc.) alongside the technology (d) to encourage people to act in ways that support the use of the system (e) (Orlikowski, 1992). Other players (individuals or representatives of affected interest groups) interpret the existing context (b), and the proposals put forward by the promoters (d), in the light of their personal and sectional interests, as well as stated organisational objectives (c).

As plans are made and implemented through the interaction of the players, people will also be interpreting and responding to the emerging new context and acting accordingly (f). They may observe that the technology has been accompanied by structural changes that allow senior managers to monitor local performance more closely. They may interpret this as a positive sign that their achievements will be noted and welcomed, or as a threat. How they react affects personal, sectional and organisational objectives, and the evolving context (g). Those promoting the project interpret that new context before deciding how to react – perhaps by adapting the context again to overcome or reassure the opposition.

Taking an interpretive perspective encourages us to consider how the main players (promoters and users) vary in their attention to contextual factors (including those

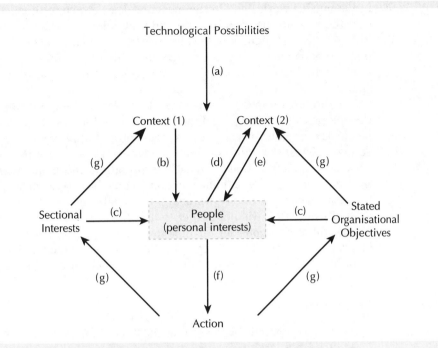

Figure 1.7 An interaction model applied to information systems

You may want to combine this work with that in Activity 1.2, as a way of organising your primary data collection on a project or assignment. It should help you practise the useful skill of analysing a situation with the aid of a theoretical model.

Think of an information systems change you have observed or about which you can collect some primary data from people who were involved. Try to gather data from at least three people in different parts of the organisation who are familiar with the project. Ask about these topics:

- *Who initiated the project?*
- *What aspects of the external context (competition, customers, etc.) stimulated them to start the project?*
- *What was their view (interpretation) of the significance of those factors?*
- *Did any aspects of the internal context (Figure 1.5/Table 1.1) stimulate them to start the project?*
- *What was their view (interpretation) of the significance of those factors?*
- *Which, if any, elements of the internal context did they try to change as part of the project?*
- *How did other people see (interpret) and react to those changes?*
- *How do people think that these reactions affected the project?*

in the outside world) and in the meanings they attach to them. The essential idea is that the relation between people and technology works both ways – as shown in Figure 1.6(c). Designers physically construct a technology in the light of what they believe management expects. Others socially construct the technology when they decide whether or how to use it. People shape institutions, and institutions then shape people.

The interaction model implies that, to a degree, people modify a system throughout the phases of design and use. As they use the system they adapt it to suit the particular circumstances. They experiment and improve. Some systems offer little scope for this: they are designed so that users must use the system as intended. Others have more scope for local interpretation. Intranets are a good example, as their content depends on human action. People have to enter, and maintain, information that makes the site worth using. If the site (part of the new context) contains little of value, staff will not bother to use it. The more flexibility that is possible, the less useful it is to consider technology as an objective, fixed entity with predictable effects. As Kimble and McLoughlin (1995) observe: 'Technology does not impact on a social context, or vice versa but, over time, each shapes the other.'

▦ Summary

- ▦ We have compared determinist, social choice and interaction models.
- ▦ The interaction model emphasises that people involved in an IS project will interpret the context in different ways and act accordingly.
- ▦ This implies that the outcomes of major IS projects are hard to predict and are likely to vary significantly from the promoters' original objectives.

1.6 The unpredictable outcomes of IS projects

Interest groups use different criteria to assess the effectiveness of a project. Some see it as a success because it is on time and within budget. These are valuable achievements, and are easy to measure. But they are essentially internal and short-term. A system may be efficient, but may not satisfy the customers. Conversely, a system may do little to improve immediate efficiency, but may provide valuable long-term experience in a new technology.

Table 1.2 describes eight dimensions which people can use to measure the success of an information system. People will view them differently, with some favouring an efficiency measure, others a customer-satisfaction measure. Views may change with time. During the project, and in its immediate aftermath, the efficiency criterion may dominate. As time passes, it becomes easier to assess the contribution of the project to the other dimensions.

The initial objectives of an IS project usually change – either explicitly or by being quietly forgotten or given a lower priority as others become more prominent. Several empirical studies (e.g. Boddy and Gunson, 1996) give examples of this from IS projects. They show that management established some objectives when they made the investment, but the outcome several years later was often quite different. Part of the reason is that projects often incorporate recent, and often incomplete,

Table 1.2 **Measures of information system success**

Dimension	Description
Project quality	Whether project was completed on time and in budget.
System quality	System's reliability, features, functions, response time.
Information quality	Is the information relevant, clear, timely, accurate?
Information use	Regularity and duration of use, number of enquiries.
User satisfaction	Overall satisfaction, enjoyment, meets expectations.
Individual impact	Productivity, work satisfaction, improved decisions.
Organisational impact	Return on investment, contribution to performance, service effectiveness.
Preparing for the future	Building organisational and technological infrastructure for the future? Is the firm more prepared for future opportunities?

Source: Based on Shenhar et al. (1997); Doherty et al. (2003).

hardware or software. More can be done than seemed possible at the start. Another is that the change is usually introduced into a business with a volatile environment. What needs to be done changes during the project. Finally, interest groups will continue to nudge the project in ways that are favourable to their view of what is best for the organisation. If their support is vital to the project, their view will influence project design.

Was the Contracting Services call centre a success or a failure? The answer would depend upon who makes the judgement, and when. Customers would have a different view again. This illustrates that opinions on success and failure in relation to IS projects are often subjective. They reflect the perspective of whoever is making the judgement. Interest groups will interpret them in different ways, as the box indicates.

MIS in Practice   Pensco – interpreting success

In their study of the implementation of an IS into an insurance company, Knights and Murray (1994) noted that, in a culture which valued success and achievement, senior management were keen to stress the success of the system. They formally launched the new system, and the new products, at a high-profile presentation. This ignored the fact that many of the original objectives had not been achieved, substantial software work had still to be done and costs were higher than expected. Customer Services staff were overwhelmed by having to process policies manually, and IS staff were demoralised by the fact that they were continually moved from one part of the project to another, to deal with the current crisis. The researchers quote a senior IS manager who had attended the public presentation:

There are two pensions projects: the one I heard about yesterday at the presentation and the one I normally hear about. (p.161)

Source: Knights and Murray (1994).

■ Summary

■ People evaluate IS projects on several measures.

■ Interest groups will pay most attention to those objectives which benefit their position.

■ Changing technology and business conditions ensure that the outcomes of a project differ from the original intention.

Contracting Services: Recovery?

Faced with the loss of an important part of the business, management quickly realised they had taken a wrong turning. In March 1998 the service director reached retirement age. His replacement made two significant structural changes. The first was to retain a smaller network of five regional branches, known in the company as 'super-branches'. The call centre would still take all calls, but the super-branches would be responsible for managing the engineers. The call centre received the call using the prepared script and passed the details immediately to the relevant super-branch. Staff there allocated the call to an engineer and managed the transaction from then on, including invoicing. The call centre retained the task of managing the performance statistics, which were a critical part of the relationship with the FM customer.

The second change was that the service director ensured that the call centre manager would in future be responsible to him. The call centre thus became a service function, supporting the relationship with customers. The IS department became an internal supplier to the call centre.

More broadly, the company acknowledged that it was now managing two different types of business: the traditional small retailer and the large supermarket chains with whom they were building facilities management work. The growing FM work prompted structural changes within the company. At first, calls from the FM customer had been handled by whichever engineer was available in the local branch. The FM customer then asked the company to provide a dedicated service, so eleven engineers were allocated to this, working for them at all times. Their employment contracts were renegotiated in conjunction with the customer, who wanted to ensure that service staff were on contracts that would provide adequate cover for the stores.

Source: Personal communication from managers in the company, and Boddy (2000).

1.7 The management challenges of information systems

It will be clear by now that implementing an information system raises organisational as well as technical challenges. Successive chapters of the book examine these, and we note them briefly here to provide an overview of the book.

■ Foundations – combining technical and organisational perspectives

Organisations invest substantial sums in information systems, yet there is little evidence that they secure an adequate return on this expenditure. Successive anecdotal reports, studies of failed projects, the work of writers such as Strassman (1999) and Brynjolfsson and Hitt (2000) combine to give a picture of unrealised opportunities.

This lack of convincing evidence about the benefits of IS investment has become so pervasive that several leading suppliers of information systems (including Microsoft, Cisco, Hewlett Packard and IBM) have funded an academic study into the problem. Founded in 2003 at the Sloan School of Management at the Massachusetts Institute of Technology it will conduct research on how to measure and improve the productivity of information work.

The director of the project (Eric Brynjolfsson) indicates clearly the likely cause: 'companies need to look at the complementary changes in work practices that accompany successful IT investment . . . You can't just buy the technology and expect it to generate productivity benefits' (*Financial Times*, 21 April 2003, p. 8). Another participant in the initiative commented: 'Technology requires changes in the way humans work, yet companies continue to inject technology without making the necessary changes. Why? It's easier to write a cheque than change the way you work' (*Financial Times*, 21 April 2003, p. 8).

These conclusions are scarcely new, as numerous academic studies reached the same point many years ago and continue to do so (see, for example, Buchanan and Boddy, 1983; Markus and Robey, 1983; More, 1990; McLoughlin, 1999). It is also clear that many practitioners are aware that systems will be more successful if organisational issues are dealt with during the development process (Doherty et al., 2003). The challenge seems to be to put this awareness into practical measures during an IS project.

Information systems and strategy

Chapter 3 examines how IS projects have been able to support broader organisational strategies and the benefits of trying to align the two. There are many examples where organisations (of which Contracting Services is a small example) have been able to develop the business successfully with the aid of computer-based information systems. Identifying and implementing new IT applications that will support the business is another management challenge.

Carr (2003) has argued in a controversial article that the use of information technology has now become so widespread that it has almost become a commodity, available to anyone able to buy it. He argues that a strategically important resource is a scarce one, not something that is widely available. This is an argument not against spending on IS as such, but for being clear about the specific applications that will have most effect in a particular business.

Identifying those powerful applications will not be easy. Different interest groups within the organisation will reach different conclusions about which IS applications will best meet organisational needs. This may reflect genuinely different interpretations of the business environment and what will best serve a particular interest. While arguments for and against a project will inevitably be presented as being 'what is best for the business', other players may well interpret these as representing at best a partial view of the situation. Those with the greatest influence over the project (i.e. whose support it most needs) will be the most successful in this.

Organising for information systems

It is clear that adapting the organisation to support a new information system remains as neglected an area as it has always been. The evidence presented in Part 3 shows clearly that companies who attempt to make at least some degree of complementary change are more likely to have a successful project than those who consider only the technology. Each chapter is intended to outline the management tasks of adapting that contextual element, in the light of emerging technological possibilities, to help people design effective IS systems.

An additional theme to note is that those promoting an IS project are more likely to achieve the outcomes they expect if the changes are consistent with each other. Similar terms are 'fit' (Miller, 1992; Miles and Snow, 1994) or 'alignment' (Sabherwal et al., 2001) – expressing the idea that a consistent (or similar) context will influence human behaviour. How people respond to the context embodying a new information system depends on how they interpret it in relation to their personal, sectional and organisational objectives. Miles and Snow (1994) suggested that achieving a high degree of fit supports performance by allowing strategies, structures and processes to be clearly articulated. People understand well-defined strategies, and can act consistently with them. Structures that align with strategy ensure people understand their tasks and responsibilities. An information system that gives people the information they need to perform their roles will support performance.

Managers are more likely to meet their goals if they can ensure that others see alignment in their organisational surroundings rather than contradictions and confusions. Achieving an acceptable degree of alignment is likely to be a difficult and subjective target – so we see it as an aspiration rather than as something that can readily be achieved.

Implementing IS and organisational change

While powerful interest groups may try to shape an IS project to enhance their local position, those managing the project (the promoter or someone responsible for implementation) also needs to maintain their support. They provide resources,

---

Contracting Services: The reaction of the small retailers

One of the reasons for the problems with the traditional customers was that staff in the call centre were used to taking FM calls, following a detailed script. The system was too complex for the small retail customers who had made up the bulk of the business. In addition the success and growth of the FM work meant that the number of calls from this source was greater than expected. Customers had to wait an unacceptable time before their call was answered. Some were concerned about the cost of the call when they heard an unfamiliar accent – even though it was a freephone number. Many turned to a local service company. A senior manager acknowledged:

Communications with the small customer were a big problem. We were under pressure to save costs but we've realised that we made a mistake in not going to the customer base and selling the idea to them properly. So when the customer rang the call centre and got a poor response he went to one of the independent service engineers. We could have sold the benefits better.

Source: Personal communication from managers in the company, and Boddy (2000), p. 34.

support, ideas, means of influence and various other resources needed to move the project forward. Other groups need to support the project by being willing to change the way they work or by taking on new tasks.

Making changes on the scale implied by the widening agenda will usually be beyond the scope of the individual or even a competent project team. Creating appropriate structures to manage these projects is a key to success, and an example of this is examined in Chapter 10.

Summary

Using the interaction model highlights four challenges in IS management:

- Identifying where best to secure business value from IS, when interest groups may have different interpretations of contextual developments,
- Aiming to secure an acceptable degree of coherence between the elements of the context,
- Maintaining the support of interest groups, especially those who interpret the project as a threat to their position,
- Managing implementation through an appropriate set of mechanisms and structures to support individual action.

Subsequent Parts of the book provide ideas, theories, examples and tools which help people deal with these issues.

Conclusions

Organisations have always depended on human and technical information systems to help conduct their business. Technological developments have greatly increased this dependence, as applications have moved from essentially background tasks to include customer-centred foreground tasks. Most organisations depend heavily on computer-based information systems, and most managers depend on accurate and timely information.

The discussion has also emphasised that while technology is central to modern information systems, it is only part of the story. Figure 1.3 (p. 11) showed that information systems include people and procedures as well as technology. Throughout the chapter we have shown that each perspective on information systems raises wider management and organisational issues. Smaller and more portable systems encourage changes in working arrangements. Advances in communication technology erode boundaries between functions and organisations. The capacity of the new technologies is such that they raise major questions of strategy – about the kind of business that a company is in, about the internal changes that technology may imply and about the processes of implementation.

CHAPTER QUESTIONS

1. Give some personal examples of data and information. What information are you missing that might be harming your performance? How should this information be generated?

2. Give some examples of the use of information systems in a business you know. What are the main reasons for this way of using such systems? What are the organisational consequences?

3. Use Figure 1.5 to describe the main changes which took place during the early stages of the Chapter Case and which contributed to the loss of customers. Then use the figure to trace the changes made as the firm recovered the situation.

4. Does the interaction model mean that management cannot accurately predict the benefits it will secure from investing in an information system? If so, what are the implications for investment decisions?

5. Describe in your own words what a 'coherent context' for an IS project would consist of. How would it differ from an 'incoherent' context?

6. Explain how the historical context affects an IS project – preferably with an illustration from a case study or other example.

7. What are the implications for those responsible for managing IS projects of the interaction model set out in this chapter?

Further reading

Chaffey, D. (2002) *E-business and E-commerce Management*, Financial Times/Prentice Hall, Harlow. Uses a wide range of informative case studies to cover the management issues raised by the Internet.

Drummond, H. (1996) *Escalation in Decision-making: The Tragedy of Taurus*, Oxford University Press, Oxford. Presents long-term case studies of major IS projects and illustrates most of the themes in this chapter as do Knights and Murray (1994) and Sauer (1993).

Knights, D. and Murray, F. (1994) *Managers Divided: Organisation Politics and Information Technology Management*, Wiley, Chichester. See note after Drummond (1996).

McLoughlin, I. (1999) *Creative Technological Change*, Routledge, London. Presents a comprehensive overview and synthesis of the many theoretical perspectives on information technology.

Sauer, C. (1993) *Why Information Systems Fail: A Case Study Approach*, Alfred Waller, Henley-on-Thames. See note after Drummond (1996).

Turban, E., Rainer, R.K. and Potter, R.E. (2001) *Introduction to Information Technology*, Wiley, New york. Emphasises the technical foundations of information systems.

References

Boddy, D. (2000) 'Implementing inter-organisational IT systems: lessons from a call centre project', *Journal of Information Technology*, **15**(1), 29–37.

Boddy, D. and Gunson, N. (1996) *Organisations in the Network Age*, Routledge, London.

Boisot, M.H. (1998) *Knowledge Assets: Securing Competitive Advantage in the Information Economy*, Oxford University Press, Oxford.

Brynjolfsson, E. and Hitt, L.M. (2000) 'Beyond computation: information technology, organizational transformation and business performance', *Journal of Economic Perspectives*, **19**(4), 23–48.

Buchanan, D.A. and Boddy, D. (1983) *Organizations in the Computer Age: Technological Imperatives and Strategic Choice*, Gower, Aldershot.

Cairncross, F. (2001) *The Death of Distance 2.0: How the Communications Revolution Will Change Our Lives*, Orion, London.

Carr, N. (2003) 'IT doesn't matter', *Harvard Business Review*, **81**(5), 41–9.

Currie, W. (1997) 'Computerising the Stock Exchange: a comparison of two information systems', *New Technology, Work and Employment*, **12**(2), 75–83.

Doherty, N.F., King, M. and Al-Mushayt, O. (2003) 'The impact of inadequacies in the treatment of organisational issues on information systems development projects', *Information and Management*, **41**, 49–62.

Drummond, H. (1996) *Escalation in Decision-making: The Tragedy of Taurus*, Oxford University Press, Oxford.

Kimble, C. and McLoughlin, K. (1995) 'Computer-based information systems and managers' work', *New Technology, Work and Employment*, **10**(1), 56–67.

Knights, D. and Murray, F. (1994) *Managers Divided: Organisation Politics and Information Technology Management*, Wiley, Chichester.

Laudon, K.C. and Laudon, J.P. (2004) *Management Information Systems: Organization and Technology in the Networked Enterprise*, Prentice Hall, Englewood Cliffs, NJ.

Leavitt, H.J. and Whisler, T.L. (1958) 'Management in the 1980s', *Harvard Business Review*, **36**(6), 41–8.

Lucas, H.C. (1975) *Why Information Systems Fail*, Columbia University Press, New York.

McLoughlin, I. (1999) *Creative Technological Change*, Routledge, London.

Markus, M.L. and Robey, D. (1983) 'The organisational validity of management information systems', *Human Relations*, **36**(3), 203–26.

Miles, R.E. and Snow, C.C. (1994) *Fit, Failure and the Hall of Fame*, Free Press, New York.

Miller, D. (1992) 'Environmental fit versus internal fit', *Organization Science*, **3**(2), 159–78.

More, E. (1990) 'Information systems: people issues', *Journal of Information Science*, **16**, 311–20.

Orlikowski, W.J. (1992) 'The duality of technology: rethinking the concept of technology in organizations', *Organization Science*, **3**(3), 398–427.

Pettigrew, A.M., Ferlie, E. and McKee, L. (1992) *Shaping Strategic Change*, Sage, London.

Sabherwal, R., Hirschheim, R. and Goles, T. (2001) 'The dynamics of alignment: insights from a punctuated equilibrium model', *Organization Science*, **12**(2), 179–97.

Sauer, C. (1993) *Why Information Systems Fail: A Case Study Approach*, Alfred Waller, Henley-on-Thames.

Shenhar, A.J., Levy, O. and Dvir, D. (1997) 'Mapping the dimensions of project success', *Project Management Journal*, **28**, 5–13.

Strassman, P.A. (1999) *Information Productivity*, The Information Economics Press, New Canaan, Connecticut.

Turban, E., Rainer, R.K. and Potter, R.E. (2001) *Introduction to Information Technology*, Wiley, New York.

CHAPTER 2

Emerging IS trends in organisations

Learning objectives

By the end of your work on this topic you should be able to:

- Explain the evolution and changing role of information systems in organisations

- Compare information systems in terms of their functions and reach

- Discuss organisational and management issues of four different IS applications that are relevant for businesses: enterprise systems, knowledge systems, CRM systems and inter-organisational systems

Siemens' e-strategy

Mr von Pierer of Siemens talks of the need to have an 'e-mindset – for me the Internet has two parts. One is technology and the other is the mindset – how we view our business.' His plan has four elements.

The first is knowledge management – of which the sharenet is an example. The second is online purchasing – e-procurement. At the moment, electronic buying accounts for 10 per cent of Siemens €35 billion annual purchases, but the plan is to raise this to 50 per cent within three years. Most of the savings are expected to come from economies of scale by pooling the demands of several purchasing departments, using a company-wide system called click2procure.

The third element is Siemens' dealings with its customers, most of whom are other companies. They can click on 'buy from Siemens' on the website home page and place orders for most Siemens' products. The automation and drives division, for example, generates some 30 per cent of its sales online. The fourth part of the strategy is to improve internal administrative processes – such as handling 30,000 job applications a year online, or expecting employees to book their business travel arrangements over the Internet.

There is more to this than paperless administration. The idea is to make sure that the whole supply chain – from customers, through Siemens and on to its suppliers – runs smoothly. Different bits of Siemens have developed e-business applications independently, which has caused problems: 'It was almost impossible to connect all these different systems in order to get information to flow from your customer to your supplier.'

The shift to becoming an e-conglomerate should also expand the number of potential customers and suppliers, explains, his colleague, Mr Goller. In principle any company with Internet access ought to be able to trade with Siemens.

'Look at the airport,' says Mr Goller, pointing out of his window. Several of Siemens' business units could sell something to such a customer. 'That', he says, 'is a big advantage of the company's wide range of activities.' But he adds: 'I don't think that in the future such a customer will tolerate four or five different views about Siemens. They want one view of our capabilities.' Even if a customer is buying things from several different Siemens divisions, it should deal directly with only one, which should act as a sort of lead manager within the company. Inside Siemens, the customer should be identified by only one code.

In all, Mr von Pierer expects to cut costs by 2 per cent in the short run and by 3–5 per cent in the medium term. Of the four elements of his strategy, he expects e-procurement to yield the quickest returns. However, they will also be the easiest. He told analysts in February,

If you want to transform a company to an e-business company, the problem is not so much e-procurement and the face to the customer. All this can be done rather fast. What is truly difficult is to reorganise all the internal processes. That is what we see as our main task and where the main positive results will come from.

Source: Based on *The Economist*, 31 May 2001, *NRC-Handelsblad*, 11 November 2000, *www.siemens.com* and *www.my-siemens.com*.

Introduction

Information systems are influenced by three forces of change: relentless business pressures, fast changing technology and rapidly evolving organizations that need the support of modern information systems. This chapter illustrates the evolution of information systems and how, if properly managed, they can change the competitive ability of an organisation.

The chapter begins by outlining the evolution of computer-based information systems from 'back office' to 'customer-facing' systems. It outlines five generic functions they perform and then describes four applications with significant implications for organisations – enterprise integration, knowledge management, customer relations and inter-organisational systems. The aim of the chapter is to illustrate the widening role of information systems in organisations.

The Chapter Case shows how Siemens uses information systems in complementary areas, and how human issues and the current organisational structures can help and hinder transformation processes. This chapter gives additional perspectives on the applications that Siemens is using, and that are widely used by other companies.

2.1 The evolution of information systems

Between 1965 and 1975 managers concentrated on automating those functions where they could make large efficiency gains. These typically included those that processed many routine transactions, such as payrolls, stock controls and invoices. Department managers often delegated responsibility for information management to an emerging IS department, which became very skilled at running large, routine and usually centralised systems. This function became very influential as managers of the main operating departments left IS matters to the specialists. The technologies did not yet affect many smaller organisations.

In the following decade automated systems spread widely. Technical developments made smaller systems possible and more attractive to managers in other parts of the organisation. Departmental managers discovered many new uses for information technology and so became familiar with issues of budgeting for hardware, requesting support, defining requirements and setting priorities. Suppliers developed systems for smaller organisations.

Since the mid-1980s the information technology environment has continued to change significantly. Technical developments have brought information systems to the foreground of corporate policy. Systems that for decades have supported core business functions, such as finance, manufacture and distribution, continue to develop and employ more modern technology. Computer-based systems have now been extended to serve many other business functions and are used to support business processes in more integrated ways. Software suppliers have expanded product lines to support functions as diverse as production forecasting, supplier rating and project management. Information systems now support managers and professional staff directly. Non-technical staff or small-business owners depend heavily on computer-based information.

The rise of the Internet since the mid-1990s has further stimulated these developments. It challenges traditional organisations to innovate their processes and to integrate their processes with those of suppliers and customers. This clearly leads to corporate transformation, reinvention of value chains and new ways of doing business.

2.2 Classifying information systems

There are several ways of classifying information systems and, although not definitive, such schemes help to understand and compare examples in a complex field. Here we use the criteria of formality, function and reach.

▨ Formality

Information systems range from those which are informal human or paper-based ones to those which are highly automated and computer-based.

Human information systems

These are informal information systems. Everyone uses sense organs to receive impulses from the environment; the brain interprets these impulses leading to decisions on how to respond. From this perspective everyone is an information system. People observe events and use this information as they manage their responsibilities. The style of 'managing by walking around' suggests that direct communication between managers and subordinates and direct observations by managers constitute an effective way of collecting and giving information.

Studying is also a human information process. The study material available is data, but the student has to remember relevant information and use it in tutorials and written examinations.

Paper-based information systems

People still use many paper-based systems as they are cheap to implement and easy to understand. Paper systems have some virtues, and the genuinely paperless office is rare. Companies often define their procedures on paper, and staff are confident with information on paper. They can file a hard (paper) copy and use it easily for audit purposes. They often use paper systems when it is important to be able to trace all stages of a transaction, and when responsibility is high. Hospital staff keep most patient records on paper. The format of paper information systems is often a piece of A4 paper with printed instructions or boxes to complete. It may be a label attached to a part being routed through a shopfloor with instructions on what work to do. A manual, paper-based attendance list kept by a lecturer is another example, as is a paper address book or a diary.

Computer-based information systems

Most information systems beyond the smallest now use electronic means to collect data and to provide information. Electronic devices often now collect the initial data – such as the bar codes and scanners that capture product details in shops. Thereafter electronic systems process, manipulate, distribute and record the data, providing paper output when required. Examples are the till receipt for the customer or a summary report on the pattern of sales. Table 2.1 lists some examples.

Table 2.1 **Examples and descriptions of computer-based information systems**

Sector and example	Description
Retailing: electronic point-of-sale (EPOS) terminals	Provide faster customer checkout, identify customer preferences and improve inventory control. This control is linked with the computer systems of the suppliers.
Financial services: automated teller machines (ATMs), telephone banking	Support 24-hour-a-day banking services. Telephone banking enables customers to make transactions from their home. Online and Internet banking.
Travel: computerised reservation systems	Enable customers to survey availability and fares, and to reserve and pay for travel directly without having to work with an agent.
Manufacturing: computer-aided design and manufacturing	Linking design and manufacturing significantly improves the time to market. Better logistics by computerised material requirements planning. Electronic data interchange (EDI) with suppliers and customers.

Activity 2.1 Information systems you use

Identify two formal but paper-based information systems that you use, or which affect you.

■ *What are their advantages and disadvantages?*

Identify two computer-based information systems that you use, or which affect you.

■ *What are their objectives?*

■ *Could you achieve those objectives without using a computer?*

■ *What are their advantages and disadvantages?*

■ *Are computer-based systems always better?*

■ Functions of IS

Markus (1984) distinguished five functions of information systems: operational, monitoring, decision support, knowledge (or expert) and communication. This still provides a comprehensive and easily understood scheme.

Operational

Early computer systems were operational ones in the sense that management introduced them to process routine transactions. This is still a major function as they rationalise and standardise transactions in an efficient, reliable and uniform way. Common examples are payroll and order entry systems.

When a student informs the administration that they have a new address, they expect the change to apply quickly and to all the files of the university. The university would use a transaction processing system. Banks and other financial institutions use operational systems to process millions of transactions (such as cheques and other payment instructions) daily in an efficient, reliable and uniform way.

Operational (or transaction processing) systems also exchange data between organisations. In retailing, such applications help retailers to control their stock and to manage the whole supply chain more efficiently. The attraction of electronic point-of-sale (EPOS) systems is that they instantly record each sale, using a laser scanner which reads the bar code on the product. There is a direct link between the shops and the computers of the firm's suppliers so that stock can be reordered automatically in line with actual sales.

Staff in operating theatres can use bar coding to 'check in' and 'check out' all the tools used during an operation to prevent any being left inside the patient. Delivering digital goods such as software or news over the Internet are operational systems.

Monitoring

This checks the performance of an activity at regular intervals. The factor being monitored can be financial, quality, departmental output or personal performance. Being attentive to changes or trends gives the business an advantage as it can act promptly to change a plan to suit new conditions.

Universities in the Netherlands use student trail systems that monitor the academic progress of students. These systems link to the national institution that provides scholarships. This information enables this institution to stop or reduce the scholarship when results are below the required standard.

Decision support

Decision support systems (DSS) help managers to calculate the consequences of different alternatives before they decide what to do. A DSS incorporates a model of the process or situation, and will often draw data from operational systems. Some examples are:

- businesses use DSS to calculate the financial consequences of investments;

- universities use them to optimise room allocation and lecturer times;

- ambulance services use command and control systems to help controllers decide which ambulance to send to an emergency (see Chapter 8 Case).

Knowledge

Certain information systems help people to make decisions by incorporating human knowledge into the system. A knowledge engineer works with one or more experts in the domain under study. The knowledge engineer tries to learn how the experts make decisions. They put this knowledge into that part of the software known as the 'knowledge base'. Examples of knowledge functions are:

- banks use knowledge systems to analyse proposed bank loans, such as The Royal Bank of Scotland example described in Chapter 5. These incorporate many years of lending experience, and less experienced staff now decide on loans;

- NHS Direct in the UK uses an expert system to enable nursing staff in a call centre to deal with calls from patients who would otherwise visit their doctor. The system proposes the questions to ask, interprets the answers and recommends advice;

■ insurance companies use knowledge systems to process applications. Aegon, a Dutch insurer, uses such a system to enable agents to make insurance contracts with clients without involving the insurer.

In the 1980s and 1990s, developers aimed to design 'expert systems' to replace human experts, but expectations are now more realistic. It is very hard to comprehend all the knowledge and experience of human experts and to reach the same quality of decision-making. Computer-based systems are not as good as people at interpreting new knowledge and experience. Many people now use the term 'knowledge systems' rather than 'expert systems' (McCauly and Ala, 1992). While knowledge systems can replace the experts to some extent, most provide support to the experts in their decision-making (Balachandra, 2000; Flores and Pearce, 2000). The system makes suggestions to the human experts, but does not take over their jobs. In this context Hirschheim and Klein (1989) distinguished between 'expert systems' (which replace people who are expert in a certain field) and 'systems for experts' (which support the human experts).

Communication

People design communication systems to overcome barriers of time and distance. They make it easier to pass information around and between organisations. Electronic mail (e-mail) is a system whereby users send and receive messages electronically, irrespective of time. Another example is the World Wide Web (www) and a third communication system example is groupware (Turoff et al., 1993). Also known as a 'workflow system' this supports cooperation among people working in teams. They provide e-mail services, diary management and record historical information about employees, customers and documents. Table 2.2 lists the components of these systems.

These five functions are not necessarily distinct as companies often integrate them – such as when they link a decision support system to an operational system. The Chapter Case shows how Siemens is integrating internal transactional systems with knowledge management and with communication systems that link them with customers and suppliers. Communication systems provide links to other employees and organisations, such as the Internet auction site, e-Bay. Such systems combine communications between suppliers, customers and the auction, and transactions between parties and monitoring.

Table 2.2 **Components of groupware systems**

Electronic communication and messaging

Information sharing

Collaborative writing, authoring and design

Workflow management and coordination

Decision support and meeting systems

Scheduling systems, calendars and diaries

Conference systems

Administration of documents

Activity 2.2 Information on new applications

The media regularly report new applications of computer software. Collect examples over the next week of new systems that seem to have implications for how people manage their organisations. Compare notes with others and decide which of these systems is likely to be of greatest organisational significance over the next two years.

■ Reach of IS

Computerised information systems vary in the geographic reach of their operation and this affects their influence on organisations.

Individual

Many people use word-processing systems, spreadsheet programs and database systems to manage their work. They can download data from company-wide systems to use on their tasks. The main advantages are that the individual can decide what to use the system for and can control the way they work. The disadvantage is that the quality of the software varies greatly. The data extracted from the corporate database is no longer current and the systems may not link easily with other systems.

Local or departmental

If separate units or departments in companies have a distinct task to perform, it may be worthwhile to have their own information system. Management often creates these as separate systems, though many are now being integrated into the systems network of the whole company. A university may use a system that provides information about courses and assessments on the local departmental network, which students can access.

Company-wide

These systems integrate departments and people throughout the organisation. In hospitals many units use centralised patient data to retrieve or update information about a patient. Such systems make it much easier for staff from various departments to treat a patient in a consistent way. If managers want to implement a hospital-wide system they will discourage the continued use of stand-alone systems, such as a doctor's list of patients held on a spreadsheet that she or he considers the definitive list.

Inter-organisational systems

Today, many systems link organisations electronically by using networks that transcend company boundaries. These inter-organisational systems (IOS) enable firms to incorporate buyers, suppliers and partners in the redesign of their key business processes, thereby enhancing productivity, quality, speed and flexibility. New distribution channels can be created and new information-based products and services can be delivered. In addition, many IOS radically alter the balance of power in buyer–supplier relationships, raise barriers to entry and exit and, in many instances, shift the competitive position of industry participants.

> ## MIS in Practice   Electronic links at Lancia
>
> The car maker Lancia delivers its models in 122 colours and delivery takes place within four weeks. A direct electronic link between the dealer, the importer and the manufacturer makes this possible. The company is also networked to its suppliers. Through these electronic links, suppliers monitor Lancia's production and ship components exactly when needed. Many of these inter-organisational systems use the Internet and provide intense sharing of knowledge, resources and business processes.

	Operational/ transactional	Monitoring	Decision support	Knowledge	Communication
Individual	A1	A2	A3	A4	–
Local/ departmental/team	B1	B2	B3	B4	B5
Company-wide	C1	C2	C3	C4	C5
Inter-organisational	D1	D2	D3	D4	D5

Figure 2.1 **Functions and reach of information systems combined**

Combining the functions of systems with their reach leads to Figure 2.1, which gives a systematic way of distinguishing information systems. A spreadsheet application in Excel developed and used by one employee would fit in box A3 while a time registration system that records working hours of employees has transactional and monitoring functions (B1–B2). Nowadays many systems, such as e-mail, groupware or customer relationship management (CRM) systems, extend beyond the company, so bringing them to levels C and D.

The significance of this is that the organisational implications of systems vary across the figure. Those in the top left-hand area – largely individual, operational – will be easy to implement and affect few staff. This book will be of little value to someone implementing an A1 or perhaps a B1 system: all they need is a technical manual. As we move towards the lower right-hand part of the diagram both technical and organisational complexity increase. This book will help people working with systems in that area.

■ Summary

■ IS take different forms, ranging from very informal or paper-based systems to highly automated computer-based systems.

- They also have different functions. We distinguished five functions: operational, monitoring, decision support, knowledge (or expert) and communication.

- Computerised IS vary in the reach of their operation and this affects their influence on the organisation: individual, departmental, organisational or inter-organisational.

In the following sections we illustrate the evolution of IS by discussing four widely used systems which support, respectively, enterprise resource planning (ERP), knowledge management (KM), customer relationship management (CRM) and inter-organisational systems (IOS). Each section describes one of these systems and introduces the organisational and management issues they raise.

2.3 Managing information flows with enterprise-wide systems

Fulfilling a customer order requires people in sales, accounting, production, purchasing and so on to cooperate with each other to exchange relevant information. However, the information systems on which they depend were often designed to meet the needs of a single function or organisational level. They were built independently and cannot automatically exchange information. Manufacturing might not know the number and types of product to make because their systems cannot easily obtain information from the systems that process orders. A common solution is to use enterprise systems (ES), also known as enterprise resource planning (ERP) systems. These coordinate activities, decisions and knowledge across many different functions, levels and business units in the hope of increasing efficiency and service.

Enterprise systems aim to create an integrated platform to coordinate internal processes. Discrete functions become integrated into company-wide business processes that flow across organisational levels and functions, as shown in Figure 2.2.

At the heart of an enterprise system is a central database that draws data from and feeds data into a series of applications throughout the company. Using a single database streamlines the flow of information. Table 2.3 shows examples of business processes and functions supported by enterprise systems. These 'modules' can be implemented separately, but promise much greater benefits when they are linked to exchange information continuously through the central database.

ERP systems give management direct access to current operating information and, among other things, enable companies to:

- integrate customer and financial information;

- standardise manufacturing processes and reduce inventory;

- improve information for management decisions across sites;

- enable online connections with suppliers' and customers' systems with internal information processing.

Currently, the leading vendors are SAP, PeopleSoft, Oracle and J.D. Edwards. Vendors tend to specialise in particular industries and some industries have standardised on a particular vendor (McKeen and Smith, 2003).

ERP systems are semi-finished products that user organisations must tailor to their own business needs. Tailoring the software using parameters provided by the

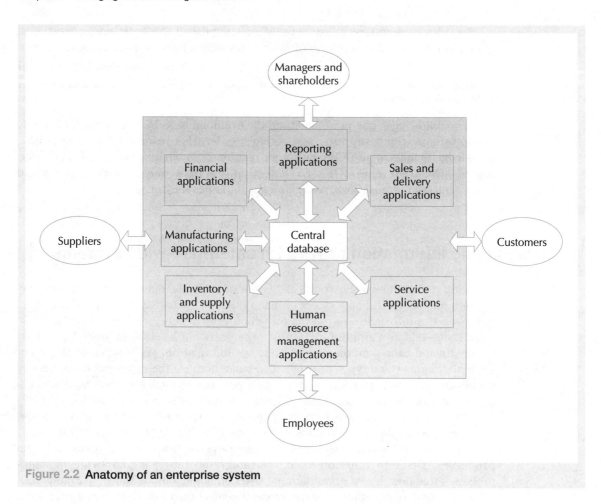

Figure 2.2 Anatomy of an enterprise system

Table 2.3 Examples of business processes supported by enterprise systems

Business function	Enterprise system
Financial	Accounts receivable and payable, asset accounting, cash management and forecasting, executive information system, general ledger, product-cost accounting, profitability analysis, profit-centre accounting, financial reporting
Human resources	Payroll, personnel planning, travel expenses, benefits accounting, applicant tracking
Operations and logistics	Inventory management, material requirements planning, materials management, plant maintenance, production planning, project management, purchasing, quality management, routing management, shipping, vendor evaluation
Sales and marketing	Order management, pricing, sales management, sales planning, billing.

vendor is called **configuration**. For example, financial software must be configured so that it knows which companies exist, which companies are subsidiaries of which other companies, the base currency of account for each subsidiary, the sales tax regimes for each subsidiary and so on. Adding non-standard features to the software by adding or changing program code is usually called **customisation**. Customisation can range from relatively simple changes, such as developing a new report, to major changes that require work on code in the software. Customisation is costly and risky, and new software releases may require recustomisation. Companies can avoid this by changing their processes to match those supported by the software – but the risk then is that the processes embedded in the system software may not suit the organisation. Changing an organisational process is itself difficult.

▧ Organisational and management issues of ERP systems

There is controversy about whether adopting an ERP system gives a competitive advantage (McKeen and Smith, 2003). A company may not benefit if using the generic models provided by standard ERP software prevents it from using unique business models that had given it a competitive edge. ERP systems promote centralised coordination and decision-making, which may not suit a particular firm. And some companies do not need the level of integration provided by enterprise systems:

> *Enterprise systems are basically generic solutions. The design reflects a series of assumptions about the way companies operate in general. Vendors of ES try to structure the systems to reflect best practices, but it is the vendor that is defining what 'best' means. Of course, some degree of ES customisation is possible, but major modifications are very expensive and impracticable. As a result, most companies installing ES will have to adapt or rework their processes to reach a fit with the system.* (Davenport, 1998, p. 125)

Another problem is inflexibility. Some analysts argue that ERP systems lock companies into rigid processes that make it hard, if not impossible, to adapt quickly to changes in the marketplace or in organisation structure (Hagel and Brown, 2001).

A study by Markus et al. (2000) shows that many ERP problems relate to a misfit between the system and the characteristics of the organisation. Enterprise systems are completely intertwined with corporate business processes and it may take years to implement them all. It is difficult to change integrated systems because a change in one part affects the other, so that the company may become inflexible and hard to change.

Koch (1999) claims that the average cost of an ERP system is US$15 million, or US$53,000 per user, including hardware, software, professional services and internal staff costs. While some companies plan for these costs, few build enough post-implementation costs into their budgets, and frequently underestimate training costs. ERP implementation should be viewed and managed as an organisational change process, rather than as the replacement of a piece of technology. It impacts strategy, structure, people, culture, decision-making and many other aspects of the company.

The following example illustrates some of these issues.

MIS in Practice   Nestlé struggles with enterprise systems

Nestlé is a food and pharmaceuticals company that operates all over the world. Traditionally it allowed local units to operate as they saw fit, taking into account local conditions and business cultures. The company had many purchasing systems and no information on how much business they did with each supplier: each factory made independent arrangements. Nestlé's management concluded that these local differences were inefficient and costly. They wanted to integrate the systems to act as a single entity, using its worldwide buying power to lower prices.

Managers therefore started a programme to standardise and coordinate its processes and information systems. The project team decided to instal SAP's financial, purchasing, sales and distribution modules throughout every Nestlé USA division. The new system would standardise and coordinate the company's information systems and processes.

A year after the project started, a stock market analyst in London doubted its success: 'It touches the corporate culture, which is decentralised, and tries to centralise it. That's risky. It's always a risk when you touch the corporate culture.' Jeri Dunn from Nestlé later agreed: at an American plant most of the key stakeholders failed to realise how much the project would change their business processes. Dunn said: 'They still thought it was just software.' A rebellion had taken place when the plant moved to install the manufacturing modules. The lower-level workers did not understand how to use the new system and did not understand the changes. Their only hope was to call the project help-desk, which received 300 calls a day. Staff turnover increased and no one seemed motivated to learn to use the system.

The project team stopped the project and removed the project leader. This person had put too much pressure on the project and the technology. By doing so the team had lost sight of the bigger picture.

Source: Laudon and Laudon (2004); Worthen, B. (2002) 'Nestlé's ERP odyssey', *CIO Magazine*, 15 May; Konicki, S. (2000) 'Nestlé taps SAP for e-business', *Information Week*, 26 June.

Chapter 4 discusses ERP systems further from a business process perspective.

CASE QUESTIONS 2.1

Read this section on enterprise systems as well as the Chapter Case (Siemens), the Nestlé example (this section) and Elf Atochem example in Chapter 4. Compare the descriptions of ERP use and implementation, listing the opportunities, advantages, disadvantages, limitations and pitfalls of such systems.

Summary

- ERP systems are software packages that enable the integration of transactions-oriented data and business processes throughout an organisation.

- Such systems have to be configured and can be customised to create a fit with the organisation. Organisational processes can also be adjusted to fit with the system.

- ERP implementation is an organisational change process, rather than the replacement of a piece of technology. It impacts strategy, structure, people, culture, decision-making and many other aspects of the company.

2.4 Knowledge management systems

Developments in information technology are of great interest to those who want to improve their organisation's ability to create and mobilise knowledge. Many businesses depend on the skill with which they are able to create and acquire knowledge and ensure that people use it throughout the organisation. Knowledge is vital to innovation and many see it as the primary source of wealth in modern economies. People in large organisations often believe that the knowledge they need to improve performance is available within the business – but that they cannot find it.

'Knowledge management' (KM) refers to attempts to improve the way organisations create, acquire, capture, store, share and use knowledge. This will usually relate to customers, markets, products, services and internal processes, but may also refer to knowledge about relevant developments in the external environment.

Managing knowledge is not new – the industrial revolution occurred when people applied new knowledge to manufacturing processes. What is new is the degree to which developments in IS make it easier for people to share data, information and knowledge irrespective of physical distance. This growing technological capacity has encouraged many managers to believe that implementing knowledge management or similar systems, to make better use of knowledge assets, will enhance performance. KM systems are a type of information system intended to support people as they create, store, transfer and use knowledge. Three common purposes are to:

- code and share best practices;
- create corporate knowledge directories; and
- create knowledge networks.

Table 2.4 illustrates how IS can potentially support each element of knowledge management – these subdivisions are of course arbitrary, and many systems will support several aspects of knowledge management.

Table 2.4 Knowledge management processes and the potential role of IS

Knowledge management processes	Knowledge creation	Knowledge storage/retrieval	Knowledge transfer	Knowledge application
Supporting information technologies	Data mining Learning tools	Electronic bulletin boards Knowledge repositories Databases	Discussion forums Knowledge directories	Expert systems Workflow systems
IT enables	Combining new sources of knowledge Just-in-time learning	Support of individual and organisational memory Inter-group knowledge access	More extensive internal network More communication channels Faster access to sources	Knowledge can be applied in many locations More rapid application of new knowledge through workflow automation
Platform technologies	Groupware and communication technologies Intranets and sometimes extranets			

Source: Based on Alavi and Leidner (2002), p. 125.

Echikson (2001) outlined how the oil company BP uses advanced information systems to enable staff in the huge global business (including those in recently acquired companies) to share and use information and knowledge. These include a web-based employee directory (an intranet) called 'Connect', which contains a home page for almost every BP employee. Clicking on someone's name brings up a picture, contact details, interests (useful for breaking the ice between people who have not met) and areas of expertise. When a manager in a BP business needed to translate their safety video into French, he used Connect to identify French-speaking employees who could do the work, rather than an external translation service. At the core of the business, decisions on where to drill are now informed by an Internet system that brings geological data to one of several high-tech facilities. Engineers view the images and make decisions in hours that used to take weeks – and help reduce the danger of expensive drilling mistakes.

It is important to recall the distinctions made in Chapter 1 about data, information and knowledge – in which we referred to knowledge as 'the expertise, understanding and experience that comes from learning' (p. 9). Many systems that people refer to as 'knowledge' management systems appear on closer examination to deal with data and information, rather than knowledge. While computer-based systems are effective at dealing with (structured) data and information, they are much less effective at dealing with (unstructured) knowledge. As Hinds and Pfeffer (2003) observe,

> systems [to facilitate the sharing of expertise] generally capture information or data, *rather than* knowledge or expertise. *Information and information systems are extremely useful but do not replace expertise or the learning that takes place through interpersonal contact.* (p. 21)

Nonaka and Takeuchi (1995) distinguish explicit from tacit knowledge. Explicit knowledge is that which people have codified, structured, perhaps written down –

MIS in Practice   Buckman Labs – successful knowledge management

Buckman Labs is a science-based company, operating around the world. The founder realised that they needed to become more effective in managing the knowledge of their 1,300 scientific staff. The company has steadily developed systems which connect codified databases around the world – containing information on current global best-practice methods, ideas and current problems. This enables scientists throughout the company to keep in touch with each other and to share knowledge electronically amongst themselves and with customers. 'This single knowledge network aims to encompass all of the company's knowledge and experience, empowering Buckman representatives to focus all of their company's capabilities on customer challenges' (p. 77).

A notable feature of the company's approach has been the extent to which it has supported technological innovation with organisational change. Initial attempts at knowledge-sharing were unsuccessful, with little activity on the system. Managers then instituted a series of changes to encourage greater use. These included producing weekly statistics showing which staff had used the system. Non-users were penalised, frequent contributors rewarded. Processes were also changed to ensure the immediate capture of information during projects.

Source: Pan (1999).

Table 2.5 **Two views of the knowledge management process**

Cognitive model	Community model
Knowledge is equated to objectively defined concepts and facts	Knowledge is socially constructed and based on experience
Knowledge is transferred through text, and information systems have a crucial role	Knowledge is transferred through participation in social networks including occupational groups and teams
Gains from KM include the recycling of knowledge and the standardisation of systems	Gains from KM include greater awareness of internal and external sources of knowledge
The primary function of KM is to codify and capture knowledge	The primary function of KM is to encourage knowledge-sharing between groups and individuals
The dominant metaphor is human memory	The dominant metaphor is the human community
The critical success factor is technology	The critical success factor is trust

Source: Scarborough and Swan (1999).

formulae, instructions, historical trends and so on. Knowledge of this form can be identified, extracted and passed on to other users. Tacit knowledge is inherent in individuals or groups, and is not written down – it is a sense about the way to do things, how to relate to each other and to situations. Because it is essentially personal and specific to the context it will often be the most useful kind of knowledge – yet it is much harder to transmit by even the most sophisticated technology.

This point has been developed by Scarbrough and Swan (1999) who argue that while technological systems deal well with data and information (explicit knowledge), tacit knowledge cannot simply be processed and passed around. Rather, it is continuously created and recreated as people work together on common problems. As they do so, interacting with each other and their work, they create new knowledge and shared understandings that are unique to that situation. They propose that while a 'cognitive' model of knowledge management is appropriate for dealing with explicit knowledge, a 'community' model is a more suitable perspective from which to consider tacit knowledge. Table 2.5 contrasts these features.

Organisational and management issues of KM systems

Presenting the community model alongside the cognitive model helps to identify the issues in the success or failure of knowledge management projects. For example, it suggests that

> *whilst it might be relatively easy to share knowledge across a group that is homogenous, it is extremely difficult to share knowledge where the group is heterogeneous. Yet it is precisely the sharing of knowledge across functional or organisational boundaries . . . that is seen as the key to the effective exploitation of knowledge.* (Scarborough and Swan, 1999, p. 11)

Systems with a technical, cognitive perspective typically fail to take account of structures and cultures that represent people's beliefs and values about what needs to be done, what should be rewarded and so on. They are likely to inhibit people from sharing knowledge in the way those who designed the system intended.

Emerging technical possibilities provide an infrastructure that enables global access to data, information and knowledge. KM tools can be valuable in exploiting knowledge in the form of experience of previous projects, technical discoveries or useful techniques. But simply reusing existing knowledge may do less for business performance than using it to create new knowledge that is appropriate for the situation. This creative process depends more on human interaction in a supportive context than on technology alone. Since most managers receive too much information it does not follow that pushing more information across such boundaries will improve performance. That depends not just on knowledge, but also on the insight and judgement to be able to apply that knowledge – which cannot be provided by an information system (Walsham, 2001, 2002).

Gupta and Govindarajan (2000) observed that

> *effective knowledge management depends not merely on information technology platforms but . . . on the social ecology of an organisation – the social system in which people operate [made up of] culture, structure, information systems, reward systems, processes, people and leadership.* (p. 72)

People will be more likely to use a knowledge management system if the culture recognises and rewards the benefits of sharing knowledge. And, for the more tacit forms of knowledge, a focus on encouraging effective communities of practice will be more effective than a focus on technology. We return to these issues in Chapters 6 and 8.

Activity 2.3 What knowledge do you need for a task?

Identify for an employee (perhaps yourself) what knowledge is created, acquired, captured, shared and used while doing a particular task.

Identify examples of explicit and tacit knowledge in this example.

Discuss to what extent a computerised knowledge system could be useful in managing that knowledge.

Discuss also whether such a system would be in your interests or in the interests of the organisation.

Summary

- Knowledge systems are directed to improving practices of organisations to create, acquire, capture, store, share and use knowledge.
- Knowledge management systems may have different forms and applications, such as data mining, bulletin boards, expert systems and workflow systems.
- Information systems can capture explicit knowledge quite easily, but tacit knowledge cannot simply be processed and passed around.
- Implementing knowledge systems is related to a range of organisational issues, including the homogeneity of the group, the structure and culture of the organisation and the objectives of the system.

2.5 Managing customer-related processes with CRM

It is more expensive to attract new customers than to retain existing ones, so many companies now try to use the power of IS to improve the way they manage their relationship with profitable customers. Marketing staff aim both to retain these customers and to earn more revenue from them.

Customer relationship management (CRM) systems are intended to build and sustain long-term business with customers. They represent a move from mass markets and mass production to customisation and focused production. CRM software tries to align business processes with customer strategies to recruit, satisfy and retain profitable customers (Rigby et al., 2002). Figure 2.3 shows three approaches to customers. The first treats all customers in the same way by sending impersonal messages in one direction. The second sends one-directional but different messages to customers, depending on their profile. The third personalises the messages, which may lead to real interaction, in the hope of increasing customer loyalty.

In many businesses the key to increasing profitability is to focus on recruiting and retaining high lifetime value customers. So the promise of CRM is to:

- gather customer data swiftly;
- identify and capture valuable customers while discouraging less valuable ones;
- increase customer loyalty and retention by providing customised products;
- reduce costs of serving customers;
- make it easier to acquire similar customers.

CRM systems consolidate customer data from many sources and try to answer questions such as:

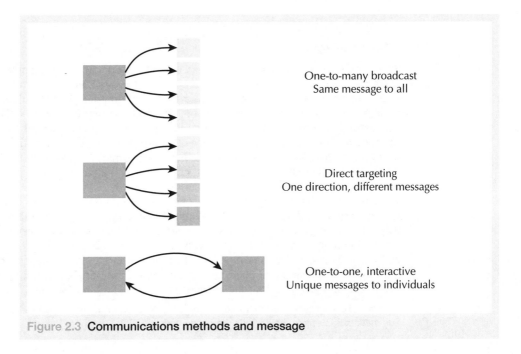

One-to-many broadcast
Same message to all

Direct targeting
One direction, different messages

One-to-one, interactive
Unique messages to individuals

Figure 2.3 **Communications methods and message**

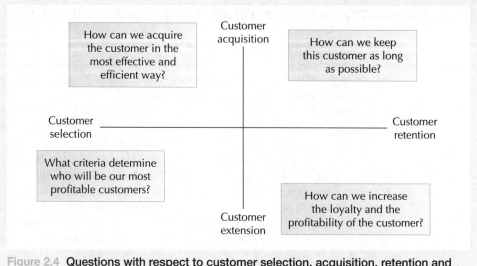

Figure 2.4 **Questions with respect to customer selection, acquisition, retention and extension**

- Who are our most loyal customers?
- Who are our most profitable customers?
- What do these profitable customers want to buy?

Firms can use these answers in their policy of customer selection, acquisition, retention and extension, as shown in Figure 2.4.

MIS in Practice   **Royal Bank of Canada**

'Gone are the days where we had mass buckets of customers that would receive the same treatment or same offer on a monthly basis,' says Shauneen Bruder, The Royal Bank of Canada's senior vice-president for North America. Instead of sending customers the same marketing information, Royal Bank has developed a CRM system for customer segmentation that tailors messages to very small groups of people and offers them products, services and prices that are likely to appeal to them. Royal Bank's customer segmentation is so effective that it can achieve a response rate as high as 30 per cent to its marketing campaigns, compared with an average of 3 per cent for the banking industry.

By querying the database, analysts can identify customers based on the products they might buy and the likelihood they might leave the bank. Clues about this include the customer's bank balance (recently being kept low), credit card payments (also reduced in amount and paid later than in the past) and deposits (which have become sporadic). These signs may highlight a profitable customer preparing to switch to another bank. Having identified such a customer, the bank's marketing department might tailor a package of banking services specifically for the customer.

Source: 'Slices of life', *CIO Magazine*, 15 August 2000; Alan Radding, 'Analyze your customers', *Datamation*, 25 September 2000; Laudon and Laudon (2004).

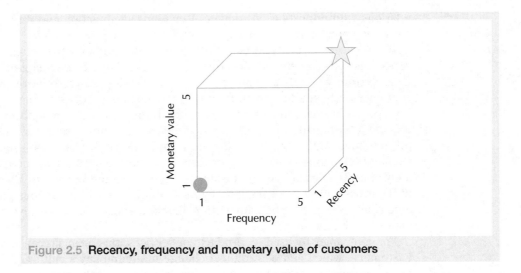

Figure 2.5 **Recency, frequency and monetary value of customers**

A common objective for a CRM system is to increase the lifetime value of customers, as measured by recency, frequency and monetary value – the RFM model. This model is based on three empirically based principles:

- customers who purchased recently are more likely to buy again compared with customers who have not purchased in a while;

- customers who purchase frequently are more likely to buy again compared with customers who have made just one or two purchases;

- customers who spend the most money in total are more likely to buy again.

Using this approach, each customer is assigned an RFM score based on recency, frequency and monetary value. Customers with high scores are usually most profitable, the most likely to purchase again and the most highly responsive to promotions. Using the RFM scores, companies can determine the lifetime value of a customer – the expected profit a customer will contribute to a company as long as the customer remains a customer. Once a company knows who their most valuable customers are, they can concentrate their efforts on satisfying those customers. Figure 2.5 illustrates the model.

Organisational and management issues of CRM systems

CRM projects result in high failure rates. A study by the Gartner group found that 55 per cent of all CRM projects fail (*www.Gartner.com*). The CRM forum claims that half of US implementations and more than 80 per cent of European implementations are considered failures (CRM-forum, 2002). In Bains' survey of management tools, CRM ranked third from bottom in terms of users' satisfaction (Bains, 2001). CRM initiatives not only fail to deliver profitable growth but can also damage long-standing customer relationships, according to a survey of 451 senior executives (Rigby et al., 2002). According to CRM-forum, only 4 per cent are software problems and 1 per cent bad advice; 87 per cent pinned failure of CRM programmes on the lack of adequate change management.

Implementing successful CRM depends more on strategy than on technology. Without a clear customer strategy a CRM system lacks direction and may disrupt relations with important customers. A customer acquisition and retention strategy has to be implemented and a segmentation analysis has to be made.

If a customer strategy is established, other dimensions, such as business processes, other systems, structure and people, have to be adapted to make the CRM system work. If a company wants to develop better relationships with its customers it needs first to rethink the key business processes that relate to customers, from customer service to order fulfilment. Such adaptations may also include job descriptions, performance measures, compensation systems, training programmes and so on. If consumers have a choice of channels – such as e-mail, web and telephone – marketing, sales and service can no longer be treated separately. A customer may place an order by phone, use the website to check the status of the order and send a complaint by mail. Multi-channel interactions pose considerable challenges if the company is to maintain a single comprehensive and real-time view of each customer.

For companies focused on products or services, this means recentring around the customer – which can be a radical change in a company's culture. All employees, but especially those in marketing, sales, service and other customer contact functions, have to think in a customer-oriented way. For example, in some call centres, employees have been measured and rewarded on how fast they resolved a customer's problem. This reflected management thinking that shorter telephone calls lowered costs. A CRM approach would concentrate efforts on customer satisfaction per call, not just call handling efficiency (Mahieu, 2002).

An important reason for the failure of CRM projects lies in narrow and poor change management. Much time, effort and money have to be spent exclusively on managing the organisational issues. It is a struggle to move from a conventional customer strategy to a CRM philosophy. CRM projects are cross-function undertakings: IT, marketing and production have to operate at the same wavelength, yet they have different orientations and cultures. Successful CRM depends on coordinated actions by all departments within a company rather than being driven by a single department.

Summary

- CRM systems are customer-facing systems for customer care and management supporting a CRM philosophy.

- CRM is primarily a customer-centric philosophy, and can be perceived as a move from mass market and industrial production to customisation and focused production.

- CRM can only be implemented successfully by managing a range of organisational issues, including establishing a strategy on which customers should be treated in particular ways. It also depends on adapting business processes, structure and skills.

2.6 Using IS beyond organisational borders

Networked information systems allow companies to coordinate joint processes with other organisations across great distances. Transactions such as payments and orders can be exchanged electronically, thereby reducing the cost of obtaining products and services. Organisations can share all sorts of business data, such as catalogues or mail messages, through networks (Laudon and Laudon, 2004). Many such systems use web technology, with labels such as extra-organisational systems, e-commerce systems, e-business systems and supply chain management systems. Since these systems cross organisational borders we refer to them as inter-organisational systems (IOS).

These inter-organisational systems can create new efficiencies and new relationships between an organisation and its customers, suppliers and business partners, redefining organisational boundaries. Firms are using these systems to work jointly with suppliers and other business partners on product design and development, and on scheduling the flow of work in manufacturing, procurement and distribution. 'Streamlining cross-company processes is the next great frontier for reducing costs, enhancing quality, and speeding operations' (Hammer, 2001, p. 84). These new levels of inter-firm collaboration and coordination can lead to higher levels of efficiency, value to customers and competitive advantage. This means that systems that transcend organisational borders may be an opportunity for some organisations but a threat for others.

IOS includes two commonly used terms:

▪ **E-commerce**, the process of selling a product or service to the customer (whether a retail consumer or another business) over the Internet; and

▪ **E-business**, the integration, through the Internet, of all an organisation's processes, from its suppliers through to its customers.

Figure 2.6 shows how the systems within a company can be linked with external parties by electronic networks.

Many businesses have used the Internet as an information system to support their distribution processes. Such **business-to-consumer** (B2C) systems offer products,

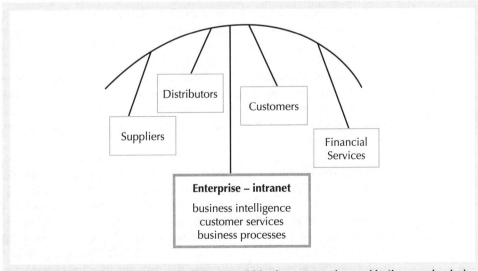

Figure 2.6 E-business: electronic linkages within the companies and in the supply chain

especially banking, publications, software, music or tickets to individual retail customers. Another way of using the Internet is to change the production system. Some companies use a website to manage information about sales, capacity, inventory, payment and so on – and to exchange that information with their suppliers or business customers. They use such **business-to-business** (B2B) systems to connect electronically all the links in their supply chain, so creating an integrated process to meet customer needs (Boddy and Boonstra, 2000).

The simplest IOS applications provide **information**, also called 'web presence'. In B2C applications, customers can view product or other information on a company website. In B2B, business customers can place their requirements on the Internet, inviting potential suppliers to seek more information. Conversely, suppliers can use their website to show customers what they can offer. Internet marketplaces are developing in which groups of suppliers in the same industry operate a collective website, making it easier for potential customers to compare terms through a single portal, providing links to many other sites (Hackbarth and Kettinger, 2000).

A further form of Internet use is for **interaction**. Customers or suppliers enter information and questions about (for example) offers and prices. The system then uses the customer information, such as preferred dates and times of travel, to show availability and costs. In B2B applications, a buyer can see a supplier's offer and ask further questions about optional features, volumes or delivery.

A third use is for **transactions**, when customers buy goods and services through a supplier's website. Conversely a supplier who sees a purchasing requirement from a business (perhaps expressed as a purchase order on the website) can agree electronically to meet the order. The whole transaction, from accessing information through ordering, delivery (in some cases) and payment, can take place electronically.

The fourth use is **integration** when it links its own information systems and (within limits) links them in turn to customers and suppliers. Dell Computing is a familiar example though there are many others. As customers decide the configuration of their computer and place an order, this information moves to the systems that control Dell's internal processes and those of its suppliers.

Finally, a company achieves **transformation** when it uses IOS to transform its internal operations as well as the value chain. It may integrate its business processes with those of suppliers and customers or use the Internet to reach the customer in more direct ways. Figure 2.7 shows these strges.

The relationship between a company and its channel partners can be changed by the Internet or by other applications of inter-organisational systems, because electronic networks can help to bypass channel partners, also called **disintermediation**. Figure 2.8 shows how a manufacturer and a wholesaler can bypass other partners and reach customers directly.

The benefits of disintermediation are that transaction costs are reduced and that it enables direct contact with customers. This also makes it possible to increase the reach of companies, for example from a local presence to a national or international presence. On the other hand, the Internet also creates the possibilities for parties to reintermediate. **Reintermediation** is the creation of new intermediaries between customers and suppliers by providing (new) services such as supplier search and product evaluation (Chaffey, 2002). Portals that help customers to find the best price and offer given specific needs are examples of electronic reintermediators. The portal performs price evaluation and helps users to link automatically to suppliers.

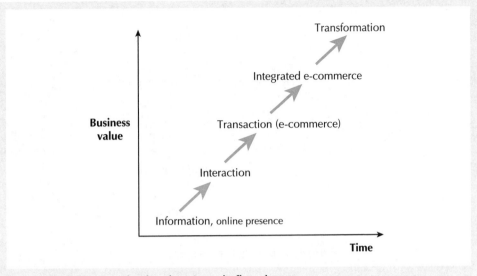

Figure 2.7 **Inter-organisational systems in five phases**

MIS in Practice   **IOS applications at IBM**

IBM aims to become the premier e-business company in the information technology industry, and also to be recognised as a leading Internet business regardless of industry. As well as providing goods and services to other Internet firms, the company uses the Internet for its own activities:

- **information** – the company website gives information about the company, including its products, employment opportunities and financial performance;

- **interaction** – prospective online purchasers can select options and configurations for their chosen machine, and receive information on price and delivery. The company places current purchase orders for suppliers on a secure Internet website to which suppliers respond;

- **transaction** – customers can order their computer or other products online; suppliers can accept orders and send invoices online;

- **integration** – the production planning system takes customer orders and automatically translates them into the components required in the following period. This passes electronically to a buyer, who in turn releases it to the Internet site. Contracted suppliers access this, and accept or decline the component order. After delivering the physical goods, the supplier converts the original electronic purchase order into an electronic invoice, which passes to IBM for electronic payment.

Source: Interviews with company managers and public documents.

Such purely Internet-based reintermediators are also called **infomediaries**. Examples of infomediaries are: search engines (e.g. Yahoo! and Altavista), malls (e.g. Barnes and Noble), virtual resellers (e.g. Amazon), financial intermediaries, forums and evaluators (who act as reviewers to provide comparisons).

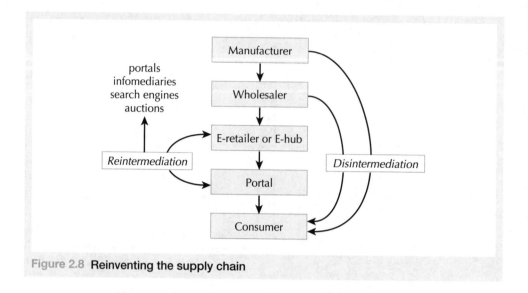

Figure 2.8 Reinventing the supply chain

Organisational and management issues of inter-organisational systems

Barua et al. (2001) and Feeny (2001) raise the question of how to allocate organisational resources for e-business by highlighting specific areas of opportunity. They emphasise that the existing products or services and existing customers must not be the only central points of orientation, and suggest that the Internet and the use of IOS may open up opportunities to reach new customers and to introduce new products or services. Straub and Kleinn (2001) build on these ideas by stating that e-commerce can have three effects:

- 1st order – towards reducing costs and increasing productivity;
- 2nd order – towards pursuing new markets and improving services;
- 3rd order – radical transformations affecting goods and services, targeting and distribution.

Porter (2001) argues that implementing IOS and Internet applications is not a substitute for strategy. He states that when all companies have embraced the Internet, the Internet itself will be neutralised as a source of advantage; companies will not survive without them, but they will not gain any advantage from them. So he emphasises that real competitive advantage comes from traditional and sustained strengths such as unique products, excellent operational activities, product knowledge and relationships. IOS should be used by companies to strengthen and 'fortify' those advantages.

A major concern of companies moving to use IOS has been to ensure they can handle the associated physical processes. These include handling orders, arranging shipment, receiving payment and dealing with after-sales service. This gives an advantage to traditional retailers who can support their websites with existing fulfilment processes. Given the negative effects of failure once processes are supported by IOS, it seems advisable to delay connecting systems to the IOS until robust and repeatable processes are in place.

Another important issue is the change management associated with e-business. The transformation to e-business affects many processes and people. The case below illustrates how unexpected problems may arise.

MIS in Practice   E-business at ABN-Amro

ABN-Amro (*www.abnamro.nl*) is a prominent international bank, its origins going back to 1824. It ranks eighth in Europe and seventeenth in the world with over 3,400 branches in more than 60 countries.

At the HQ and main offices the bank employs financial staff who offer very specialised services to companies. The bank also offers most standard financial services to the general public, like bank accounts, mortgages, insurance, loans and stock trading. Traditionally, this bank had many branches, including some in small villages. The commercial staff had personal contact with the more profitable customers and maintained these relationships in a personal way. Now they are reorganising and reducing their branches in order to make these offices more cost-effective. Because of this, the bank expects that its customers will use the Internet and call centres to obtain standard services.

ABN-Amro faces a number of problems during its transition to online banking:

- Some, mainly well-educated customers appreciate online banking and the services of the centralised call centres, but others expect a more personalised service. A key quality of ABN-Amro is that it has always been able to provide personalised and specialised services to companies and wealthy individuals.

- ABN-Amro already offers a wide range of services over the Internet, but many customers are reluctant to use them. The less profitable customers in particular use the services at the branches more than the bank would like.

- Customer retention has gone down significantly since the reorganisation of branches and the introduction of online banking. The bank targets companies and wealthy individuals, but since these customers use the Internet, they can switch easily to other providers, especially to new single-channel Internet entrants who offer just a few products with low costs and low prices. Since the deregulation of financial services, and the advent of the euro, many new foreign entrants have entered the market with great ease.

- The bank does not know enough about customers to offer them a correctly targeted service. Since many customers are shopping from one financial service provider to another, customer information is dispersed among competitors. This makes it difficult to focus on potentially profitable customers.

- Many employees feel quite unhappy about their employer. Many staff have been laid off, and others have had to move to other branches, losing their contacts with customers and colleagues. Performance indicators are used to monitor the short-term performance of staff; employees who do not meet these criteria may be penalised by higher management. These problems affect the atmosphere at the bank.

- Back-office activities were decentralised in the past, but the bank is concentrating this work at a single processing centre in each country. Another option is to outsource the processing operation completely to a service provider. This change has created a lot of confusion among people who are now working at regional processing centres.

Kanter (2001) argues that the move to e-business for established companies involves a deep change. She found that top management absence, shortsightedness of markerting people and other internal barriers are common obstacles. She quotes an executive:

We have internal opposition from parts of the organisation that are threatened by the Internet. The sales force is obviously not keen on deploying the Internet with channel partners, which means reduced sales to them. (p. 92)

Based on interviews with more than 80 companies on their move to e-business, her research provides 'deadly mistakes' as well as some lessons. These include:

- Create experiments and act simply and quickly to convert the sceptics.
- Create dedicated teams and give them space and autonomy. Sponsor them from the wider organisation.
- Recognise that e-business requires systemic changes in many ways of working.

CASE QUESTIONS 2.2

Review the Siemens case at the beginning of this chapter and discuss the following issues:

What are the main elements of the e-strategy plan?

How are these elements related to each other?

What are the main reasons and possible benefits implementating this plan?

What are the organisational consequences of this plan?

What does it mean for external stakeholders of Siemens?

What may this plan mean for the role and function of Siemens in the long run?

Summary

- A major management issue is the extent to which the Internet provides opportunities to improve or expand the existing business, while at the same time threatening that business by opening it to new competitors.
- When management has decided to use the Internet to develop e-commerce or e-business, strategies have to be developed as to how this will be realised. Such a strategy will have external elements (e.g. customers, suppliers, competitors) and internal elements (e.g. how to redesign the business process and the organisational structure) to support this new strategy.

Activity 2.4 A research project

If you have the opportunity in an assignment or a project, you may be able to identify:

- current main information systems used for the operational processes;
- trends and possible future changes with respect to IS use;
- the familiarity with and the relevance of ERP systems, knowledge management systems, CRM systems and inter-organisational systems.

You can obtain this information by interviewing different people, including users, managers and IS staff. Ask also about the degree of satisfaction with current IT use and familiarity with new IT and change.

Conclusions

Organisations have always depended on information systems to help conduct their business. Technological developments have greatly increased this dependence, as applications have moved from essentially background tasks to include foreground, customer-centred tasks. Most organisations depend heavily on computer-based information systems. In many, such systems are the basis of their business. Equally, most managers depend on accurate and timely information. We have outlined several perspectives on information systems and shown how some modern technological developments have increased the power and versatility of information systems.

The discussion has also emphasised that, while technology is central to modern information systems, it is only part of the story. Figure 1.3 showed that information systems include people and procedures as well as technology. Throughout the chapter we have shown that each perspective on information systems raises wider management and organisational issues. Smaller and more portable systems encourage changes in working arrangements. Advances in communication technology erode boundaries between functions and organisations. The capacity of the new technologies is such that they raise major questions of strategy – about the kind of business that a company is in (Chapter 3). Although the cost of the basic technology is falling, the cost of implementing new systems continues to rise. How can managers decide if the investment is worth the cost (Chapter 5)?

Looking inward, modern systems encourage companies to consider redesigning the processes through which they deliver their strategies (Chapter 4), with significant implications for the human side of organisations (Chapter 8). There are structural questions too – since information can flow more freely, it breaks down established boundaries (Chapter 6) and raises questions about the place of the information systems function itself in the organisation (Chapter 7). Finally, in Chapters 9 and 10 we examine many of the implementation issues that people have to manage in projects and programmes.

CHAPTER QUESTIONS

1. Which functions of information systems are becoming more important? Explain your answer by giving examples.

2. Information systems are increasing their reach. What are the reasons for this and what are the consequences for businesses?

3. What are the advantages and disadvantages of local systems?

4. What are the main motives for organisations in implementing knowledge systems, enterprise systems, customer relationship management systems and inter-organisational systems?

5. What are the limitations and possible pitfalls of knowledge systems, enterprise systems, customer relationship management systems and inter-organisational systems?

Further reading

Alavi, M. and Leidner, D.E. (2002), 'Knowledge management and knowledge management systems: conceptual foundatons and research issues', *MIS Quarterly*, **25**(1) 107–36. Accessible introduction to the topic from an IS perspective.

Chaffey, D. (2002) *E-business and E-commerce Management*, Financial Times/Prentice Hall, Harlow. Uses a wide range of informative case studies to cover the management issues raised by the Internet.

Davenport, T.H. (1998) 'Putting the enterprise into the enterprise system', *Harvard Business Review*, **76**(4), 121–32. Worthwhile treatment of the main management issues of ERP systems.

Davenport, T.H. and Prusak, L. (1998) *Working Knowledge*, Harvard Business School Press, Boston. Useful overview of knowledge management with many practical examples, as well as a review of the strengths and limitations of such systems.

Gartner Group website contains regular updates of developments in IS applications discussed in this chapter. Visit it at *www.crm-forum.com*.

Rigby, D.K., Reichheld, F.F. and Schefter, P. (2002), 'Avoid the four perils of CRM', *Harvard Business Review*, **80**(2), 101–9. Discusses pros and cons of CRM and the main pitfalls of relationship management systems.

References

Alavi, M. and Leidner, D.E. (2002) 'Knowledge management and knowledge management system: conceptual foundations and research issues', *MIS Quarterly*, **25**(1), 107–36.

Bains, J.W. (2001) *Survey on Management Tools*, KPMG, London.

Balachandra, R. (2000) 'An expert system for new product development', *Industrial Management and Data Systems*, **100**(7), 317–28.

Barua, A., Konana, P., Whinston, A. and Yin, F. (2001) 'E-business operations: driving e-business excellence', *Sloan Management Review*, **43**(1), 36–44.

Boddy, D. and Boonstra, A. (2000) 'Doing business on the Internet: managing the organisational issues', *Journal of General Management*, **26**(1), 18–35.

Chaffey, D. (2002) *E-business and E-commerce Management*, Financial Times/Prentice Hall, Harlow.

Davenport, T.H. (1998) 'Putting the enterprise into the enterprise system', *Harvard Business Review*, **76**(4), 121–32.

Echikson, W. (2001) 'When oil gets connected', *Business Week e-biz*, pp. 19–22.

Feeny, D. (2001) 'Making business sense of the e-opportunity', *Sloan Management Review*, **43**(1), 41–51.

Flores, B.E. and Pearce, S.L. (2000) 'The use of an expert system in the M3 competition', *International Journal of Forecasting*, **16**(4), 485–93.

Gupta, A.K. and Govindarajan, V. (2000) 'Knowledge management's social dimension: lessons from Nucor Steel', *Sloan Management Review*, **42**(1), 71–80.

Hackbarth, G. and Kettinger, W. (2000) 'Building an e-business strategy', *Information Systems Management*, Summer, 78–93.

Hagel, J. and Brown, J.S. (2001) 'Your next IT strategy', *Harvard Business Review*, **79**(10), 105–13.

Hammer, M. (2001) 'The superefficient company', *Harvard Business Review*, **79**(9), 82–91.

Hinds, P.J. and Pfeffer, J. (2003) 'Why organizations don't "know what they know": cognitive and motivational factors affecting the transfer of expertise', in M.S. Ackerman, P. Volkmar and V. Wulf (eds), *Sharing Expertise: Beyond Knowledge Management*, MIT Press, Cambridge, Mass.

Hirschheim, R. and Klein, H.K. (1989) 'Four paradigms of information systems development', *Communications of the ACM*, **32**(10), 1199–214.

Kanter, R.M. (2001) 'The ten deadly mistakes of wanna dots', *Harvard Business Review*, **79**(1), 91–100.

Koch, C. (1999) 'ERP-Quake!', *CIO: The Magazine for Information Executives*, **13**(2), 38–9.

Laudon, K.C. and Laudon, J.P. (2004) *Management Information Systems: Managing the Digital Firm*, 8th edn, Prentice Hall, Upper Saddle River, NJ.

McCauly, N. and Ala, M. (1992) 'The use of expert systems in the health care industry', *Information and Management*, **22**(3), 227–35.

McKeen, J.D. and Smith, H.A. (2003) *Making IT Happen: Critical Issues in IT Management*, Wiley, Chichester.

Mahieu, Y. (2002), *Note on Customer Relationship Management*, Ivey Management Services, London, Ontario.

Markus, M.L. (1984) *Systems in Organizations*, Pitman, London.

Markus, M.L., Axline, S., Petrie, D. and Tanis, C. (2000) 'Learning from adopters' experiences with ERP: problems encountered and success achieved', *Journal of Information Technology*, **15**(4), 245–66.

Nonaka, I. and Takeuchi, N. (1995) *The Knowledge-creating Company*, Oxford University Press, Oxford.

Pan, S.L. (1999) 'Knowledge management at Buckman Laboratories', in H. Scarbrough and J. Swan (eds), *Case Studies in Knowledge Management*, IPD, London.

Porter, M.E. (2001) 'Strategy and the Internet', *Harvard Business Review*, **79**(2), 63–78.

Rigby, D.K., Reichheld, F.F. and Schefter, P. (2002) 'Avoid the four perils of CRM', *Harvard Business Review*, **80**(2), 101–9.

Scarbrough, H. and Swan, J. (eds) (1999) *Case Studies in Knowledge Management*, IPD, London.

Straub, D. and Klein, R. (2001) 'E-competitive transformations', *Business Horizons*, **44**(3), 3–12.

Turoff, M., Hiltz, S.R., Bahgat, A.N.F. and Rana, A.R. (1993) Distributed group support systems, *MIS Quarterly*, **17**(4), 399–417.

Walsham, G. (2001) 'Knowledge management: the benefits and limitations of computer systems', *European Management Journal*, **19**(6), 599–608.

Walsham, G. (2002) 'Knowledge management and – as organizational communication – what knowledge management Systems Deliver?', *Management Communication Quarterly*, **16**(7), 267–73.

PART 2

IS and strategy

This part deals with issues of strategy, evaluation and process redesign. Chapter 3 examines the interaction between strategy and information systems. The discussion is based on established models of the strategy development process. The chapter also considers the concept of strategic alignment, and concludes with an analysis of some of the practical complexities of forming an information system strategy.

The focus of Chapter 4 is on how companies have used computer-based systems to modify their business processes. Established functional boundaries often add cost and delay to the task of delivering products and services. Modern systems make it possible for people to break down these boundaries by passing information electronically to those who need it, irrespective of their location or affiliation. However, the task is complex and depends on a good understanding of different approaches to business process redesign and being aware of organisational interactions.

Chapter 5 considers an issue of concern to many senior managers: how to evaluate the benefit of investing in information systems. The dilemma which all managers face is that, while they can usually predict the costs of an information system, they are much less certain about the benefits. The chapter outlines briefly the principles, and the weaknesses, of conventional investment appraisal methods. It then introduces some alternative methods that give more weight to non-financial criteria.

CHAPTER 3

Using information systems to reinvent strategy

Learning objectives

By the end of your work on this topic you should be able to:

- Describe and explain the possible strategic role of information systems

- Analyse how information systems can affect an industry and relate this to company strategy

- Explain different ways of using information systems for strategic advantage, and assess the implications

- Outline how IS can play different roles in different organisations

- Use models to analyse the possible strategic advantage of IS to a business

- Explain the risks of using IS strategically

- Explain the possible roles of the Internet, and describe the dimensions of an Internet strategy

The Aalsmeer Flower Auction

Aalsmeer Flower Auction offers globally active growers, wholesalers and exporters a central marketplace for the trading of flowers and plants. It gives them access to a range of marketing channels, and financial, information, storage and logistics facilities. Within the floricultural value chain, growers are the initial suppliers. Demand comes from exporters, importers, wholesalers, cash and carry stores and retailers. Within this chain, auctions play a mediating role between suppliers and buyers – they bring together supply and demand and so determine prices. These sometimes establish world prices, since many parties throughout the world use them as price indicators. Another role of the auction is that it increases efficiency by breaking large consignments from growers into smaller amounts for buyers.

This chain was originally dominated by growers who were able to sell what they produced in a steadily growing market. The auction was able to determine how to conduct business, and took a fairly passive role.

Three developments began to threaten that comfortable position:

1. The emergence of alternative, electronically driven flower markets.

2. The auction met the needs of growers, not those of retailers. To satisfy changing consumer tastes the retailers asked for fresher products, more varieties, smaller quantities and multiple deliveries each week. They felt that demand should have more influence on supply.

3. Mergers and acquisitions among retailers increased their size and power. At the same time growers became more professional, which led to a more formal way of doing business and interest in new, perhaps electronic, ways of selling.

The board of the Aalsmeer Flower Auction felt that they had to react to these changes if the business was to survive. This included the possibility of using electronic networks to support its business processes and to connect with suppliers and buyers. Initial objectives of these e-business activities were to enable innovation, redefine the value chain, reduce transaction costs, strengthen the link with wholesalers and retailers and to increase market share.

The director of commercial affairs, John Stevens, was responsible for developing e-business applications. In 1997, he formed a group of ten employees with backgrounds in IT, marketing and logistics and led by Marianne Groothuis from marketing. To keep this group open-minded, creative and ambitious, they worked in a building outside the auction complex. Within its own atmosphere and in relative autonomy, this 'e-selling' group developed e-business applications.

This case shows how changes in the external environment, including changing customer needs, actions of competitors and new technologies, raise questions to organisations of how to respond strategically and how new strategies should be translated into new information systems. This chapter addresses this relation between strategy and IS use. The IS response of the company will be set out throughout the chapter.

Introduction

Developments in technology and greater competition mean that managers see information systems as a matter of strategic importance to their organisation. They no longer buy information systems just to provide background administrative support. That role remains important, but many managers also consider information systems alongside the broader strategy of the organisation. This strategic use of information systems (Earl, 2002; Applegate et al., 2003) is a development of great significance to the future of organisations and their management.

In seeing IS in this way, managers look beyond technological issues. They consider what the computer-based systems becoming available will mean for the organisation and its customers. They focus not on technical features, but on what matters to their customers. They look beyond short-term matters to longer-term questions such as whether they can use an information systems investment to:

- serve customers in a better way;
- reduce costs and work more efficiently;
- differentiate products or services;
- offer new or better products or services;
- lock in suppliers or buyers;
- raise barriers to market entrants;
- improve employee satisfaction.

Considering these strategic questions helps managers to avoid being driven by fashion. The technical possibilities are unlimited, and without a clear sense of strategy managers can be tempted to demand the newest technology. With a sense of strategic direction they can discuss IS firmly within that framework. The Aalsmeer Flower Auction case study illustrates how computer-based systems can help managers realise objectives that improve competitiveness and respond to environmental changes.

The chapter begins with the strategy development process, and shows how managers have used IS to change the way they compete. We then examine the strategic alignment concept – the case for seeking a fit between the nature of a company and its information system. That leads to an analysis of the way companies can use the Internet to support, or change, their strategy. Finally, the chapter considers the practicalities of formulating an information strategy. The overall aim is to help the reader conduct a coherent analysis of the role of information systems in a company's strategy.

3.1 Issues in developing an IS strategy

Planned or emergent IS strategies?

One theory is that managers develop strategy consciously, and that the strategy they follow corresponds to what they intended and planned. An alternative is that strategies 'emerge' in the sense that only in part do they reflect stated intentions. Some of the strategies which managers intend are not implemented: the unrealised strategies. Other strategies are realised – but were unintended and followed from the cumulative effect of successive operational day-to-day decisions. Thus, realised strategies combine the results of structured plans and informal ad hoc events (Mintzberg et al., 2003; Spil, 2003), as shown in Figure 3.1.

'Emergent strategy' expresses the idea that people have a broad long-term vision, but take only small steps towards that vision. There is space for uncertainty, experiments and participation. Since developing IS strategy is an uncertain process the emergent strategy style will often be more realistic and satisfactory than the strategic planning style. In most organisations, the realised strategy is somewhere between these positions (Fuller-Love and Cooper, 2000).

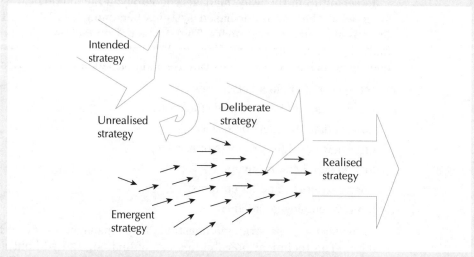

Figure 3.1 **Deliberate and emergent strategies**
Source: Mintzberg et al. (2003).

Decisions in relation to information systems and information strategies also have emergent characteristics. Research by Boonstra (2003) indicated five issues affecting how managers make IS decisions:

■ whether there is scope to *design* a solution;

■ whether distinct alternatives have to be *searched* for;

■ the *urgency* and *necessity* of the decision;

■ whether it can be *subdivided* to allow a more gradual process (planned versus incremental); and

■ the number and power of *stakeholders* involved.

Depending on these factors, IS-related decisions can be straightforward and planned or messy, complicated and time consuming.

■ IS and strategy interrelated

We use terms like 'strategy', 'strategic advantage' or 'the strategic use of IS' to describe the broad choices facing companies concerning which products to offer and which markets to target. These decisions are fundamental for their success. Competitive advantage is what a company seeks to gain from the way it positions a product or service in relation to competitors. This may emphasise, for example,

■ the needs of specific customers (a niche market);

■ a wide distribution network;

■ a unique product in terms of price (cost leadership) or quality (differentiation).

Computer-based information systems can contribute to an organisation's strategy. They are like any other capability – human resources, finance or marketing. They are all resources which managers can incorporate into their strategic planning.

		Competitive advantage	
		Lower cost	Differentiation
Competitive scope	Broad target	COST LEADERSHIP	DIFFERENTIATION
	Narrow target	COST FOCUS	DIFFERENTIATION FOCUS

Figure 3.2 Generic strategies
Source: Porter (1985).

Developments in information and communications technologies have introduced a new dimension to the strategy development process. We can illustrate this with Porter's well-known model, shown in Figure 3.2 (Porter, 1985; Porter and Millar, 1985; Porter, 2001). Companies can use information systems to achieve *cost leadership* by using, for example,

- computer-aided manufacturing to replace manual labour;
- stock control systems to cut expensive inventory; or
- online order entry to cut order processing costs.

They can support a *differentiation* strategy by using:

- computer-aided manufacturing to offer flexible delivery;
- stock control systems to extend the range of goods on offer at any time;

They can support a *niche/focus* strategy by using:

- computer-aided manufacturing to meet unique, non-standard requirements;
- online ordering to allow customers to create a unique, customised product by selecting from a range of features.

Another useful starting point to relate general business strategies with IS can be the Treacy and Wiersema (1995) classification of three 'generic strategies':

- **Operational excellence**: competitive advantage lies in a reliable and fluent organisation of operational processes. Effective process design and a small number of product variations are important. Organisations that follow an operational excellence strategy do not focus on developing innovative products or customer communication, but on effective, reliable and cost-controlled business processes. Examples are McDonald's and easyJet.
- **Product leadership**: competitive advantage lies in focusing on product improvement and product innovation. Product leaders try to offer the best product in their class and use new technologies to improve their products. Examples are Bang & Olufsen, Nike, Apple, Mercedes and Porsche.
- **Customer intimacy**: competitive advantage lies in focusing on customers and providing a unique 'customised' service for every customer. Focus is on the identification and understanding of customers' needs. Examples are private banks, and consultants such as Ernst & Young and McKinsey.

The Treacy and Wiersema framework is different from, but related to, Porter's model. Operational excellence is close to cost leadership, and product leadership and customer intimacy are both different forms of differentiation. The main idea is that companies can use IS to strengthen or adapt their competitive advantage – indeed it is one of the main reasons why managers invest in such systems. The Case Questions below relate these ideas to the Aalsmeer case.

CASE QUESTIONS 3.1

What are the major strengths and the main competitive advantage of the Aalsmeer Flower Auction?

What were the strategic reasons for Aalsmeer's e-business initiatives? Relate these reasons to the Porter or Treacy and Wiersema models.

Are the e-business initiatives (as described throughout this chapter) aligned with current strategies or do they imply changing those strategies?

What threats may the e-business activities hold for Aalsmeer?

What is the direction of the link between strategy and information systems? One possibility is that managers shape the strategy of the firm and then ensure that their investments in information systems support that strategy. Figure 3.3 shows this.

This is a 'strategic choice' model. The information system is the dependent variable. An example of this would be when supermarkets use bar code systems to enter transaction data quickly and accurately. This supports their strategic objective of reducing costs and improving quality.

An alternative model is that information systems can themselves offer a firm new strategic possibilities. Figure 3.4 shows this possibility. This is a 'technological imperative' model (Venkatraman, 1998). Strategy is now the dependent variable. An example would be when a small firm uses the Internet to sell goods or services to consumers directly all over the world. That would not be possible for such a firm if the enabling technology (the Internet) did not exist.

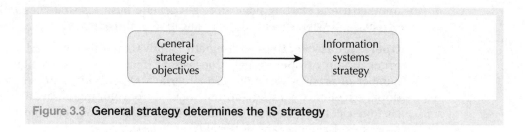

Figure 3.3 **General strategy determines the IS strategy**

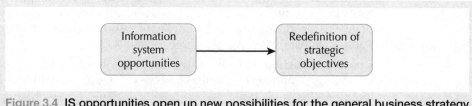

Figure 3.4 **IS opportunities open up new possibilities for the general business strategy**

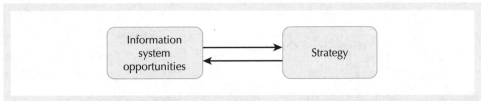

Figure 3.5 **Information systems and strategies affect each other: the interaction model**

A third possibility is that the two affect each other – what we call the *interaction model*. That is when companies have a strategy and look for ways in which they can use information systems to support that strategy. In doing so they develop their ability to manage advanced information systems. They are then able to see how they can use newly developed systems to reach a new set of customers, and adapt their strategy accordingly. Figure 3.5 shows this position.

The boxes below describe two examples of this interaction.

MIS in Practice **Novotel**

The company has the strategic objective of putting the customer first, and is determined to relate every action to satisfying the customer's needs. It has for many years used information systems to support this strategy. As the Internet became available, managers analysed how best to use it to support their strategy. They identified several possible applications. In setting priorities the main factor was the impact on satisfying existing customers and attracting new customers. They decided to give priority to having a presence on the Internet, an easily accessible website, an online reservation system and useful information for customers. They gave lower priority to web-based buying operations. (*www.novotel.com*)

MIS in Practice **Strategic use of IS at Fortis**

Fortis is an international supplier of financial services based in the Netherlands and Belgium. The IS department at the headquarters of Fortis supports the various business units by identifying IT applications which may support the company's strategy. By relating strategic objectives to IT opportunities, Fortis tries to create coherence between IS and strategy. Based on such an analysis, IS planning, design and implementation takes place. The following table shows a simplified example of the company's approach.

Strategic priorities	Internet	Call centres	Expert systems	CRM systems	Improving ATMs with new services
Service improvement	x		x	x	
Enabling multi-channelling	x	x			x
Cost reduction	x	x			x
Relationship management		x		x	
From product to customer focus	x		x	x	

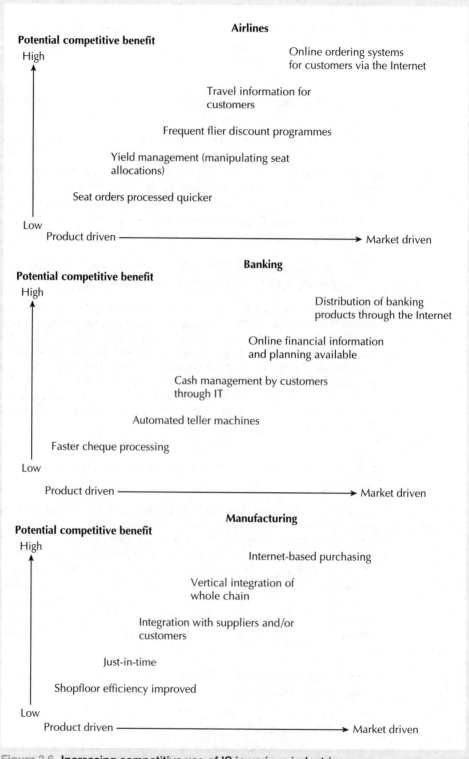

Figure 3.6 **Increasing competitive use of IS in various industries**

By relating strategic priorities and possible IT applications, management can make more informed decisions. This is an example of an application of the interaction model: IS support the strategy but possible IT applications can also be used to add or change strategic priorities.

Figure 3.6 shows how companies in different industries have used information systems to develop their strategies. The horizontal axis shows the balance between an internal (product) and an external (market) focus. The vertical axis shows the potential competitive benefit. Those applications with the greater competitive potential are usually more expensive – so the risk is greater. The figure summarises how different IS applications relate to strategic considerations. Early applications tended to be internally focused and of limited competitive advantage. More recently the emphasis has switched to:

- market-centred applications, through which companies use information systems to improve customer benefits; and
- systems which transcend organisational boundaries and connect firms electronically with suppliers, customers and other business partners.

Summary

- Realised strategies (IS as well as organisational) combine planned and unintended elements – often described as emergent.
- Managers can use IS to support their strategy (such as cost leadership or differentiation).
- The relationship between IS and strategy may be deterministic, strategic choice or interactive in nature.

3.2 IS from a strategic perspective

Earl (2002) gives a comprehensive account of tools with which to analyse the relationship between strategy and IS. Here we use the Five Forces model originally developed by Michael Porter, which enables us to assess the possible impact of IS on the competitive position of a firm. Figure 3.7 is based on Porter's framework and shows that IS represents an opportunity to secure a strategic advantage by using it to strengthen one or more of these forces. Similarly, it represents a competitive threat if other organisations are able to use IS more effectively in these ways.

Information systems and the threats from potential entrants

Managers can apply IS to this force by using it to reduce the threat from new entrants by raising barriers, or by using it themselves to enter new markets.

Using information systems to raise entry barriers

The Aalsmeer Flower Auction is trying to strengthen its position by linking customers electronically with the auction. This electronic link makes it easier for customers to do business and harder for new entrants to compete so strengthening Aalsmeer's position as the main auction in this field. The box gives two other examples.

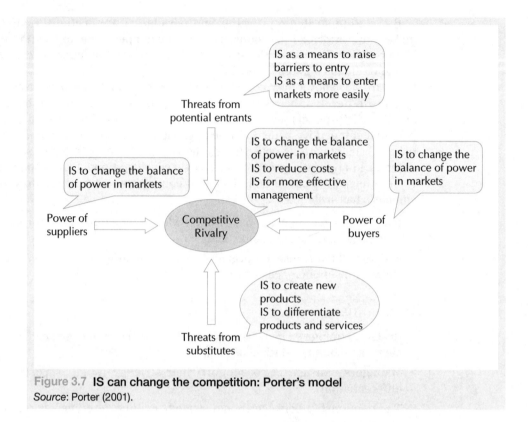

Figure 3.7 IS can change the competition: Porter's model
Source: Porter (2001).

MIS in Practice	Barriers to entry

Large retailers use computer-based systems such as bar coding and electronic point-of-sale terminals to control their inventories. These systems are linked with those of their suppliers. Since it is mainly the larger retail chains who can afford such systems, this gives them a strong negotiating position in relation to their suppliers. Smaller companies or potential entrants are deterred by the relatively high cost of building these links.

Many car manufacturers have information systems linked to importers and dealers. When a customer buys a car, the dealer can immediately enter the specifications into the system. This enables the dealer to access a great deal of information from the manufacturer, such as delivery time and available options, and pass it to the customer.

In the IS industry itself, 'setting the standard' is very important to gaining a strong position. Most customers want to use industry standard hardware or software, such as Microsoft word-processing software, Intel computer chips and Netscape Internet browsers. It is very hard for new entrants to overcome these entry barriers, leading to a 'winner takes all' situation in many sectors of the market.

Using IS to enter markets more easily

Information systems can also be used to enter markets that were not previously accessible. The Chapter Case shows how the Aalsmeer Flower Auction developed an

Internet portal (*www.floweraccess.com*) to reach retailers. Without Internet technology, retailers were the exclusive customers of wholesalers and cash and carrys who could not be reached and influenced by Aalsmeer. Direct contacts with retailers provided Aalsmeer with useful information about final customers that may help growers to adjust their supply more precisely to customer needs.

MIS in Practice   Bertelsmann enters new markets

A well-known example is that of Bertelsmann (*www.bertelsmann.com* and *www.bol.com*), a German publishing company. It rapidly entered the book market in many countries. The company did this not by opening book shops but by offering a very wide range of books and related material in its Internet store. Within a few years it was the biggest bookseller in the world. It uses the Web to enter markets that were very hard to enter on such a large scale without this technology.

The Bertelsmann case shows that information systems can help companies to enter markets much more easily. These markets could be widely dispersed or isolated in other ways before the advent of this technology. This is a chance for newcomers but at the same time a threat to established companies. This development occurs in many markets, such as books, CDs, software, hardware, clothes, artwork, cars and auctions.

MIS in Practice   Caterpillar Tractors

This case describes how Caterpillar Tractors claims to use an information system to support its maintenance function and its market position.

A part on a Caterpillar machine operating at a copper mine in Chile begins to deteriorate. A district centre that continuously monitors the health of all the Caterpillar machines in its area by remotely reading the sensors on each machine automatically spots a problem. It sends an electronic alert direct to the portable computer of the local dealer's field technician. The message specifies the identity and location of the machine, and includes the data that sparked the alert and its diagnosis. The technician validates the diagnosis and determines the service or repair required and which parts and tools are needed. Then the technician logs into Caterpillar's information system, which links dealers, Caterpillar's parts distribution facilities, Cat's, its suppliers' factories and large customers' inventory systems, to determine the best sources of the parts and the time when each source can deliver the parts to the dealer's drop-off point.

Next, the technician sends a proposal to the customer by computer, and the customer responds with the best time to carry out the repair. The technician then orders the parts electronically from the factories or warehouses that can supply the parts in time. At the factories and warehouses, the message triggers the printing of an order ticket and sets in motion an automated crane that retrieves the parts from a storage rack. Then the parts are on their way to the dealer's pick-up site.

The repair completed, the technician closes the work order, prints out an invoice, collects by credit card and electronically updates the machine's history. That information is added to Caterpillar's databases, which helps the company spot any common problems that a particular model might have and thereby continually improve its machines' designs.

Source: Fites (1996).

■ Information systems and the threat of substitutes

Companies can use information systems to alter this force by differentiating their products, or by creating new ones with which they can threaten competitors.

Using information systems to differentiate products and services

The Caterpillar case shows the company using the information system mainly to improve the speed and quality of customer service. When the system notes a deterioration the service starts immediately and the expensive machine will be repaired soon, saving the customer money. Other companies use the Internet to create and orchestrate active customer communities. Examples include Kraft (*www.kraftfoods.com*), Intel (*www.intel.com*), Apple (*www.apple.com*) and Harley Davidson (*www.harley-davidson.com*). Through these communities the companies become close to their customers. They can learn and innovate with product or service improvements that would otherwise be impossible.

The Research Summary box below explains why it is essential for information service providers to differentiate their products.

Research Summary   Versioning information

Shapiro and Varian (1999) suggest that selling information to a broad and diverse set of customers is one of the new products that information systems can provide. CD phone books and travel information are examples. What makes information goods tricky is their 'dangerous economics'. Producing the first copy of an information product is often very expensive, though subsequent copies are very cheap: the fixed costs are high and the marginal costs are low. Because competition tends to drive prices to the level of marginal costs, information goods can easily turn into low-priced commodities. This often makes it impossible for companies to recoup their investments, leading to failure.

To avoid that fate, the authors recommend that companies create different versions of the same information by tailoring it to the needs of different customers. Such a 'versioning' strategy can enable a company to distinguish its products from those of the competition and protect its prices. It is a form of mass customisation with higher value for customers and producers of information. They suggest that information can be differentiated by:

■ restricting the time or place at which a customer can access information;

■ offering more or less depth of detail;

■ offering the ability to store, duplicate or print information; or

■ offering more or less actual information.

The power of versioning is that it enables managers to apply tried-and-true product-management techniques in a way that takes into account both the unusual economics of information production and the endless malleability of digital data.

Source: Shapiro and Varian (1999).

Using information systems to create new products and services

Telephone and Internet banking are relatively new phenomena that have only become possible with new systems. The same is true of companies that use the power of database technology to offer new services in CRM and direct marketing.

Wide Internet access has generated a huge increase in businesses offering new services. These include electronic auctions, search engines, electronic retailers, electronic hubs (Dutta and Segev, 1999; Kaplan, 2000; Timmers, 2000) and Internet providers. Caterpillar created new maintenance services.

Information systems and the bargaining power of suppliers

Increasing power of suppliers

Suppliers can increase their power by using information systems to track much more closely the costs of providing services to customers. They can set prices accordingly, or decide that they do not want a particular piece of business. For example, airlines use yield management systems to track actual reservations against traffic forecasts for any flight, and then adjust prices for the remaining seats to maximise revenue. Stepanek (1999) reports how Weyerhaeuser, an international forest products company, uses an Internet-based system to manage orders from its distributors. This allows the company to manage its internal processes more efficiently, and also to assess much more accurately the value of each order and the overall performance of its distributors. This enables it to refuse unprofitable orders and to be more selective about which distributors it supplies. Customer relationship management systems enable companies to track customers' requirements accurately, which may increase the suppliers' power (see also Chapter 2).

Decreasing power of suppliers

Information systems can also be used the other way around. Customers can use information systems to strengthen their position in the marketplace at the expense of suppliers' power. In February 2000, Ford, in association with GM and Daimler Chrysler, set up 'Covisint' (*www.covisint.com*) an online marketplace and private exchange. Covisint's objective was to offer Ford and other auto manufacturers collaborative product development, procurement and supply chain tools that could substantially reduce costs and bring efficiencies to their business operations. Suppliers to the industry function in a tiered structure. At the bottom are level 3 suppliers who make a simple component and pass it to a level 2 supplier who combines it with others into a larger component. That goes to a level 1 supplier who completes and delivers the full assembly. Traditionally the car makers dealt with the level 1 supplier, who then passed the order down to the others. Besides taking time, this method forced suppliers at each tier to keep extra inventory just to make sure they were not short of components. Before Covinsint, the level 1 suppliers were in a powerful position with respect to the car manufacturers as well as the level 2 and the level 3 suppliers. They used this position to charge high prices and to utilise information about demand and supply in their own interest. Introducing Covinsint opened the component market to a wider range of suppliers and helped to reduce the power of level 1 suppliers.

Inter-organisational systems can be used to cooperate as well as compete with business partners, whether suppliers or customers. Powerful parties tend to urge less powerful ones to adopt their systems.

Information systems and the bargaining power of buyers

A good example of the balance of power being altered is when retail chains use modern communication technologies to make electronic links with their suppliers.

Such systems reduce inventory costs and warehouse expenses and improve fulfilment time and information flows. The retailer's computer continually monitors its suppliers' finished goods inventories, factory scheduling and commitments against its schedule. The purpose is to ensure the stores always have adequate stocks. A supplier who is unwilling to join the system is likely to lose business. The box shows how Wal-Mart used this.

MIS in Practice   Wal-Mart

For many years Wal-Mart had not only set up computer links between each store and the distribution warehouses, but through an electronic data interchange (EDI) system, it also hooked up with the computers of the firm's main suppliers. The distribution centres themselves were equipped with miles of laser-guided conveyor belts that could read the bar codes on incoming cases and direct them to the right truck for their onward journey. The final step was to buy a satellite to transmit the firm's enormous data-load. The whole system, covering all the firm's warehouses, cost at least $700m, but it quickly paid for itself.

The first benefit was just-in-time replenishment across hundreds of stores. The company has since refined this further, using computer modelling programs to allow the firm to anticipate sales patterns. The second benefit was cost. According to Sam Walton, the company's founder, Wal-Mart's distribution costs were under 3 per cent of sales, compared with 4–5.5 per cent for the firm's competitors – a saving of close to $750m in that year alone.

Perhaps the system's finest hour came when Procter & Gamble proposed setting up a 'partnership' that involved not just data-sharing through EDI but joint management of the whole relationship between the two companies. P&G uses this to tailor the production to Wal-Mart's demand. The two firms say they both benefit – a faster and more predictable stock-turn can help the manufacturer too. But as other retailers adopted similar distribution systems, it became clear that one of the partners benefited more than the other. P&G went through a round of plant closures and lay-offs, while Wal-Mart's profits kept on growing. Wal-Mart's distribution system gave it a great competitive advantage.

Source: Based on 'Riding the storm', *The Economist*, 4 March 1995, p. 64.

More generally, buyers can use the Web to access more suppliers and to compare prices for standard commodities much more widely than was practical with earlier technologies.

Activity 3.1   Research on IS strategy

Choose a major and important information system from a company you know and interview a manager about that system. Try to identify:

- the initial (strategic) objectives in acquiring and using that system;
- whether the system meets or exceeds the expectations in relation to those objectives;
- whether the system aligned with the strategy or also impacted and changed the strategy.

Use the Porter model and the value disciplines of Treacy and Wiersema to determine the degree of fit of the system with the strategy.

■ Information systems and competitive rivalry

Two ways of using information systems to strengthen competitive rivalry are by reducing costs and more effective management.

Using IS to reduce costs

Online inventory systems and e-procurement enable radical changes in manufacturing supply systems. This greatly reduces inventory levels and the costs associated with them. Car manufacturers are only invoiced for components when the completed assembly leaves the factory. When the system knows that a specified number of headlamps have been used, it passes the information to the component supplier. The supplier sends an (electronic) invoice for the components used, and supplies replacements. These inter-organisational systems reduce the costs of inventory working capital.

The Internet enables large companies to transfer their purchasing operations to the Web. Secure websites connect suppliers, business partners and customers all over the world. This makes it easier for new suppliers to bid for a share of the available business, makes costs more transparent and improves the administrative efficiency of the supply process.

Using IS to enable more effective management

A travel agent's branch accounting system can now provide detailed patterns of business to managers, enabling them to monitor trends more closely and to take better-informed pricing and promotional decisions. Another example is Ahold, a Dutch retailer, which achieved much greater performance in the supply chain by using IS to manage its customer database. Management information systems can expand the span of control of individual managers, which can support the flattening of organisations.

These examples show that information systems may become opportunities for creating, supporting or changing generic strategies. On the other hand, competitors have similar opportunities – there are also costs and risks associated with using information systems in this way.

■ IS can also be a threat

New entrants in the financial services sector have very quickly been able to introduce telephone banking through call centres. They were able to take advantage of the fact that they did not have an established branch network and so could use the new technology very quickly. The technology worked to the disadvantage of established banks with many local offices. They found it costly to close branches. The technology was an advantage to the new, a disadvantage to the old. This illustrates a more general point that, for all the potential opportunities, IS can also be a threat.

Information systems enable new competition

Computer-based information systems represent opportunities for one business and threats to another company. In retailing, large chains have benefited at the expense of smaller shops, large suppliers have benefited at the expense of smaller ones and large retailers have more power over suppliers. Any use of IS by one company to enter a new market, reduce costs and so on is a potential threat to a competitor. The competitor loses out if it has not seen the possibility or has managed implementation less effectively. The London Stock Exchange is threatened by the fact that modern technology allows major institutions to trade shares directly, rather than use the market institution. The problem is increased by the fact that competing exchanges have implemented new information systems more effectively. They are likely to gain a larger share of a smaller market.

Information systems place new demands on management time

Implementing a major system takes a great deal of management time – a cost that managers rarely include when evaluating investments. They require managers to look inward at (important) operational problems of staff, system design, security. The danger is that they do not look at (even more important) issues of how to use the systems for strategic advantage. In other words, managers are often balancing between a 'problem orientation' and an 'opportunity orientation'. Senior management frequently underestimates the resources required to implement new information systems, especially of managing the many organisational implications.

Implementing an information system successfully is difficult

Many research reports comment on the difficulties of implementing information systems. This is especially true of systems that involve many stakeholders with different interests, or those that are innovative in other respects. Implementation often takes place in an uncertain environment, from a competitive as well as from a technological point of view. These uncertainties make it difficult to plan a change over a longer time. At the same time, the stakes are getting higher in terms of costs, people and other resources.

Dependency on technology suppliers and consultants

Managers often buy in expertise for development, operations and consultancy. These suppliers become the main experts of a company's IS resource. This dependency can be misused. Their lack of knowledge and insight in the organisation causes major problems. They have difficulty in negotiating successfully with the external providers and crucial company knowledge becomes the asset of other companies.

Activity 3.2   Online newspapers?

Many publishers of newspapers face the development of Internet newspapers. Most are traditional newspapers but also new entrants publish Internet newspapers. Use Porter's model (Figure 3.7) to analyse how this development influences the competitive environment for publishers of newspapers.

   What opportunities and threats arise from this development?

Summary

- From a strategic point of view IS brings important business opportunities, such as raising barriers to newcomers, ability to enter markets, changing the power

Aalsmeer Flower Auction: continued

The first e-business application of Aalsmeer Flower Auction was named FlowerAccess (*www.floweraccess.com*). This was an ordering system which enabled retailers to place orders online to wholesalers, who would then pass these to growers. The growers would transport the products to the wholesalers, who put the orders together and took them to the retailer.

Marrianne Groothuis and her team visited a large number of growers, wholesalers and retailers to demonstrate the system and its potential benefits. This initially led to 60 participating growers, 7 wholesalers and 1,200 retailers (across Europe). The wholesalers received the total supply of all FlowerAccess growers and offered this to retailers. Based on information that the system generated, growers were able to adjust their supply in line with demand.

Aalsmeer traditionally had no business relations with retailers, so FlowerAccess could be interpreted as an attempt to redefine the value chain. By using FlowerAccess, Aalsmeer tried to increase its grip on the value chain as a whole by including retailers in the system. By being the first with such a system, Aalsmeer aimed to dominate the market and discourage others from entering the market.

Unfortunately, only 20 per cent of the 1,200 connected retailers made regular use of FlowerAccess. The amount of flowers ordered was too small for the growers to continue participating in FlowerAccess. It accounted for less than 1 per cent of the total auction turnover and had clearly not lived up to expectations.

balance in a beneficial way, developing new products or services in order to differentiate, reducing costs and implementing a more effective management style.

- IS can also be a threat for the same reasons as mentioned above – competitors can always do the same.

3.3 Aligning IS with corporate strategy

As information systems have become more central to the strategic development of firms, it becomes essential for managers to consider the alignment, or degree of fit, between IS and strategy. Questions to consider include why alignment is important, the value of the contingency approach to alignment and the contribution of the interaction approach.

The case for alignment

Many writers have suggested that information systems need to 'fit' the organisation or unit in which they are used. Lockamy and Smith (1997) proposed that managers should aim for a good fit between current information systems and customers, IS strategy and the organisation. They advise managers to ensure that:

- strategy is driven by customer needs and expectations;
- processes selected for redesign by IS create value for the customer; and
- IS supports those processes in a way which supports the strategy.

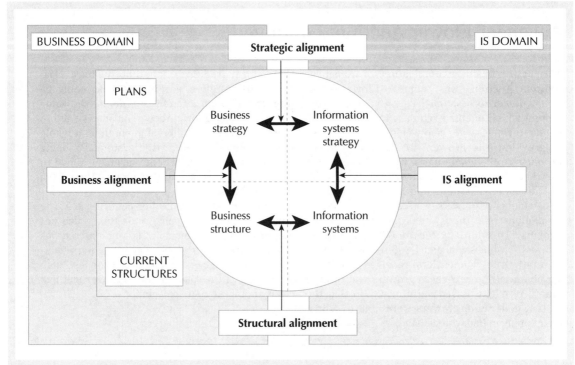

Figure 3.8 Alignment between IS and organisation, in plans and in operations
Source: Lockamy et al. (1997); Sabherwal et al. (2001)

This is the central idea of 'strategic alignment': the search for the right fit between these variables. Figure 3.8 shows this. The business domain influences the IS domain and vice versa. The plan influences current practices and current practices influence the plan.

We describe the alignment between business and IS strategies as '*strategic alignment*', between business and information systems as '*structural alignment*', between IS strategy and information systems as '*IS alignment*' and between business strategy and business structure as '*business alignment*'.

Much literature treats alignment as a static end-state, but in real life the search for alignment is a moving target and an emergent process. The business environment continues to change after alignment is achieved. If business strategy or structure is changed in response, the other elements should be altered in a synchronised fashion in order to maintain alignment (Sabherwal et al., 2001)

The concept of alignment can be a good starting point for the diagnosis of organisations. In that case, the analyst can, for example, determine whether the business structures, the IS strategy and information systems are aligned with the company's strategy (or the other way around).

The contingency approach to alignment

What factors should shape the nature of that alignment? One approach uses the idea, long popular in organisational theory, that the fit should reflect the situation in

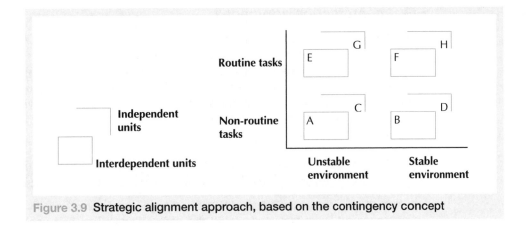

Figure 3.9 **Strategic alignment approach, based on the contingency concept**

which the unit is operating. The theory, reflected in Figure 3.9, is that some basic characteristics of organisations influence how they use information systems within their core operations. The variables are:

■ the primary tasks of the organisation: routine or non-routine;

■ the degree of interdependency between those doing these tasks: high or low;

■ the environment of the organisation: stable or unstable.

Figure 3.9 expresses these variables on three dimensions, giving eight types of (pure) organisations.

When the environment is relatively stable and there are many routine tasks (for example, an energy supplier, a water supplier or a tax administration), companies will use information systems mainly to support the primary processes. They will focus on providing integrated, structured, well-balanced, reliable and sustainable systems. These systems will provide information to managers in a fixed and focused way.

In an unstable environment of non-routine tasks (for example, consultancies, R&D departments, software houses), information systems have to be flexible and adaptive. These systems are often unstructured and 'open'. Intranets, groupware systems and flexible decision support systems will be more helpful in such environments than structured and integrated data processing systems. The employees as well as the customers expect a flexible and supportive information environment they can easily adapt to changing circumstances.

Relatively independent units can develop their information environment – one which is most supportive to the needs and characteristics of that particular business unit. However, when units have to collaborate and exchange information regularly (interdependency), they will move towards more integrated systems.

The model suggests that there is no 'one best' or 'general' or 'best-practice' approach to using information systems. Effectiveness depends on selecting the form of system best suited to the situation. This implies that managers should not follow fashion, but ensure that their systems match the present and evolving nature of their organisation. The contingency approach challenges approaches that seek a universal solution or that pay most attention to current fashion.

■ An interaction approach?

On the other hand, do not interpret the model too mechanically. As presented, it ignores other variables such as cultural, political and historical features. It also stresses only one aspect of the external conditions. The best solution probably depends on both internal and external conditions, and how managers see and interpret them. To use it in a mechanistic and deterministic way is an oversimplification. In addition, people can use information systems to influence these variables, as the example in the box shows.

MIS in Practice   Changing alignment – from a D firm to an A

A small consultancy firm, located in one building in a medium-sized city, had about ten management consultants and a small staff of four people. They had a good reputation in the region, based on personal relationships between the consultants and their clients. The consultants all had their own personal style. IT was only used for word-processing and the financial data processing. It resembled a 'D firm': non-routine, independent and stable. Its IT systems fitted that description.

However, when the owner and director retired, the consultancy firm was taken over by a big international consultancy. That firm imposed a common working style, based on its 'generally accepted standards'. Project management and groupware systems were implemented to share the knowledge and experience of the worldwide operating firm. Positions were more tightly regulated and consultants from other areas were brought in. The business expanded to more than 40 consultants. The environment became more unstable, interdependency became higher and tasks were still non-routine. It was now a typical 'A firm'.

This example shows that changing circumstances and conditions, but also IT applications like groupware and project management systems, can change the characteristics of companies.

People in the original company developed a way of working and used information systems to support that. A change in circumstances brought new people into the business, and they introduced new information systems. These required people to work in new ways. We see an interaction between people, how they see the environment and the kinds of systems they use.

Activity 3.3 Evidence on the contingency approach

Find an example of a company for each position in Figure 3.9 (A–H).

■ *Are these positions stable or changing?*
■ *If they have changed, what were the drivers of this change (for example, technology, competition, customer expectations)?*

■ Summary

■ There is no best way to organise and use information systems. Many alternatives are available and it depends on the business and its environment which combination fits best with the company.

- The challenge for managers is to align information systems in an optimal way with their business and to use them to support strategy and organisation.
- Important factors in alignment are: processes (routine or non-routine), inter-dependency between units (high versus low) and environment (stable or unstable).
- The form of information system will also reflect how people see other factors, such as the culture, politics and history of the organisation.

3.4 E-business strategy

Clearly the Internet raises many new questions under all the headings we have discussed so far. Some industries are strongly affected by the Internet, while others are less so. All need to consider the possible effects, by asking strategic questions such as:

1. Which business processes and business functions can be improved by using the Internet? (See Chapter 4.)
2. How can the Internet change competition?
3. How can Internet-related activities be positioned in a firm?

Aalsmeer Flower Auction: continued

The next e-business initiative of Marrianne Groothuis and her e-selling team was FlowerXL, an Internet-based ordering system aimed at wholesalers. Aalsmeer had established links with wholesalers, and they hoped that this system would complement and strengthen the existing value chain. Because Aalsmeer knew the wholesalers, they were able to design the system to their needs and expectations. FlowerXL appeared to have more potential than FlowerAccess.

Twelve months later Marrianne Groothuis again reported that sales through FlowerXL were quite limited. Like the retailers, wholesalers also based their business on personal and informal contacts that were maintained at the auction hall. From the perspective of many wholesalers, an exclusive Internet-based ordering system under-mined this informal information exchange.

The directors of Aalsmeer concluded that a successful e-business system should be integrated into the existing business and be complementary and supportive rather than replacing the traditional business. This view dominated the next stage of e-business at Aalsmeer Flower Auction.

CHAPTER CASE: PART 3

CASE QUESTIONS 3.2

Read the alternative Internet strategies set out in the following paragraphs.

Which of them has Aalsmeer followed?

Were any of the others a realistic alternative strategy?

What problems has Aalsmeer experienced in implementing its chosen strategies?

■ Applying the Five Forces model

The Internet tends to make competition more intense due to its global and ubiquitous characteristics. This section illustrates how the Internet affects the competitive landscape in many industries by using Porter's industry analysis model (Porter, 2001).

Internet and the threat of new entrants

It is very easy for businesses to enter the Internet and by doing so enter a market. Fewer physical facilities are needed and all energy can be spent on web presence and other directly business-related activities. Some Internet-based businesses, such as search engines and electronic auctions, are creating completely new markets. Such companies have few competitors in the early stages of business development and are able to gain first-mover advantages. Others are entering established markets and may challenge existing businesses. Examples of markets affected by and being transformed by new Internet entrants are travel, stockbroking, books, CDs and many business-to-business markets.

MIS in Practice   easyJet

The low-cost airline has a strategy which includes a sharp focus on customer needs, using technology wherever possible and adapting processes to suit market conditions. When it began to operate it took reservations on the telephone, so paid no commissions to travel agents. Its emphasis on technology meant that as the Internet became available it rapidly adapted its business model to offer online reservations. It took their first online reservation in April 1998. By 2004, over 95 per cent of reservations were made online – probably the highest proportion of total sales for any established business. Its success in using the Internet has led the company to launch a further range of online services, such as easyRent (car rental) and easyMoney (financial services). (*www.easyjet.com*)

GoCargo is an exchange for the container shipping industry, which is expanding from a relatively small spot market to a far larger contract market and learning just how complex that is. Eyal Goldwerger, founder of GoCargo, quickly saw that old-style service contracts were not about to disappear. So he built a staff, based in New York, of 60 multilingual industry specialists and traders who could codify terms, certify shippers and carriers and otherwise make this handshake business safe for Internet trading. As GoCargo got better at this, it started to turn into a real business. Contracts now amount to nearly one-third of the exchange's total volume. The site has 12,000 members and conducted more than 5,000 live auctions in 1999/2000 (*The Economist*, 21 October 2000).

GoCargo is an example of an Internet-based newcomer which challenges the established 'handshake' business. Its market share of the worldwide container volume rose from 0 per cent in the fourth quarter of 1999 to 30 per cent in the second quarter of 2000.

Internet and the threat of substitutes

The Internet can also be used as a substitute for certain products. An example is the market for news and information. Many people use the Internet as a primary or an additional source. In certain areas, such as for information about finance and sport, but also for advertisements for houses, job vacancies and second-hand cars, websites and Internet newspapers have become a substitute for television and paper-based newspapers.

Certain products or services are more easy to substitute than others. When products or services are

- digitisable (e.g. software, music, news, information, but not bricks, cars),
- standardisable (e.g. insurance, cars, commodity goods, but not works of art),
- portable (e.g. information, but not amusement parks), or
- low touch (e.g. books, music, but not shoes, vegetables)

they are often easy to substitute by Internet-based suppliers.

Internet and the bargaining power of suppliers and buyers

Internet-based electronic marketplaces are illustrations of changes in the power of suppliers and buyers. Such marketplaces are examples of changes in the supply chain in some industries. Such changes can be reintermediation, which is when a new party creates a position because of its value-adding activities. On the other hand, disintermediation, the removal of links from the value chain, also takes place by the Internet. When somebody orders a book from Amazon, bookshops, wholesalers and importers of books are disintermediated. This all means that the Internet can affect the reason for the existence of some companies to a high extent.

Internet and the intensity of rivalry

Because of the uncertainty in markets about the role of the Internet in the future, many businesses are very keen to observe how their competitors use the Internet in the marketplace. This can be illustrated by the competition in the financial services industry. Many banks and insurers introduced the Internet to support and to inform their customers; now, many types of transactions can be conducted online. They often use the Internet, combined with call centres, to offer a 24-hours-a-day service, while at the same time they close branches and reduce staff. They use the Internet to improve and differentiate services and at the same time to reduce costs. Many banks and insurers are trying to figure out how far they can go with these policies without frustrating customers. Some are now complementing their Internet activities by offering wealthier and more profitable customers a personal account manager, who can offer them more complex products.

Dell, which was the first PC manufacturer to use the Internet to take customer orders, is one example. Competitors have long imitated the practice, but Dell, first to gain the Internet audience, gained more experience than other PC manufacturers on the e-commerce vehicle and still sells more computers via the Web than its competitors (Oz, 2002, p. 45)

Positioning Internet activities within the company

Having decided how to adapt their strategy to take account of the Internet, companies then need to decide how the Internet relates to their existing business (Figure 3.10). Will the Internet be the exclusive channel (e.g. to sell or to buy) or will it be complementary? The possibilities are:

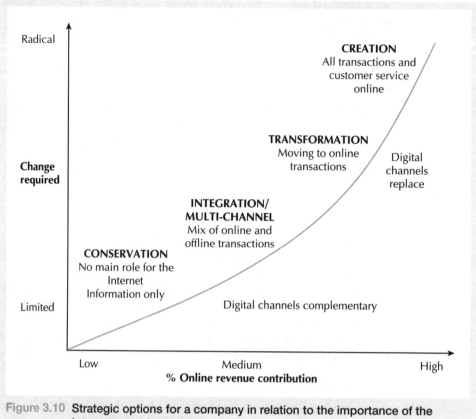

Figure 3.10 Strategic options for a company in relation to the importance of the Internet as a channel
Source: Based on Chaffey (2002), adapted.

CONSERVATION	Brick – continue to operate without Internet or information only
SEPARATION	Brick or click – separate units for Internet business
INTEGRATION/MULTI-CHANNEL	Brick and click – Internet combined and integrated with existing firm,
TRANSFORMATION	From brick to click – from existing to new form
CREATION	Clicks – setting up a business which only uses electronic channels

Separation: brick or click

This is when a company sets up a separate Internet operation beside its established activities. This can be an option if the Internet operation targets different customer segments or a different product mix than the non-Internet operation. Some travel agencies have set up Internet-only ventures, often with another brand name, while continuing with their traditional branches.

Integration: brick and click

If a company decides to integrate the Internet activities in the existing business, it can combine various facilities and offer multiple channels to customers. At many banks, customers can use the call centre, the Internet or the branch. Advantages of this approach are that traditional customers are not put off by a new medium and can become used to it gradually. The company can also attract new customers at the same time. Many established retailers such as Toys 'R' Us, Tesco and Boots are taking the same approach, using the Internet to complement conventional channels. They recognise that their existing strengths, such as a trusted brand name, established customers and a distribution and payment infrastructure, can be essential supports to an Internet venture, while start-up companies need to create them from scratch.

Transformation: from brick to click

This means a gradual move from non-use of the Internet to becoming a complete Internet company. One example is the major German insurance company Gerling (Loebbecke and Jelassi, 1997), which is following a strategy of gradually moving its business onto the Internet. In its customers' perception there is one office. In reality they are linked to whichever office has free capacity at that moment. They also work with 'virtual employees' who do the same work at home as is done in the office (see also Warner and Witzel, 1999).

Creation: clicks

This option describes new businesses based entirely on the Internet. Such entrepreneurial creations do not carry the burden of traditional structures and distribution channels, so they avoid the problems of transformation that face bricks-and-mortar rivals. They tend to have young, Internet-literate customers, and have clearly been able to attract substantial amounts of venture capital. Their disadvantages include lack of established reputation, brand name or order-fulfilment processes.

These issues related to the Internet show how information systems developments raise fundamental and strategic questions for companies. Established companies are sometimes slower in their reaction to such innovations than newcomers, but they are increasingly challenged to transform their business to electronic channels.

Activity 3.4 Analysing an Internet strategy

Choose a firm that is currently using the Internet and analyse its Internet strategy (use Encyclopaedia Britannica (below) if you wish). Use the three questions at the start of this section (p. 83) to help organise your answer.

■ *Which strategy did they follow – separation, integration, transformation or creation?*

■ Summary

- ■ The Internet gives completely new opportunities for businesses to reach new groups of customers and to develop new products and services.
- ■ The Internet confronts existing businesses with fundamental strategic questions of how to deal with this new technology while giving entrepreneurs chances to set up new businesses using the Internet extensively.

> ## MIS in Practice   Encyclopaedia Britannica
>
> Until the early 1990s, Encyclopaedia Britannica enjoyed brisk sales, and many still consider it the world's best encyclopaedia. However, while other organisations decided to move their books from paper to compact discs, the University of Chicago (which held the rights to the Britannica) was slow to do so. By 1992, consumers, including many people who would not buy traditional encyclopaedias, bought more encyclopaedias on CD-ROM than in book form – they are cheaper and easier to search. So while competing encyclopaedias such as Encarta and Grolier sold well, Britannica quickly lost market share.
>
> When the Web rush started, management of the 233-year old organisation decided to go online. Initially, management offered the encyclopaedia on the Web for subscribers. Apparently, the strategy did not bring in the expected revenues. In 1999, management changed its strategy: it offered the encyclopaedia on-line, free of charge, hoping that *Britannica.com* would become a portal: a site where people start their daily journey on the Web.
>
> Portals can attract paid advertising if they can get enough traffic to their sites. But the strategy did not work as traffic at the site continued to fall. Then management contemplated offering both chargeable and free parts of the encyclopaedia. Perhaps the new strategy will have done the trick.
>
> *Source*: Asbrand, 2001; *www.britannica.com*.

■ Strategic issues with respect to the Internet include: the organisation of the value chain, the approach of current and/or new customers, and the positioning of Internet activities within the company – as the exclusive channel or complementary to the old way of doing business.

3.5 Opportunities and problems of IS planning

Having studied how managers formulate their IS strategies, Macmillan (1997) found that managers typically identify these problems:

■ IS investments are unrelated to business strategy;

■ pay-off from IS investments is inadequate;

■ too much 'technology for technology's sake';

■ poor relations between IS users and IS specialists;

■ designers' low insight into users' preferences and work habits.

Such problems indicate the value of in-depth thinking about information systems planning, yet many companies lack the necessary expertise. Senior management often lacks current IS knowledge and has other priorities. This encourages them to delegate IS strategy to internal or external experts. These experts lack business knowledge – but are keen to implement the latest technologies. The result can be increasing costs without a corresponding benefit – so that senior management becomes even less interested in IS strategy. This sequence of events is shown in Figure 3.11.

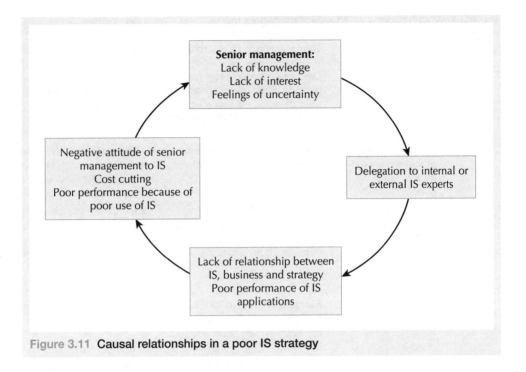

Figure 3.11 Causal relationships in a poor IS strategy

Ross and Weill (2002) provide useful guidelines to senior management regarding which IT decisions they should be making. Table 3.1 summarises their suggestions.

Their main suggestion is that it is a principal task for senior management to define a clear IS policy and, derived from that, to decide how to fund, organise and control the execution of IT responsibilities.

All these arguments suggest a need for flexible and open methods for defining information strategies. Rigid and detailed long-term plans can become out of date too quickly. The higher the uncertainty the more open to adaptation a strategy should be. Based on a firm's strategic priorities and insight in the degree of alignment, an information systems plan can be developed. An IS plan is a road map indicating the:

- direction of system development;
- rationale;
- current situation;
- management strategy;
- new technological developments;
- implementation plan; and
- budget.

Modern IS planning is integrated into the overall organisational strategic plan. IS planning should not come from IS managers but from senior management, business unit managers, line managers and users. There are several prerequisites for IS planning (Oz, 2002). Senior management must:

Table 3.1 **What happens when senior managers ignore their IT responsibilities**

	IT decision	Senior management's role	Consequences of abdicating the decision
Strategy	How much should we spend on IT?	Define the strategic role that IT will play in the company and then determine the level of funding needed to achieve that objective.	The company fails to develop an IT platform that furthers its strategy, despite high IT spending.
	Which business processes should receive our IT budget?	Make clear decisions about which IT initiatives will and will not be funded.	A lack of focus overwhelms the IT unit, which tries to deliver many projects that may have little value or cannot be implemented well simultaneously.
	Which IT capabilities need to be company-wide?	Decide which IT capabilities should be provided centrally and which should be developed by individual businesses.	Excessive technical and process standardisation limits the flexibility of business units, or frequent exceptions to the standards increase costs and limit business synergies.
Execution	How good do our IT services really need to be?	Decide which features – for example, enhanced reliability or response time – are needed on the basis of their costs and benefits.	The company may pay for service options that, given its priorities, are not worth the costs.
	What security and privacy risks will we accept?	Lead the decision-making on the trade-offs between security and privacy on the one hand and convenience on the other.	Overemphasis on security and privacy may inconvenience customers, employees and suppliers; underemphasis may make data vulnerable.
	Who do we blame if an IT initiative fails?	Assign a business executive to be accountable for every IT project; monitor business metrics.	The business value of systems is never realised.

Source: Ross and Weill (2002).

- recognise IS as an indispensable resource;
- understand that IS is a complex resource that must be planned and controlled;
- regard IS as an essential resource for the whole company;
- regard IS as a source for strategic advantage and for control of processes.

Ideally, an IS plan is developed by focusing on the mission and a long-term vision of the company. Derived from this, goals and objectives are set and the strategic plan of necessary information systems and the tactical steps to develop them are made. Strategic IS plans should not be rigid, since most strategic plans are dynamic and revised frequently. Changing competitive environments and technologies are the main reasons for revising strategic IS plans on a biannual basis.

Strategic IS plans have to be translated into tactical objectives and result in action. At this stage, projects are defined and assigned resources, including staff and funds, for execution.

Figure 3.12 sets out one highly simplified view of the relationship between information systems and a broader strategy. The basic idea of an information strategy is that it should be derived from the general corporate strategy. As we discussed

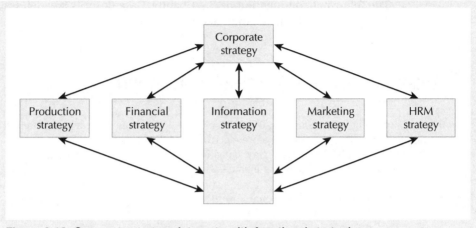

Figure 3.12 **Corporate strategy interacts with functional strategies**

MIS in Practice   GCO

GCO (*www.gco-fryslan.nl*) is a consultancy (120 employees) that helps primary and secondary schools to improve their educational and management processes. Two years ago, it changed its strategy from providing a product-focused service to becoming a more client-focused organisation. This means that it wants to service its customers by providing integrated and client-focused support rather than offering a set of different service products. This strategic reorientation led to a need for new information systems.

Consultants needed systems that collect and use customer knowledge. For that reason, GCO implemented a customer relationship management system to capture its customer knowledge in an integrated way. It also integrated that system with a knowledge system designed to share experiences of different projects among consultants. In this way a strategic IS plan was logically derived from the new strategy.

before, the link can easily go the other way. It is even more likely that the relationship between IS and strategy is interactive, with each affecting the other. Strategy shapes the information system, but equally the information system shapes strategy. Other complexities are shown in Table 3.2.

Table 3.2 **Complexities in forming an information systems strategy**

Complicating factors	Description
Links to other functional areas	Enterprise resource planning (ERP) and similar systems link functions and have expectations of IS. It is hard to change just one part.
Potential IS developments	Infinite possibilities for changing the way the firm works, and for the strategy it follows. Strategy needs to remain fluid.
Interaction	Changes in IS and organisations affect each other, making it hard to see cause and effect.
Lack of expertise	Managers lack IS knowledge; IS experts lack business knowledge.

The following continuation of the Chapter Case describes which issues are faced by Aalsmeer while implementing and continuing its new strategy.

Aalsmeer Flower Auction: continued

The management of Aalsmeer believe that the auction still has a long way to go before electronic networks are used in the optimal way. Questions and challenges they are considering include:

- How can we promote acceptance and use of electronic channels, internally and externally?
- How can Aalsmeer gain market dominance without threatening wholesalers and growers?
- Should e-business be a separate activity or integrated within the organisation?
- Is e-business the future and should Aalsmeer go through a transformation process or is it only one of many channels which should be integrated?

- How do the e-business initiatives fit with the other electronic means that have entered the floricultural sector in recent years (e.g. the introduction of standard EDI messages between growers, auction, exporters/wholesalers)?
- How can e-business enhance the strategy of the auction to disconnect product information from the logistic processes?
- How can the different e-business initiatives function as catalysts for future electronic systems?

Long-term research by Smits and van der Poel (1997) in six information-intensive organisations in the Netherlands found that information strategies go through different stages. They concluded that these stages mean that the adoption process of information technologies in organisations is a learning process. Managers and IS staff, as well as users of new technologies, are interacting and negotiating to find some sort of a balance. The stages also suggest that the tasks and responsibilities of managers are changing over time. In the early stages they have to be very open and communicative with respect to the new system, but, as it becomes routine, more control and efficiency are needed. But soon another system appears, and again an open attitude is needed.

Bensaou and Earl (1998) compared styles of IS management in Japan and the West (United States and Europe). The most striking results to come from this research were that:

- The Japanese executives had not considered developing a special IS strategy. They design processes and use IS to facilitate those processes in the best way. This leads in practice to more incremental (small-step) approaches and 'short-term success' rather than risky long-term plans.
- The western approach is more directed to the implementation of the newest technology while the Japanese bias is more to the appropriate technology, whether it is advanced and new or simple and old.
- In Japan, there is a broader knowledge about IS issues among managers; many of them have to work two or three years in the IS department in order to get hands-on experience; job rotation is more normal.
- The western model places more emphasis on a deliberate IS strategy, based on clear analysis, a preference for the newest technology and a division between

experts and users. The Japanese model follows an intuitive path using the appropriate, technology rather than the newest, and a more integrated approach.

Summary

Some guidelines for improving the effectiveness of IS strategy would include:

- Understand the complex impact of different kinds of IS. Develop iterative and adaptive modes of planning in situations where IS plans influence and are influenced by the broader strategy.
- Recognise the importance of IS on strategy by appointing to senior positions people with a broad experience of applying IS to business.
- Strive towards a balance between IS opportunities and problems of managing IS. Some top management teams spend more time managing current problems (e.g. troubles with systems, people, outsourcing) than on developing a clear direction for IS, which may in itself solve some of the problems.
- Educate employees in the potential opportunities and effects of modern IS. This may be especially important among middle and senior managers.

Conclusions

The theme of this chapter appears quite straightforward: how IS can support an organisation's strategy. An observer who sees business organisations as rational, well-informed decision-making bodies blessed with foresight would have no problem in advising how managers should do the job. Yet, as the chapter has unfolded, we have shown how much more uncertain and provisional the link between IS and strategy is.

Right from the start we continued the theme of the interactive approach, in which IS affects strategy and strategy affects IS. We then examined the ways in which IS can be used to affect all aspects of the five forces driving competitive behaviour. This is made more difficult by the continuing developments in technology, where a decision that seems right today may well seem to have been a mistake in a few months' time. Rapid developments in Internet technology are opening up new opportunities and threats for many businesses – so much so that current prescriptions will date very quickly. The Internet is changing consumers' expectations, and is encouraging new entrants into many markets – as well as increasingly strong responses from established players. So technology is one of the driving forces of a volatile competitive landscape in many industries. This means that IS strategies have to be adaptive and flexible.

Above all, IS is not an isolated part of the organisation. It interacts not just with broad strategy, but with most other functional areas of the business – which may have different expectations of IS. This suggests that developing an IS strategy can at best be a cautious, provisional approach, with an emphasis on learning and reflection, and a willingness to change course if business requirements change, as they inevitably will.

CHAPTER QUESTIONS

1. How can information systems play a role in the competitive position of a firm? Illustrate your answer by giving five examples.

2. Implementation of computer-based information systems can be an opportunity but also a threat. Explain when and why it can be a threat and illustrate your answer with two examples.

3. How does the Internet play a role in changing the competitive landscape in many industries? What is an Internet strategy and what choices have to be made when a firm formulates an Internet strategy?

4. Give examples of how information systems can hinder strategic objectives of organisations.

5. Products or services and characteristics of organisations play a role in the way they use information systems. Explain (a) how a product or service can be critical and (b) how the characteristics of a firm can play a critical role in using IS.

6. Many managers find it very difficult to formulate an information strategy. Give four possible reasons for this. Give suggestions or guidelines to deal with these difficulties in practice.

Further reading

Gottschalk, P. (1999) 'Strategic processes: implementation of formal plans – the case of information technology strategy', *Long Range Planning*, **32**(3), 362–72. Explores the planning problems of IT strategies. IT opportunities may change during implementation and the plan may hinder flexibility.

Levy, M. and Powell, P. (2000) 'Information systems strategy for small- and medium-sized enterprises: an organisational perspective', *Journal of Strategic Information Systems*, **9**(1), 63–84. Article focuses on specific problems and opportunities of using information systems for strategy advancement.

Ross, J.W. and Weill, P. (2002) 'Six IT decisions your IT people shouldn't make', *Harvard Business Review*, **80**(11), 84–91. A clear plea for general managers to take the lead in a small number of critical strategy and execution challenges but to get out of the way when it comes to more routine aspects of IT management.

Shapiro, C. and Varian, H. (1999) *Information Rules: A Strategic Guide to the Network Economy*, Harvard Business School Press, Boston. An authoritative analysis of the effects of the Internet, drawing on well-established economic principles to develop some fundamental and valuable lessons.

References

Applegate, L.M., Austin, R.D., McFarlan, F.W. (2003) *Corporate Information Strategy and Management: Text and Cases*, McGraw-Hill/Irwin, Boston, Mass.

Asbrand, D. (2001) 'Britannica.com: look under M for Mess', *The Industry Standard*, 14 March.

Bensaou, M. and Earl, M. (1998) 'The right mind set for managing information technology', *Harvard Business Review*, **78**(5), 119–28.

Boonstra, A. (2003) 'Structure and analysis of IS decision-making processes, *European Journal of Information Systems*, **12**(3), 195–209.

Chaffey, D. (2002) *E-Business and E-Commerce Management*, Financial Times/Prentice Hall, Harlow.

Dutta, S. and Segev, A. (1999) 'Business transformation on the Internet', *European Management Journal*, **17**(5), 466–76.

Earl, M.J. (2002) *Management Strategies for Information Technology*, Prentice Hall International, Hemel Hempstead.

Fites, D. (1996) 'Make your dealers your partners', *Harvard Business Review*, **74**(2), 84–92.

Fuller-Love, N. and Cooper, J. (2000) 'Deliberate versus emergent strategies: a case study of information technology in the Post Office', *International Journal of Information Management*, **20**, 209–23.

Kaplan, S. (2000) 'E-hubs: the new B2B marketplaces', *Harvard Business Review*, **78**(3), 97.

Lockamy, A. and Smith, W.I. (1997) 'A strategic alignment approach for effective business process reengineering: linking strategy, processes and customers for competitive advantage', *International Journal of Production Economics*, **50**, 141–53.

Loebbecke, C. and Jelassi, T. (1997) 'Concepts and technologies for virtual organizing: the Gerling journey', *European Management Journal*, **15**(2), 138–46.

Macmillan, M. (1997) 'Managing information systems: three key principles for general managers', *Journal of General Management*, **22**(3), 12–23.

Mintzberg, H., Quinn, J.B. and Ghoshal, S. (2003) *The Strategy Process: Concepts, Contexts, Cases*, Financial Times/Prentice Hall, Harlow

Oz, E. (2002), *Management Information Systems*, Thomson, Boston.

Porter, M.E. (1985) *Competitive Advantage: Creating and Sustaining Superior Performance*, Free Press, New York.

Porter, M.E. (2001) 'Strategy and the Internet', *Harvard Business Review*, **79**(2), 63–78.

Porter, M.E. and Millar, V.E. (1985) 'How information gives you competitive advantage', *Harvard Business Review*, **63**(4), 149–62.

Ross, J.W. and Weill, P. (2002) 'Six IT decisions your IT people shouldn't make', *Harvard Business Review*, **80**(11), 84–91.

Sabherwal, R., Hirschheim, R. and Goles, T. (2001) 'The dynamics of alignment: insights from a punctuated equilibrium', *Organization Science*, **12**(2), 179–97.

Shapiro, C. and Varian, H. (1999) *Information Rules: A Strategic Guide to the Network Economy*, Harvard Business School Press, Boston, Mass.

Smits, M.T. and van der Poel, K.G. (1997) 'The practice of information strategy in six information intensive organizations in the Netherlands', *Journal of Strategic Information Systems*, **6**(2), 129–48.

Spil, S. (2003) 'Dynamic and emergent information systems strategy formulation and implementation', *IT Management*, **9**(3), 22–37.

Stepanek, M. (1999) 'How an intranet opened doors', *Business Week*, 26 July.

Timmers, P. (2000) *Electronic Commerce: Strategies and Models for Business-to-Business Trading*, Wiley, Chichester.

Treacy, M. and Wiersema, F. (1995) *The Discipline of Market Leaders*, Harper Collins, New York.

Venkatraman, N. (1998) 'IT agenda 2000: not fixing technical bugs but creating business value', *European Management Journal*, **16**(5), 573–85.

Warner, M. and Witzel, M. (1999) 'The virtual general manager', *Journal of General Management*, **24**(4), 71–92.

CHAPTER 4

Using information systems to rethink business processes

Learning objectives

By the end of your work on this topic you should be able to:

- Understand the role of IS in supporting changes to business processes

- Explain how IS enables people to rethink business processes within and between organisations

- Apply some approaches to process innovation

- Identify the human and organisational issues which arise in IS-enabled process change

- Contribute to sound decisions on such change by understanding the management dilemmas

Redon

Redon is a city council in a western country and has approximately 200,000 inhabitants. In this country, city councils are responsible for local economic policy, attracting companies, parts of the infrastructure and for services directed to local residents and companies, such as licences and permits. Municipalities are partly funded by the central government but also collect local taxes from residents and companies. Some services are standardised and simple (e.g. car licences) while others are complicated (attracting companies to settle). Redon is vertically organised, which means that 20 rather isolated departments provide services.

The Redon tax administration is responsible for collecting local taxes, which add about €100m to the revenues of the municipality, mainly through a property tax. It has about 120 employees who work in a highly computerised environment. The organisation structure includes main departments such as valuations, levy, collection and remissions and support departments such as finance, HRM and IS.

Some years ago, management realised that changes were needed and they had to use IS more effectively. The city council wanted better information, while the tax unit itself faced internal problems:

■ contacts with local taxpayers were not effective – they saw the system as bureaucratic and frustrating;

■ there was a large backlog of assessments and objections;

■ it made mistakes because of using incorrect data;

■ the process for dealing with each customer involved many departments – valuations estimated building values, another department assessed the tax, a third collected the tax and yet another arranged payments and remissions.

The information systems were designed to serve internal needs, such as recording historical data. Every department had its own IS policy, though the IS department had connected some systems to enable them to use each other's data.

An external consultancy analysed the organisation and identified the following problems:

■ the functional structure was oriented towards procedures ratter than customers;

■ taxpayers were all treated in the same way in spite of their differing needs;

■ the functional structure and rigid rules led to complex procedures even in simple cases;

■ the information systems were not integrated, which led to unreliable data and too many mistakes;

■ there were no clear standards against which to measure the administration's performance.

This chapter discusses how problems such as those faced by Redon can be dealt with by taking a new view of operational processes and by using IS to support those processes. Later in this chapter there is an interview with one of the directors and a description of how staff in the organisation responded to the problems.

Introduction

Early information systems supported separate business functions. These often worked well for the function concerned, and encouraged managers to apply computer-based systems more widely. However, these independent systems produced inconsistent and often unreliable data. The next step was to link the systems with one joint database. This included (ideally) consistent data about all the separate functional areas and often led to more efficient, reliable and accessible information systems – but management was still using the technology to support existing business processes. The way of doing business and organising work did not fundamentally change.

Developments in information systems technology, and some prominent experiments by new companies using this technology, led others to think more radically. They saw that modern information systems could enable business to work in a fundamentally different way (Galliers and Baets, 1997; Grover and Malhotra, 1997; Sauer and Yetton, 1997). In the management literature, people such as Hammer (1990) and Davenport (1993) also advocated a completely new approach. They called this 'business process re-engineering' or 'business process redesign'. Other terms representing similar ideas for linking separate aspects of a business include enterprise resource planning (ERP) systems and customer relationship management (CRM) systems.

This chapter elaborates this perspective, showing how people can use information systems to organise processes more effectively. This includes inter-organisational as well as internal processes, since the Internet and other networks make it easier to link all the processes within a value chain. This may blur the boundaries between organisations and changes the value chain of a business. Figure 4.1 illustrates these stages.

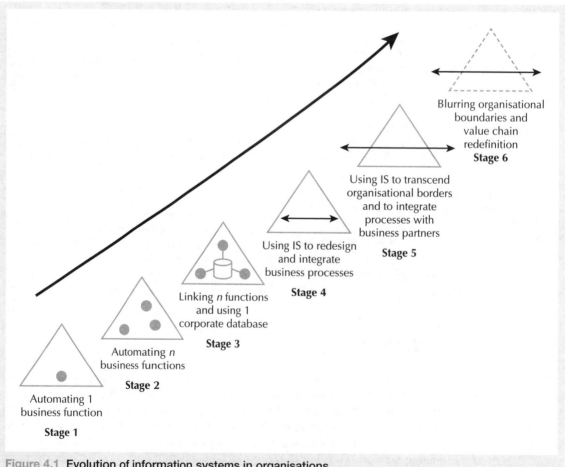

Figure 4.1 Evolution of information systems in organisations

The Chapter Case is about a local authority tax department that has begun to make changes in the direction shown in the figure. It used to have many isolated processes and unconnected systems – which led to a wasteful system that provided a poor service to local residents. It then tried to work in a more customer-centred way by redesigning its processes and supporting them with modern information systems. That experience illustrates many of the themes in the chapter.

The first main section defines the topic more precisely, while the next section describes some approaches to innovating business processes. We then explain how IS can play an important role in process innovation. Next, we consider the managerial and organisational aspects, and the chapter concludes by discussing some management dilemmas in process innovation. The overall aim is to understand the managerial issues when people use information systems to change business processes in and between organisations.

4.1 Rethinking and innovating business processes

Day-to-day pressure and the force of habit mean that the established way of doing things becomes the only way. It is hard to think about these processes with an open mind. People in an established department, say purchasing, see themselves as specialised, experienced and knowledgeable. Purchasing is their job. Suppose that someone suggests that production operators could, with the assistance of modern information systems, order the materials that they use. Purchasing staff are likely to resist the suggestion instinctively, whatever the possible merits. This illustrates a central challenge of rethinking and innovating business processes – an independent position, an open mind and a critical attitude to things that people take for granted are all needed.

What is a business process? Teng et al. (1994) define it as 'a set of logically related tasks performed to achieve a defined business outcome'. A business outcome is a product or service which is delivered to a customer (internal or external). The business process is the chain of tasks from purchasing to manufacturing to selling and delivering.

Different functional departments usually perform these linked tasks. They specialise in one step, such as design or purchasing, and design internal systems to make that part of the process efficient. The difficulties arise at the boundaries as the product or service moves between departments. This can become a source of trouble and wasted time which Goldratt and Cox (1992) illustrate in an amusing way. Boundary troubles lead to misunderstandings and time-consuming meetings since nobody fully owns the complete process or takes responsibility for it. Departments optimise their partial responsibility. Purchasing tries to buy goods under optimal delivery conditions. Manufacturing focuses on an optimal use of production facilities. Sales tries to meet all the expectations of its customers. The result will often be a slow process, full of mistakes and with more attention to internal procedures than to customer value. It is also very difficult to connect the different information systems.

These problems led to the argument that people should manage organisations from a process view rather than a functional view. This would lead to customer-directed processes that would improve quality and lower costs, supported by information technology. One of the earliest advocates of process innovation (Hammer, 1990) said: 'we should re-"reengineer" our businesses: use the power of modern information technology to radically redesign our business processes in order to achieve dramatic improvements in their performance'. Similarly Teng et al. (1994) wrote: 'redesign or reengineering is the critical analysis and radical redesign of existing business processes to achieve breakthrough improvements in performance measures'. What these authors emphasise is the notion of discontinuous thinking. They advocate recognising, and breaking away from, the historical rules and assumptions that underlie current operations.

Information technology is important in process innovation, but it is not the only place to start. Critical evaluation of business practice and creative thinking can also lead to process innovations, as the ITEC example shows.

MIS in Practice   ITEC

ITEC, a company which repairs and maintains computers in printing companies, provides an example of process innovation without using IT. When there is a fault, someone in the printing office calls the company. An engineer comes to diagnose the problem and estimates the time needed to do the repair and the costs. If the customer accepts the estimate the engineer orders the parts and repairs the computer. ITEC later sends an invoice for payment. The whole process is often time-consuming and leads to many complaints. The company therefore analysed the breakdowns. They found they could speed up the process by selling customers a pack of the spare parts most likely to be needed. Customers who bought such a pack got an immediate repair in 90 per cent of all cases. This simple process redesign improved efficiency and satisfied customers.

However, computer-based systems such as enterprise resource planning (ERP) systems can strengthen the case for radical process change. They make possible what was previously impossible, and the Internet has opened up yet more possibilities.

Managers usually make process innovations by combining separate processes and designing the remaining ones to be more efficient. They often find that most of the

---

MIS in Practice   Port of Rotterdam

The Port of Rotterdam (*www.portofrotterdam.com/UK/*) controls approximately 100 km of waterway. This process starts at sea as each ship reports its approach to the harbour. That information is used for traffic control, tariffs and special arrangements for dangerous cargoes. Not long ago the harbour had 126 departments, each with its own IT systems, and used more than 100 applications. 'That became unmanageable,' says Chris van de Weerd, IT manager at the Traffic Management department.

At the start of this year we moved from a departmental structure to a process-based organisation. This move also led to an IT audit and a redesign of our information systems architecture. Now we only have a few information systems which support the arrival and departure of any ship. One of these systems is a knowledge system which helps to analyse all relevant data and to determine whether a ship needs a pilot to enter the harbour.

time in a process is taken up waiting for the next process to start – a sure sign that it involves too many departments.

While the principles are easy to understand, the practice is more difficult, since process innovation involves significant changes in responsibilities and a more explicit orientation towards the customer. The changes also need to be aligned with broader strategy. They might involve closer cooperation with suppliers and customers as there are further benefits in innovating processes between, as well as within, organisations. Finally, new information systems will support the new processes. They are challenging projects to manage, and the failure rate is high.

■ Summary

■ Changing environments and new IT generates ideas for process redesign.

■ IT enables a process orientation (as opposed to functional ways of organising).

■ Process changes potentially affect all aspects of the organisation, including IS.

4.2 Approaches to innovating processes

Consultants and researchers have developed principles and methods for innovating business processes.

■ Organising process innovation

Process innovation usually takes place as a project within an established organisation, with staff seconded from several units to work with external consultants. Figure 4.2 shows a common sequence of activities.

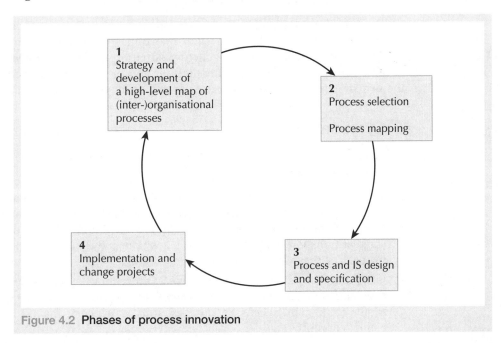

Figure 4.2 **Phases of process innovation**

Most authorities take the view that a company should start with a view of the organisation (or business unit) as a whole and a clear strategic vision of the business and the environment. Business processes should not be (re)designed in isolation, so, first, a high-level map of the (inter-)organisational processes has to be constructed. From that map, particular processes or subprocesses can be prioritised for innovation.

Common criteria are:

- the health of the process (unhealthy processes are dysfunctional and prone to error, with extensive information exchange, redundancy of work and iteration of tasks);
- the criticality of the process (processes can be ranked in order of importance relative to the competences and the performance of the organisation. Which processes have the greatest potential for improvement?);
- the feasibility of innovation (it is more feasible to change some processes than others, either on technical grounds, e.g. a new software package, or organisational, e.g. readiness to change).

Then the process innovation can be designed, specified and implemented.

Systematic design or clean sheet?

Within this view on the organisation of process innovation there are two different methods (Peppard and Rowland, 1995):

- systematic design: identify and analyse existing processes, evaluate them critically and plan major improvements;
- clean sheet approach: fundamentally rethink the way that the product or service is delivered and design new processes from scratch.

The first approach will probably get more support from staff who are actively involved in processes and may lead to certain improvements more quickly. The danger is that starting from the current situation may limit radical thinking. The second approach is more fundamental but can probably be carried out only with the help of external advisers because of the bias of staff inside a company.

Systematic approach

If a company decides to follow a systematic design approach, Peppard and Rowland (1995) suggest asking four questions:

1. Is it possible to eliminate process steps? Many processes contain unnecessary steps and consequently cause unnecessary waiting times. For example, insurance claims move between departments and have a waiting time in each one. Every stage of transport, and each activity, takes time and effort. Managing and monitoring each of these steps is also time-consuming.

2. Is it possible to simplify process steps? Often, unnecessary forms and too many procedures are used. Nowadays many firms use the Internet to enable the customer to key in necessary data to start a process that is an example of simplification.

3. Is it possible to integrate process steps? Some tasks which are separated and executed by different people or different departments can easily by done by one. This often makes it easier to manage a process and divide responsibilities more clearly.

4. Is it possible to automate process steps? For example, can dangerous or boring work be eliminated, and is there scope for eliminating duplication in capturing and transferring data?

Process mapping and modelling

Kim (1995) developed an approach that models a process and then uses this model to analyse the process (see Figure 4.3). This method can be used for both the systematic design and clean sheet approaches. Kim distinguishes three constructs:

1. Event: a perceived change of status at one point in time that is of interest to the organisation.

2. Process: an activity or series of activities performed by the customer or between the customer and organisation over time, often as a response to the triggering events.

MIS in Practice   A hospital process

John Smith arrives at the hospital with stomach ache at 1.30 p.m. He has to go to the reception desk first to register. He has to fill in a form, verify his insurance status, wait his turn and pay the doctor's fee in advance (as required by this particular healthcare scheme). After receiving a consultation slip from the reception desk, he has to go to the internal medicine department on the second floor. It is now 2 p.m.

At the second floor reception, John gives his form to a nurse and waits for his turn. This is normally at least an hour even when he has an appointment. Consultation with the doctor lasts about fifteen minutes. The doctor diagnoses food poisoning and prescribes some medicine. John takes the prescription to the cashier's desk in reception, pays the bill and goes down to the pharmacy in the basement. After waiting another half an hour, he receives his medicine.

By the time he leaves the hospital, it is already 4 p.m., too late to return to work. John wonders if anything can be done to speed up this slow process.

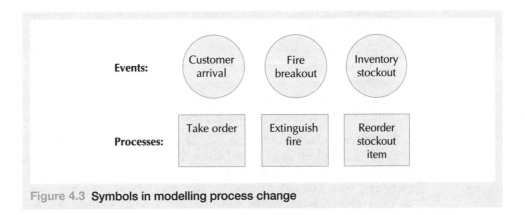

Figure 4.3 **Symbols in modelling process change**

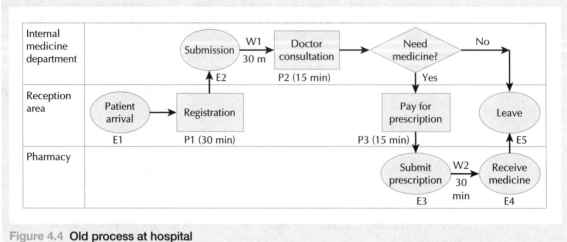

Figure 4.4 **Old process at hospital**

3. Wait: a significant average delay before the start of an event or a process due to a queue or other unfavourable conditions of the organisation.

In the hospital example below the approach will be explained by describing the old process and the design of a new one.

Figure 4.4 models this process in a diagram, which helps us to analyse the process flow. We can use the model to give an accurate picture of the present situation and to identify how it can be improved. We also need to consider whether those improvements should be made radically or incrementally.

Each process (boxes P1–P3) can be divided into subprocesses – Figure 4.4 only shows the broad picture. The challenge is to improve the process by cutting lead times and reducing the number of people involved without causing quality problems. Kim mentions the following principles for designing processes:

1. Start with the most critical process.

2. Reduce the number of process steps by eliminating unnecessary ones.

3. Transform processes into events. In Figure 4.4 the registration process can turn into an event by issuing each patient with a smart card containing personal health and bank account information.

4. Minimise the travel distance. When the chain moves up and down a 'red flag' is raised. The number of involved parties should be as small as possible.

5. Make processes and events parallel. In Figure 4.4, process P1 and process P3 can be done simultaneously while event E3 can be done by the doctor during the consultation.

6. Reduce the waiting time before process but eliminate it before event. Events take hardly any time and it is irritating and often unnecessary to have to wait.

To illustrate what can be done, Figure 4.5 shows the improved process.

These suggestions are derived from Teng's process-modelling approach. He suggests that a process has to be as short as possible (less time) and as narrow as possible (fewer people). Comparing the old and the new processes we can see that IS (card readers, smart cards, networks and databases) make it possible to:

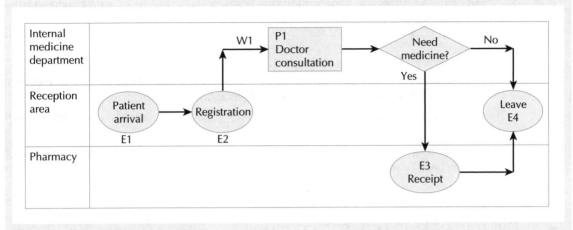

Figure 4.5 **New process at hospital**

- change the registration process (old P1) into an event (new E2);
- remove the wait (old W2) into an event (new E3);
- remove the payment process (old P3) by integrating it in the receipt event (new E3).

This illustrates how computer-based information systems open many opportunities to rethink a process and bring significant reductions in process steps and waits.

Activity 4.1 Analysing a process

Use Kim's method to describe a process in an organisation.

Use Peppard's four questions to analyse this process.

This analysis can be characterised as a systematic approach. An alternative would have been the clean sheet approach to process design. Make a list of the advantages and disadvantages of the two approaches.

Indicate the consequences for the information systems of each alternative. Discuss also consequences for other factors, including people.

This method can stimulate discussions about 'old' and 'new' processes. A clear scheme of the old situation shows how things really are and how much time and how many steps they take. A danger is that it is close to 'systematic design': it improves the situation without designing a fundamentally new process, disconnected from the

CASE QUESTIONS 4.1

What stimulated managers at Redon tax administration to start redesigning processes?

Which processes did they change?

How did they change the processes, in terms of the Peppard and Rowland approaches?

How will this kind of process change have consequences for the information systems they use?

old situation. However, in designing processes, a clear scheme of a proposed alternative makes a good discussion possible.

■ Summary

- ■ Process innovation can take place by analysing the old processes or by designing a new process from scratch; both have advantages and disadvantages.
- ■ In doing a systematic design, asking 'can we eliminate, simplify, integrate or automate' can help to stimulate ideas.
- ■ Modelling and analysing old and new processes (e.g. with Kim's modelling approach) can help in making new designs.

4.3 The role of IS in process change

Information systems and process change provide a further illustration of the interaction model. One perspective is that managers should first redesign their processes and then implement IS to support them – as in Figure 4.6(a).

The alternative view is that rapidly developing information technologies are themselves often driving business process change. Davenport (1993) gives examples of computer-based information systems – what he calls a 'disruptive technology' – enabling new processes. He suggests that the power of information systems is to set new 'rules', which enable change in the way people and organisations work – as shown in Table 4.1.

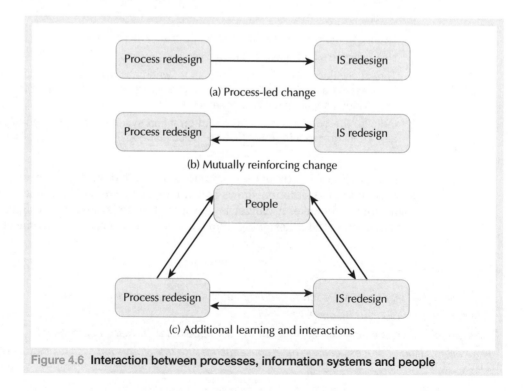

Figure 4.6 **Interaction between processes, information systems and people**

Table 4.1 **How information systems can change the rules**

Old rule	Disruptive technology	New rule
Information can appear in only one place at one time	Shared databases	Information can appear simultaneously in as many places as it is needed
Only experts can perform complex work	Expert systems	A generalist can do the work of an expert
Managers make all decisions	Decision support tools	Decision-making is part of everyone's job
Field staff need offices where they can receive, store, retrieve and transmit information	Wireless data communication and portable computers	Field personnel can send and receive information wherever they are
You have to find out where things are	Automatic identification and tracking technology	Things tell you where they are

Source: Based on Davenport (1993).

The Internet is the driving force behind many of the electronic marketplaces that are changing purchasing processes so radically. As these markets develop, people need to update their processes – and they need more advanced systems to support these new processes. So process change and IS are becoming mutually reinforcing factors – as shown in Figure 4.6(b).

A further interaction, of great practical significance, is that, as people use information systems to improve their processes, they learn what is possible. This helps them to become more confident in breaking out of the old mindset. They are more willing to abandon the traditional ways of thinking which, as we remarked at the outset, can block attempts at process change. They can see new possibilities of process change – which will require further new systems. The ChemTec example in Chapter 8 illustrates this, and the additional interaction is shown as Figure 4.6(c).

The continuing Chapter Case illustrates the interaction between information systems and business process and organisational change at the tax administration.

The case illustrates how IS enables process innovation and strategic change. It reduces the number of steps, departments and people involved, and supports individuals by helping them to access data and make well-informed decisions quickly. The information systems are built around points of contact with customers instead of around functions that are just a small part of a process. Information systems follow from the chosen organisational design and become increasingly cross functional and inter-organisational. In this case, the information systems have enabled these new ways of organising. That does not always happen, and depends on management decisions on each of these elements.

Davenport (1993) suggests that there are many opportunities to use information systems to support fundamental process changes. He distinguishes nine categories of impacts, which are shown in Table 4.2.

This table illustrates that IS enables organisations to work on a wider geographic scale and in a more consistent, controlled and reliable manner. Customers can be anywhere (Internet), employees can be anywhere (groupware, Internet, portable systems) and processes can be controlled more effectively (workflow management systems, expert systems).

Redon: continued

To overcome their problems, the administration started to define their products, services, markets and customers. They learned that groups of taxpayers have different needs and expectations. Companies expect a more personalised approach – such as an account manager at the tax administration with whom they can discuss their tax position. They expect that person to be able to give advice. Taxpayers expect a simpler form, and the possibility of sending it via the Internet. They also appreciate a call centre they can phone to get answers to tax questions.

Managers used this idea to restructure the organisation around customer groups. There are line departments, each dealing with one group of customers – big companies, medium/small companies or local residents. Within the company departments, staff deal with particular companies. Work processes and information systems reflect these differences.

The local residents department deals with large numbers, and needs to be reliable and timely. A workflow management system helps managers to control the speed and reliability of customer contacts. There is also a call centre (with an e-mail option) to answer taxpayers' questions quickly. The system is easy to use and supports staff by including a feature which suggests the questions they should ask the citizen. An interactive website allows people to submit their tax forms and check progress electronically, which saves time for everyone.

The company-directed departments needed an advanced 'company information system' to record relevant company data in an orderly manner. External systems, such as that at the chamber of commerce, had to feed into this system, so it was connected to the Internet. The account managers had very specific demands in terms of screen layouts and drilldown features, so an expert system was provided that helps them deal more consistently with complex tax problems.

Company account managers, call centre agents and people who deal with local residents were trained to be effective, efficient and customer-oriented. Many had to be re-educated from being a tax expert to being a customer-directed account manager.

Table 4.2 **How information systems can support business process change**

Category	Description	Example
Integrative	Coordinating and integrating tasks and processes	With all the relevant information easily available at one time and place, bank staff can help customers with different needs
Geographical	Transferring information over long distances	Using the Internet, businesses can perceive the whole (connected) world as their marketplace, rather than a limited region
Automational	Eliminating or reducing human labour	In the retail industry, many inventories are connected electronically with suppliers in order to automate the stock control completely
Analytical	Support decision-making by better analysis of information	Decision support systems help users to develop different scenarios and make better decisions
Informational	Providing information in right amounts at the right time	Information systems can be helpful in providing managers with information in the form of, e.g., exception reporting
Sequential	Changing the process sequences or enabling parallelism	Because information is available at many places at the same time, people can work simultaneously on the processing of an order
Intellectual	Capturing and distributing intellectual assets	Expert systems, for instance in financial services, can distribute corporate knowledge to financial advisers
Tracking	Monitoring processes	Point-of-sale systems to constantly monitor inventory levels
Disintermediation	Eliminating intermediaries	IT can replace the information previously supplied by the intermediary (e.g. wholesalers)

Source: Davenport (1993).

Clearly, Table 4.2 identifies links between process innovation and broader strategy and choices for companies about whether to perform certain processes themselves or outsource them, supported by information systems. Whether companies can realise the potential in practice depends on how well managers deal with the elements in Figure 1.5 (p. 16).

Lockamy and Smith (1997) suggest two principles in using information systems to innovate business processes:

- systems must facilitate easy access to process information across functional boundaries;
- the assessment of IS for use in process design must be conducted within the context of the wider IS strategy (see Chapter 3).

These two principles suggest that information systems enable the innovation of processes based on a strategic vision of the organisation. IS can bring that vision to life. The next section illustrates this by describing three examples of process change enabled by IS: ERP, e-commerce and Internet procurement.

CASE QUESTIONS 4.2

How have information systems supported the process change at Redon?

What related changes have there been in culture and structure?

Who might see these changes as a threat? Why? What are the consequences for the change management?

Summary

- IS will often support or drive process change.
- IS can (among other things) be used to facilitate easy access to process information across functional boundaries.
- A management issue is to relate IS used to support process design to the overall IS strategy.

4.4 Examples of IS-enabled process change

Enterprise resource planning

Many companies now use information systems for enterprise resource planning (ERP) (see also Chapter 2). An ERP system helps coordinate all facets of business, including planning, manufacturing, sales and finance (Laudon and Laudon, 2004). ERP systems eliminate expensive links between isolated IT systems in different business functions. Within an ERP system, sales representatives can easily enter online orders from customers and verify inventory levels. Manufacturing and purchasing files are automatically updated. If the system has a link to the Internet, customers can check the progress of an order.

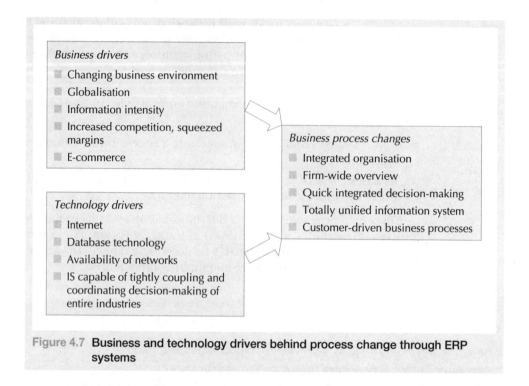

Figure 4.7 **Business and technology drivers behind process change through ERP systems**

Implementing an ERP system implies changing processes. Vendors advise changing these radically before putting such a system in place. Information flows cross functional borders and different units can access the same data. Enterprise systems are usually implemented in stages, with the most essential modules first (often finance, purchasing, manufacturing and marketing). Many organisations choose to extend their system to suppliers and customers (often using the Internet) so that it becomes an inter-organisational system. In this 'extended enterprise' borders become unclear and several partners use the same database and information systems.

Figure 4.7 shows business and technology drivers that lie behind the wide acceptance of ERP. They lead to an integrated business from an information flow point of view. Customers trigger a chain of activities (a business process) when they make a transaction. People in companies who share responsibility for a process have an overview and can make decisions more confidently. Technology, as mentioned in the figure, makes this possible. But, as Figure 1.3 (p. 11) shows, people and procedures are also part of the system and their response will affect the outcomes of process innovation.

The following example illustrates the implementation of an ERP system at Elf Atochem and shows the strong relation between strategy, process change and IS.

While ERP has many advantages, there are also disadvantages. These include possible inflexibility and the difficulty of securing a fit between the system and the characteristics of the business. Many managers say that they have to adapt their business to the ERP system rather than vice versa to make the system work. The system forces the company to organise its processes in a prescribed way – which may lose a distinct advantage.

Elf Atochem North America is a chemicals subsidiary of the French company Elf Aquitaine. Following a series of mergers in the early 1990s, managers were hampered by the fragmentation of critical information systems among its 12 business units. Ordering systems were not integrated with production systems; sales forecasts were not tied to budgeting systems or to performance measurement systems. Each unit was tracking and reporting its financial data independently. As a result of the many incompatible systems, operating data were not flowing smoothly through the organisation and senior management was not getting the information needed to make sound and timely business decisions.

The company's executives saw that an enterprise system would be the best way to integrate the data flows. Looking beyond the technology, the executives saw that the real source of Elf Atochem's difficulties was not the fragmentation of its systems but the fragmentation of its organisation. Although the 12 business units shared many of the same customers, each unit was managed autonomously.

Management decided to focus on four processes: materials management, production planning, order management and financial reporting. These cross-unit processes were the ones most distorted by the fragmented organisational structure. Moreover, they had the greatest impact on the company's ability to manage its customer relationships in a way that would both enhance customer satisfaction and improve corporate profitability.

Elf Atochem also made fundamental changes to its organisational structure. In the financial area, for example, accounts receivable and credit departments were combined into one. This enabled the system to consolidate a customer's orders into a single account and issue a single invoice. It also allowed managers to monitor overall customer profitability – something that had been impossible to do when orders were fragmented across units.

Source: Based on Davenport (1998).

This brings us to a more general point: IS can also constrain real process innovation. Information systems that are expensive legacies of the past are difficult to adapt and limit the ability of organisations to change their processes radically. New systems, such as ERP, can urge organisations to arrange their processes in a specific way without leaving enough space for creativity and for doing things differently. Managers who are aware of these dangers can, however, ensure that they try to obtain the benefits of such systems, without the limitations.

Using the Internet for e-commerce

Another example of IS-enabled process change is the use of the Internet (see also Chapter 2). This opens up enormous possibilities for the transformation of processes. Most organisations now have an Internet presence through their website, which has to reflect a strategic vision about how the business will use the Internet. If the site is going to manage transactions with customers, reliable methods for handling them need to be organised. This implies a new design of that core business process.

When organisations decide to use the Internet, they also have to decide between combining it with non-Internet activities or transferring all their operations to the

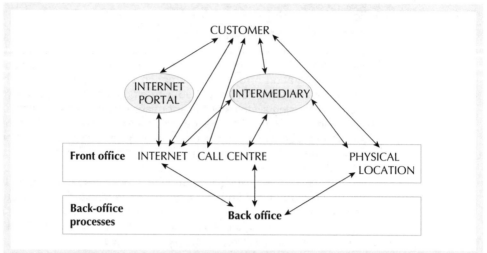

Figure 4.8 **Multi-channel approach: customers choose their own channel for every transaction**

Internet. The companies taking the former (multi-channel) route have to combine processes consistently and clearly for their customers (see Figure 4.8).

Organising such complicated processes in order to have an efficient and reliable fulfilment is a major focal point for many project managers. An important concern for companies that move (a part of) their processes to the Internet has been to ensure they can handle the associated physical processes, such as handling orders, arranging shipment, receiving payment and dealing with after-sales service. This gives an advantage to traditional retailers who can support their websites with existing fulfilment processes. Effective B2B applications require that the business processes between customers and suppliers fit with each other. This has been a bigger task than many expected.

Due to the advent of mobile phones (so-called m-commerce) and other devices, the number of channels that people may use to contact companies and place orders is growing. This means that the forefront of customer contact increases in variety and options, while back-office systems are needed to collect all relevant information and make it available to all front-office contact points, such as call centres and branches.

Activity 4.2 Change at a bank

A traditional bank decides to change its operations by offering call centre and Internet services to its customers. It also wants to attract new customers.

▪ *What ideas can you generate from Table 4.2 on how the bank could use IS to support these changes?*

▪ *What are the implications of the options in Figure 4.8 for process redesign?*

▪ *What will the proposed changes mean for the structure of the organisation, the employees and the customers?*

Innovating procurement processes

Procurement refers to all activities involved with obtaining items from a supplier; this not only includes purchasing, but also inbound logistics such as transportation, goods-in and warehousing before the item is used (Chaffey, 2002). Since the advent of the Internet, procurement is increasingly perceived as a business process that can be used to achieve significant savings and other benefits. A traditional procurement process includes activities and process steps such as:

- search for goods;
- fill in paper request;
- send to buyer;
- into buyer's in-tray;
- buyer enters order number;
- buyer authorises order;
- buyer prints order;
- order copied to supplier and goods-in;
- delivery from supplier;
- order copy to accounts;
- three-way invoice match;
- cheque payment.

This process can be characterised by a long cycle time and by many process steps that all lead to a slow, expensive flow of activities open to errors. Hammer (2001, p. 84) says about traditional procurement processes:

> It's the mirror image of your supplier's order-fulfillment process, with many of the same tasks and information requirements. When your purchasing agent fills out a requisition form, for instance, she is performing essentially the same work that the supplier's order entry clerk performs when he takes the order. Yet there's probably little or no coordination between the two processes.

Information systems can be used to reduce the number of steps and to reduce the number of people involved (see section 4.2 – e-procurement is the electronic integration and management of all procurement activities (Chaffey, 2002). An important driver for e-procurement is of course cost reduction; in many cases the costs of ordering exceed the value of the products purchased. Direct cost reductions are achieved through efficiencies in the process that may result in less staff time spent in searching and ordering but also in reduction of inventory costs by lower cycle times. Other advantages include: improved budget control, quality improvement and elimination of errors, increased buyer productivity (now they can concentrate on more strategic issues), lower prices through company-wide standardisation and control and better management information (Turban et al., 2000).

A typical e-procurement process may include the following process steps:

- search for goods;
- order on the Internet;

MIS in Practice   E-procurement at IBM

An IBM purchasing manager reported about the company's e-procurement system:

[Our Internet procurement system] has eliminated a lot of transactional activity – raising orders, printing orders, fax, paper trails all over. Previously most suppliers were receiving purchase orders by paper. They would then look at what we wanted, write that on the paper and send it back to us, and we would key it into our system – a lot of manual activity. That is now completely automated – an order goes electronically to the supplier . . . they send back an electronic message saying they can deliver. We receive the goods into the system, and there is a match between the physical and the electronic, which triggers the payment process.

Source: Personal communication.

- delivery from supplier;
- receive invoice;
- cheque payment.

These steps can be automated, however, if company systems are integrated with supplier systems.

There are a number of organisational risks and impacts related to e-procurement. One issue is that the integration of company systems with those of suppliers demands trust and a long-term partnership with the supplier. Building up such a relationship may take years and will not always be perceived as desirable, since system integration with a supplier may lead to dependency.

Another internal issue is that e-procurement has huge implications for the procurement staff; it may for instance lead to redundancies or redeployment. When e-procurement process is operational, procurement staff have to focus on more strategic activities, such as contract management. An implication for other employees is that they may all get authorisations for procurement, which may lead to a dispersion of tasks and responsibilities. It may also create a number of complicated security issues, since many people become involved in this process.

Summary

- Implementing an ERP system is an example of IS-based process change because it integrates information resources and redesign processes. Managers should think carefully about which modules of ERP will be implemented, given the strengths and limitations of such systems.

- Doing business over the Internet by electronic commerce is another example of (inter-organisational) process change. Implementing such a change has huge implications and demands a new process design.

- The Internet can also be used to enable electronic procurement. This may lead to ongoing improvements in the buying procees. The organisational issues are associated with dependency on suppliers, the reorganisation of the procurement function and the involvement of other members of the organisation with the e-procurement process.

4.5 Managing process innovation

Many authors on process innovation emphasise the radical organisational change with information technology. They suggest a strong reduction of process steps and lead times by making fewer people responsible for the process. Critics argue that this approach is too narrow and fails to address important issues, particularly those concerning organisational change and politics. Process innovation projects usually have wide consequences (Willcocks and Smith, 1995):

- work units change, from functional departments to process teams;
- jobs change, from simple tasks to multi-dimensional work;
- people's roles change, from controlled to empowered;
- focus of performance shifts, from activity to results;
- values change, from protective to productive.

If such changes are not managed carefully and consciously, problems may arise, going from indifference and passivity to stronger forms of resistance. A potential danger is that the focus of the project team is on the development or adaptation of the IS behind the process change and the design mechanics of the new process. Human issues can easily be ignored, which may lead to problems during implementation and operations.

The Chapter Case interview below with one of the directors of the Redon tax administration unit provides an illustration of the view of a manager on process innovation. The interview suggests that business process change is a challenging activity – mainly because of the need to manage the interactions between the various organisational elements. Markus (1994) researched the organisational issues that surround process innovation by interviewing more than 50 management consultants. The objective was to identify which process innovation projects have a good chance of succeeding. From the interviews various positive and negative starting points arose. These are summarised in Table 4.3.

Table 4.3 **Positive and negative starting points for process change**

Positive starting point for process innovation	Negative starting point for process innovation
Senior management support	No sponsor or wrong sponsor
Realistic expectations	Technical focus
Independent and cooperative staff	Low-level support
Project directed to growth and development rather than cost reduction and savings	Too many changes at the same time
Joint vision and mission	Project leader without authority
Continuing communications	Poor financial conditions
Full-time project team with competent members	Fear and lack of optimism
Resources	Animosity to IT

Source: Markus (1994).

115

Redon: Interview with a director

Why did you decide to reorganise the processes of your administration?

When I started as a director in this unit, I was confronted with an organisation which received an enormous amount of written objections to tax assessments (more than 15 per cent of all the assessments resulted in a formal objection). Many of these objections were the result of mistakes on our side. Another problem was that we did not differentiate between types of customers: big companies were treated in the same way as individuals. Such a working procedure results in annoyances and other problems.

Can you describe your ideals with respect to your organisation?

My ideal is a customer-directed and efficient organisation. Customers have to be treated in an appropriate way: there are big companies, small companies, different kinds of individuals (e.g. prosperous people, students, immigrants) and they all need to be treated suitably. Employees have to manage themselves and take responsibility for their work and their errors. They have to deal with taxpayers and cooperate proactively with colleagues.

Customer-focus in a tax administration?

Yes. Our starting point is compliance: this is a strategy where those subject to tax (customers) are treated in a just and careful way in order to create a relationship beneficial to the customers as well as to us. By treating customers well, they become more cooperative in paying tax.

How can you realise customer focus?

We try to shorten lead times, to increase accessibility by phone, to set up websites, to have account managers and to create help-desks to assist people with their forms. People are more willing to pay taxes (though as little as legally possible) when we treat them in a friendly and efficient way.

Is this only a matter of culture?

No, it is not only a matter of culture. The structure of the organisation, the working processes and the automated systems also have to contribute to such a change. An integrated approach is needed; this is much more important than simply changing cultural aspects, parts of the structure or the IT system. The complexity of such a change is that organisational issues, human issues and technological issues all play an important role. To manage these aspects similarly makes such change rather difficult, but also challenging.

So this is a far-reaching renovation?

Yes, it can be compared with a house. When the circumstances and the needs of the residents change they have to renovate the house. In many cases, an outsider sees the need before the residents. They live there and have dealt with the problems for years. Translate this to an organisation: from time to time it is necessary to change the functions and processes to make the organisation more customer-directed. This is because the needs of the customers change or because there are new possibilities (for example IS) of organising things in more effective ways.

Markus concluded that if there are more negative than positive starting points, it is better to improve these conditions rather than to start IT-enabled process innovation. The Chapter Case shows how the context of change influences the outcome.

▣ Summary

- Process design projects are broad projects where different dimensions demand explicit attention. These dimensions include: IS, politics, people and financial resources.

- The human side especially demands a lot of attention because of the implications it may have for people: their work units and their jobs may change.

Redon: continued

The account of the tax administration of Redon shows how some units of the municipality are changing their processes, using IS and the Internet to make it possible. Some are now well advanced in using the Internet to improve their services – the tax administration is one. Other departments only have a 'brochure ware' website or no website at all. The municipality lacks an overall vision of how to transform and use IT including the Internet to become more efficient and more customer-focused.

The home page of Redon's website makes policy documents and reports available and provides information and links to department websites. It is also possible to submit specific questions, e.g. about policies and procedures, by the Internet, but the response is slow because there is no clear procedure on how to deal with them. This often leads to complaints.

Another possible problem for Redon is that many employees have a quite bureaucratic, department-centred attitude and find it difficult to collaborate effectively with other departments and to perceive the services from the local residents' point of view.

CASE QUESTIONS 4.3

What approach did the tax administration follow in relation to process change (use the models in this chapter to organise your answer)?

What are the advantages and disadvantages of that approach?

How would you assess the approach from the point of view of the city council as a whole?

What would you advocate: a department-by-department approach to process change or a council-wide strategy? Relate your answer to the findings in Table 4.3.

■ This implies that process design projects need to take account of the challenging task of managing not only the technical aspects but also the interactions between the many organisational elements.

Conclusions

In this chapter we have outlined the idea of process innovation and how it is being enabled by developments in computer-based information systems. Some advocates of process redesign take a mechanistic approach: they perceive the design of a process as an engineering task rather than as a socio-technical problem. Such a focus on information technology and the mechanics of the process design, while important, can easily be overemphasised. The cases and other material presented in this chapter show that real organisational innovations involve people, jobs, skills and structures as well as the latest software.

The central theme of this chapter has been interaction. This was introduced at the start, showing the mutual interaction between IS and process innovation. We then extended it to include people's interaction with both of the other elements, and later brought in wider issues of strategy and culture. The evidence is clear: effective use of information systems to innovate processes depends on managing a range of interactions; it is not a narrow technical project. These issues are examined elsewhere in this book – Chapter 3 (strategy), Chapter 6 (organisation) and Chapter 8 (people).

Many process innovators believe that such projects must be conducted from the top down, but this opinion can be challenged. The detailed understanding of process design and customers often resides with the people who do the work. In many cases resistance to new work designs has occurred when people do not want their jobs defined by someone else. There is growing empirical support for the view that changes with more of a bottom-up character may be more successful, besides which such major changes will have a strong political element as vested interests try to shape the direction of the project.

A related issue is whether process change should be conducted as a radical one-off approach or a continuous and incremental activity. How managers resolve this dilemma will depend on factors such as the urgency of the problem and the readiness of the organisation for radical change. Some will stress the urgency of pressures from the market, while others will want to take time to ensure the commitment and support of influential stakeholders. Whichever approach is taken, those implementing it will confront some challenges – not dissimilar from those experienced by the managers in the tax administration. The ideas and techniques outlined in Chapter 9 (projects) and Chapter 10 (programmes) may be of some help.

CHAPTER QUESTIONS

1. Why might IS drive process change? What other factors can also be drivers?
2. What phases of IS use in organisations can be distinguished, and what could be the next phase?
3. What are the main failure factors in IS-driven process change? How can managers deal more effectively with these factors?
4. To what extent is the use of the Internet for transactional purposes an example of process innovation? What management issues arise because of that?
5. What are the advantages and disadvantages of a diagramming method (e.g. Kim, 1995) to analyse processes?
6. What are the advantages and disadvantages of using ERP systems to enable process change?
7. What has to be managed in an IS-enabled process change project?

Further reading

Chaffey, D. (2002) *E-Business and E-Commerce Management*, Financial Times/Prentice Hall, Harlow. Introduces many forms of e-business and e-commerce as forms of process innovations that transcend organisational borders.

Hammer, M. (2001) 'The superefficient company', *Harvard Business Review*, **79**(9), 82–91. Discusses how a process view can be extended to processes among organisations.

Timmers, P. (2000) *Electronic Commerce: Strategies and Models for Business to Business Trading*, Wiley, Chichester. Explores how the Internet provides opportunities and business models for business transformation.

References

Chaffey, D. (2002) *E-Business and E-Commerce Management*, Financial Times/Prentice Hall, Harlow.

Davenport, T.H. (1993) *Process Innovation: Reengineering Work through Information Technology*, Harvard Business School Press, Boston, Mass.

Davenport, T.H. (1998) 'Putting the enterprise into the enterprise system', *Harvard Business Review*, **76**(4), 121–32.

Galliers, R.D. and Baets, W.R.J. (1997) *Information Technology and Organizational Transformation: Innovation for the 21st Century Organization*, Wiley, Chichester.

Goldratt, E.M. and Cox, J. (1992) *The Goal: A Process of Ongoing Improvement*, Gower, Aldershot.

Grover, V. and Malhotra, J.K. (1997) 'Business process reengineering: a tutorial on the concept, evolution, method, technology and application', *Journal of Operations Management*, **15**(3), 193–213.

Hammer, M. (1990) 'Reengineering work: don't automate, obliterate', *Harvard Business Review*, **68**(4), 104–28.

Hammer, M. (2001) 'The superefficient company', *Harvard Business Review*, **79**(9), 82–91.

Kim, Y.G. (1995) 'Process modelling for BPR: event process chain approach', *Proceedings of the 16th International Conference on Information Systems*, NorthHolland, Amsterdam.

Laudon, K.C. and Laudon, J.P. (2004) *Management Information Systems: Organization and Technology in the Networked Enterprise*, Prentice Hall, Englewood Cliffs, NJ.

Lockamy, A. and Smith, W.I. (1997) 'A strategic alignment approach for effective business process reengineering: linking strategy, processes and customers for competitive advantage', *International Journal of Production Economics*, **50**(2/3), 141–53.

Markus, M.L. (1994) 'Preconditions for BPR success', *Information Systems Management*, **11**(2), 7–14.

Peppard, J. and Rowland, P. (1995) *The Essence of Business Process Reengineering*, Prentice Hall, Englewood Cliffs, NJ.

Sauer, C. and Yetton, P. (1997) *Steps to the Future: Fresh Thinking on the Management of IT-based Organizational Transformation*, Jossey-Bass, San Francisco.

Teng, J.T.C., Grover, V. and Fiedler, K.D. (1994) 'Business process reengineering: charting a strategic path for the information age', *California Management Review*, **36**(3), Spring, 9–31.

Turban, E., Lee, J., Chung, H. (2000) *Electronic Commerce: A Managerial Perspective*, Prentice Hall, Upper Saddle River, NJ.

Willcocks, L. and Smith, G. (1995) 'IT enabled business process reengineering: organizational and human resource dimension', *Strategic Information Systems*, **4**(3), 279–301.

CHAPTER 5

Assessing the costs and benefits of information systems

Learning objectives

By the end of your work on this topic you should be able to:

- List the main elements in the cost of an information system, both direct and indirect

- List the main elements in the benefits of an information system, both tangible and intangible

- Give the primary reasons for inaccurate IS project evaluation

- Describe alternative methods of evaluating information systems that take organisational factors into account

- Explain how organisation structure can influence the process of evaluation

Evaluating IS at a utilities company

In 1981 a state-owned utilities company became a public limited company. It faced competition for the first time, and needed to become more efficient and responsive to customers. To support these changes the company invested heavily in IS throughout the 1980s and developed a more commercial management structure and culture. The value of managing information as a resource was identified for the first time. One consequence was that senior management challenged the business value and contribution of the company's IS.

The company had relied on evaluation processes that were cost-focused and used accounting frameworks. Managers identified many shortcomings in these, including:

- they used only financial measures, especially costs;
- the process treated projects in isolation from other current developments;
- they ignored the human or organisational implications of projects;
- the standards for formulating a business case varied between divisions;
- there were no mechanisms to monitor and track the expected benefits.

Between 1989 and 1996 senior managers introduced evaluation techniques and processes that would address these problems. Methods were developed that included both the tangible and intangible benefits of IS proposals, and linked these to strategic objectives. Managers were made accountable for the delivery of the project objectives and responsible for delivering the benefits. The method for tracking benefits had to be included in any proposal. Tools were developed to assist managers to make realistic estimates of costs, benefits and risks, and to standardise the building of business cases.

These new evaluation processes had limited success. They moved the company in the direction of treating IS as an asset and promoted the notion of business/IS coordination. It helped the organisation to make a cultural shift from a public bureaucracy to an entrepreneurial business.

On the other hand, the new methods were not universally adopted and many stakeholder groups rejected their credibility. Even when the new methods were introduced they were often quickly superseded by yet more proposals. The problem was not one of ideas, but of application.

The chapter examines the problem which all companies face in using conventional, financially based IS project evaluation methods. It also examines various alternative techniques that some propose, which may be used to complement earlier methods.

Source: Based on Serafeimidis and Smithson (2000).

Introduction

People in organisations are rarely short of ideas and proposals that promise to enhance their information systems. Suppliers of hardware, software and communications systems vie with each other in promising that their systems will dramatically enhance performance, usually implying that doubters will become extinct. From business process re-engineering (BPR) to enterprise resource planning (ERP) to customer relationship management (CRM), the conveyor belt of three-letter acronyms presents managers with the challenge of deciding between competing IS investment proposals. They will probably base this choice on estimates of what the project is likely to cost and potential benefits to the organisation. This is simple to say, but difficult to put into practice.

The costs and benefits of IS projects are notoriously difficult to determine accurately:

■ The cost of the Libra project to provide a national system for 385 courts in the UK had soared from £146m to £390m. Despite spending more than twice what they expected, the court service still did not have a working system (*Computer Weekly*, 11 November 2003).

■ Over 50 per cent of systems projects fail to meet their expected rate of return due to fundamental flaws in predicting initial costs (*Financial Times IT*, July/August 1999, p. 10).

■ A study of 365 executives revealed that as many as half of all IS projects exhibited significant cost and schedule overruns. In 1995, American companies spent an estimated $59 billion in cost overruns on such 'runaway' projects and another $81 billion on cancelled software projects (Johnson, 1995).

What went wrong with these projects? Why are the costs and benefits of information system projects so difficult to predict and control? This chapter reviews the most common reasons.

People have many motives for evaluating project proposals. It is a means of making objective decisions about competing proposals. It also helps to establish the value of information systems to the organisation and its growth (Farbey et al., 1993; Willcocks, 1994), and to rank alternatives (Hawgood and Land, 1988; Clemons, 1991) when formulating an IS strategy (Peters, 1994; Baker, 1995).

These are not the only uses. Hirschheim and Smithson (1987) pointed out that formally appraising a project proposal can serve as the first stage in a feedback function that assists organisational learning. It can also be part of the political game – a way of gaining legitimacy for a project which promoters desire for other reasons. If the culture of the organisation is one that values rationality people need to support their proposals with apparently rational information, to give an appearance of playing by the rules (Gregory and Jackson, 1992; Powell, 1992; Farbey et al., 1995). A radical view is that the issues are so complex that it is simply impossible to quantify the costs and benefits of IS projects accurately. Attempting to do so merely gives a comforting delusion of predictability in a fundamentally unpredictable world. Those who take this approach suggest that managers should instead focus on other criteria that demonstrate the overall value to the organisation (Bannister and Remenyi, 2000).

The Chapter Case traces the evolution of IS evaluation in an energy company as it moved from being a state-run business to one operating in a competitive market. It shows how managers developed alternative ways of assessing IS proposals and how others within the business reacted to these changes.

The chapter begins by outlining the elements of the formal–rational evaluation techniques. This appears simple – until we describe the problems with the approach. The following section details the wider considerations required when estimating the costs and benefits of information systems. Several alternative evaluation methods are described that take a more holistic approach to evaluation by incorporating human and organisational perspectives. Finally, we consider some organisation design issues that influence the effectiveness of IS projects. The aim is to identify the factors that influence the evaluation of information systems and what that means for those managing such projects.

5.1 Formal–rational methods for evaluating IS proposals

Traditional methods of project evaluation express the idea that the costs of an investment need to be related to the benefits which the investment brings. The costs tend to be incurred now, while the benefits come later. So the calculation needs to take account of the timing as well as the amounts of costs and benefits. The longer the delay in receiving the financial benefits, the greater the risk – which also needs to be included. Having made those calculations for the projects under consideration, managers then have an apparently rational basis upon which to decide between them. The more the estimated payback from the investment in a project appears to be, the more likely managers are to approve it. To illustrate the principles involved some common techniques for making these calculations are outlined below; Laudon and Laudon (2004) includes a much fuller discussion.

Payback period

This method calculates the number of years required before the cumulative financial returns equal the initial investment. If a company invests £10m, and expects to receive returns of £2m each year, the payback period is 5 years. A shorter payback period is more attractive as it means the investment is at risk for less time. The difficulty is that this ignores the fact that some investments will produce returns for longer periods than others.

Return on investment

This method calculates the return on the investment (ROI) by estimating the annual benefits to be achieved over the life of the project, and dividing that number by the amount invested. The annual benefit is calculated as the expected cost savings, additional revenue or whatever other benefits people expect. In the example above, the annual benefit of £2m would give an ROI of 20 per cent.

Discounted cash flow

Payback and ROI are simple and easy to understand. The difficulty is that neither takes account of the timing of the costs and benefits. A project which brings immediate benefits is worth more than one in which the benefits occur much later – but ROI calculations would not show this. Similarly a project with a short payback period would be preferred over one in which the benefits took longer to repay the investment. This ignores the fact that the second project, while slow to deliver, may produce benefits for a much longer period.

To overcome these problems, accountants have developed more sophisticated appraisal methods, which take account of the fact that money itself has a value. In the discounted cash flow (DCF) method, costs and returns are calculated over the expected whole life of the project, but then adjusted for the fact that distant returns are worth less than those that are received soon.

All methods depend on identifying and estimating the costs and benefits of the project, and the major elements of these are outlined in the next section.

5.2 The costs of information systems

People make different interpretations of the cost of IS. Those in the finance function tend to consider the purchase invoice. Those in the IS department will think more about support and maintenance costs. Users will look at training and business process costs. Organisations have great difficulty establishing the true cost of their information systems. Viewing IS as a product that can be purchased, plugged in and forgotten fails to capture the cost impact of all but the most simple stand-alone applications. The complex and costly systems being implemented today – many of which transcend organisational boundaries – require a rigorous approach to cost estimation.

One method is to calculate the total cost of ownership (TCO) of an information system, rather than the more obvious purchase price. TCO refers to the activity of taking a holistic view of costs over the lifetime of an investment, rather than viewing the purchase price in isolation. This is difficult but essential. Knowing exactly what a system costs to buy and run is the first step on the road to reducing those costs.

The manager preparing a project proposal needs a checklist of the likely costs. This needs to include both the costs of initial purchase and the longer-term costs of implementation, ownership and change. The following pages indicate costs that people may overlook, but which add to TCO.

■ Cost of purchase

For most information systems the acquisition cost consists mainly of hardware and software. These costs dominate formal–rational evaluation techniques but become a smaller part of the true cost as systems become more integrated into organisation processes.

Hardware costs

- The front end – user interfaces and peripherals (monitors, keyboards, control equipment, printers, scanners, etc.);
- The middleware – networking equipment (cabling, routers, switching devices, encryption devices and other communication linkages);
- The back end – processing equipment (servers, mainframes, desktop PC units, etc.).

When considering the total cost of a large project, it may also be worth separately considering any elements of the new system that could be described as infrastructure. These are elements that can be used by more than one system. For example, a national cable network for a bank's automated teller machines (ATMs) might also be used for a future communications system such as intranet or video-conferencing links. The desktop computers given to office workers for word-processing could also be used for e-mail. Logically the infrastructure costs would be shared across such other projects, and so affect relative costs and benefits.

Software costs

- Developments costs if built in-house, package and licence costs if bought-in;
- Operating system software;

- Application development tools;
- Security and encryption packages;
- Networking and communication software;
- Systems management software;
- Database and database management software;
- Front-end packages such as office applications (e.g. word-processing, spread-sheets), data analysis packages, presentational software, management information systems, browsers.

Implementation, ownership and change

Information systems inevitably interact with other aspects of the organisation. This brings with it a variety of implementation costs which, while significant, are hard to measure. They include:

- Re-engineering current business processes;
- Decommissioning and disposing of existing systems;
- Staff communication and training;
- Customer communication and training;
- Costs of parallel running during the rollout period;
- Error correction and compensation for quality 'dip' during initial use of the new system.

Those proposing and approving projects frequently ignore or underestimate these costs. Doing so puts an extra burden on staff during implementation – which adds yet further cost elements.

Having purchased and implemented a new system, managers must understand the cost of maintaining and supporting it throughout its active life cycle. Costs of ownership will include:

- **Support**: help-desk functions, user manuals, retraining of staff
- **Disaster recovery**: duplication of facilities at alternative sites to ensure continuity of operation in the event of major problems at the main site.
- **Staff**: recruiting development staff, training developers, maintainers and users.
- **Maintenance**: Hardware and software incur costs of minor enhancements, bug-fixes and requests for change. Is the product high-quality/low-maintenance, or low-quality/high-maintenance? Availability and cost of spare parts? For how long? Availability and cost of suitably skilled technicians and help-desk staff?
- **Obsolescence**: Does the product comply with an industry standard with an established history and a foreseeable life? If not, the product may soon be impossible to maintain or upgrade.
- **Upgrade**: Both hardware and software are likely to need upgrading – to meet new communication standards, regulatory changes, new market requirements, expanded applications or new processes. Having bought a particular software package, it is hard to avoid paying for successive upgrades. This in turn may require additional hardware capacity.

In times when markets, technologies and regulatory requirements change rapidly, change itself becomes a major, if rarely considered, cost category. How rapidly will the IS department be able to adapt the information system to changes that were impossible to forecast when it was designed? Some points to consider are:

- Interoperability of hardware: Can the proposed hardware platform operate with other platforms, operating systems, networks, peripheral equipment? Flexibility in this area allows future merging of systems, changes of operating platforms, software applications, etc.

- Openness of software: Can the software be easily and cheaply modified, or linked to other systems? Open, modular, object-oriented software is normally preferable to a single-platform, specialised one-use system architecture.

Summary

- The true costs of a new IT system extend well beyond the purchase costs of the hardware and software, covering the costs of implementation, ownership, change and infrastructure.

- Costs associated with the impact of the new system on staff, customers, suppliers and other stakeholders must be considered.

- Long-term costs are difficult to foresee, but choices in the design of the system influence their scale.

CASE QUESTIONS 5.1

Why would you have expected the company to use formal–rational evaluation methods?
What benefits would it gain from their use?
What problems may it have experienced in using them in the new business conditions?

5.3 The benefits of information systems

No useful business case can be based on cost alone. Often the more important issue is not what is spent, but what is received in return and when it will appear. When working out the benefits of an investment, the project manager needs first to consider what business benefits senior managers or the project sponsor are expecting to achieve from the investment. Ideally these will derive from, or at least contribute to, the wider strategy (Chapter 3). Managers with high growth targets will be most interested in systems that increase sales capability, while those fighting for survival in a competitive market may prefer one that cuts costs.

Having established the benefits that managers expect from a new system, they need to be quantified if policy requires a formal–rational assessment of the proposal. However, while staff can estimate immediate costs reasonably accurately, benefits are a different matter. These will arrive in the future and will be affected by factors beyond the control of the project team. Even more than with costs, people make subjective judgements about the benefits of a system. They will inevitably make different judgements, based on their interpretation of the future course of the business or their position in relation to the project. Those most in favour will naturally be most optimistic about the potential benefits both tangible (directly quantifiable) and intangible (difficult to quantify).

▓ Tangible benefits

Direct cost savings

Often, the most obvious benefit is that an information system can save costs by automating processes and so replace people. More accurate and timely distribution of work (e.g. using document imaging or telephone call routing systems) can decrease operator waiting time and lead to efficiency-based cost reductions. Fewer staff can mean lower property costs. In practice these are usually less than expected owing to:

- agreements with trade unions preventing job losses;
- staff time savings may be spread over several locations, limiting the ability to reduce staffing at any one location;
- time saved only counts as a benefit once people have moved to other profitable work.

Quality improvements

A major benefit is the ability of a computer-based system to reduce errors when it replaces a manual system. While people can provide a personal and flexible service, they can also make mistakes and act inconsistently. Customers become annoyed if they are treated differently each time they use a service or see others receiving more favourable treatment. Errors are also expensive since they need additional effort to find and correct, and may result in compensation payments or lost business.

Other aspects of quality include:

- Which customers see benefits from consistent, standardised processing?
- What reduction in reworking and compensation costs will be achieved?
- What revenue may accrue if we reduce the number of customers lost?
- How much less money will be spent in servicing warranty agreements?

Avoiding cost increases

A modern information system can save an organisation from a future increase in costs. Like a car, an ageing system will incur high maintenance costs just to keep it going. Breakdowns disrupt operations and annoy customers – and spares become harder to find. Most organisations replace their PCs after about five years, as maintenance costs then rise sharply. If a new system will avoid these costs, this should be in the evaluation.

Revenue increases

Those advocating a new system will emphasise the prospects of increased sales through offering new services, delivery channels, promotional activities or market penetration. These can be real benefits – but are likely to be optimistic. They are also notoriously difficult to validate, since any change in sales is usually the result of a variety of factors, not necessarily connected to the new system.

MIS in Practice	RBS Manufacturing Division – using IS to reduce costs

The Royal Bank of Scotland (RBS) Group Manufacturing Division is responsible for the operational areas of the Bank that support the income-generating business areas. It has three functional areas: Technology (IT operations and development), Operations (account management, lending, telephony, payments) and Services (purchasing, property, other support units). As the primary back-office 'engine room' for the world's 5th largest bank, Manufacturing provides operational services to over 20 branches serving 20 million customers across a variety of delivery channels (branches, Internet, ATMs, telephone, etc.).

Since 1999, RBS income has increased by an average of 14 per cent a year. During this period the number of people employed in Manufacturing has remained static (about 20,000) or even decreased when transfers from other divisions are taken into account.

How has Manufacturing driven such significant cost reductions at a time of growth?

One way has been by basing its IS strategy on the idea of 'build once, use many times'. This means developing a single IT platform to support the many different financial brands and delivery channels across RBS. By building newly acquired business areas, and the growing needs of existing businesses, into the same IT platform, Manufacturing has established a very large system with big economies of scale. By developing common processes for the different brands, this large platform operates very efficiently while meeting the different demands of the businesses.

Manufacturing's scale has allowed it to develop large information processing centres specialising in account management, lending, telephony, payments or credit cards and handling large volumes of transactions from low-cost buildings. Using integrated information systems to drive efficient processes, Manufacturing staff are dramatically increasing their productivity. In one year (2002–03) staff in payments centres handled a 30 per cent increase in payments per head. Furthermore, these increases in productivity are being achieved while RBS employee opinion surveys indicate one of the highest rates of staff morale in the industry.

In its report to market analysts in October 2003, Manufacturing promised to continue increasing efficiency. Initiatives under way include the introduction of Image and Workflow technology, improved customer query management systems, improved fraud detection, simplified account-opening processes and further consolidation of the IT platform.

Source: Information from managers and staff in Manufacturing.

Staying in business

Sometimes introducing a new system is simply essential if the organisation is to continue. In a highly regulated environment, it may be necessary to be able to operate in a certain manner just to be allowed to continue to provide the service. Suppliers to Wal-Mart (Chapter 3) and many other retail chains have had to implement new information systems to manage their relationship with the customer, or lose the business. Major engineering companies require their suppliers to be able to receive drawings and specifications electronically. Those unable to do so have to merge with those who can.

The companies that in the mid-1970s invested in automatic and electronically controlled machine tools were well positioned to explore the microprocessor-based revolution in capabilities that hit during the early 1980s. Because operators, maintenance personnel and process engineers were already comfortable with electronic technology, it was relatively simple to retrofit existing machines with powerful microelectronics. Companies that had earlier deferred investment in electronically controlled machine tools fell behind: they had acquired no option on these new process technologies.

Source: Kaplan (1986).

Intangible benefits

The tangible benefits can be quantified to some degree, but still with a wide margin for interpretation. Other benefits, the intangible ones, are those which people cannot usually quantify. Table 5.1 lists some of these.

Brynjolfsson and Hitt (2000) propose that a large part of the benefits of IS investments come from intangible benefits such as variety, convenience and service – which are hard to measure quantitatively. Nevertheless, these lead ultimately to an economic contribution substantially greater than the initial investment costs.

Table 5.1 **Some intangible benefits of information systems**

Possible improvements	Description
Communications	Between staff and suppliers, customers or investors
Staff morale	Staff may see improvements in their role or working environment
Customer satisfaction	Brings repeat business and reduces the cost of sales
Reputation	New systems may send positive signals to the market about commitment to innovation
Customer management	Using customer data in advanced information systems may improve reaction to customers' needs
Value chain management	Building direct system links between partners in the value chain can improve responsiveness and reduce costs
Flexibility	IS often enable an organisation to react more quickly and easily to changes in the marketplace
Organisational learning	IS enable lessons from current practices to spread more widely; staff can also learn about external events, and be better placed to take advantage of new developments
Differentiation	As discussed in Chapter 3, an important strategic use of IS is differentiation; it is hard to quantify the benefits, as we cannot know how soon competitors will match it

Activity 5.1 Identifying and assessing benefits

Choose an organisation with which you interact regularly – e.g. a bank or a supermarket.

- *What benefits could it gain from using IS to improve quality of service that you would value?*
- *How easily could it quantify these benefits in monetary terms?*
- *What three intangible benefits (see Table 5.1) could it achieve with the help of IS?*

Summary

- Information systems have a wide-ranging set of tangible and intangible benefits that need to be carefully considered from an organisational perspective.

- Overemphasis on costs (which tend to be immediate and certain) and underemphasis on benefits (which tend to be in the future and uncertain) would lead to overly conservative decisions.

5.4 Creating a balanced portfolio of project types

Large organisations typically undertake several related projects at once so they need to evaluate individual projects as part of a wider programme (see Chapter 10). The programme will contain projects representing different types of activity, such as:

- Upgrading a network connecting different locations to a more modern platform that will provide capacity for new applications across all business areas.

- Building a new web-based system for presenting product features to customers, collecting order and payment details and passing them to the operational area to complete the transaction.

While both projects provide vital functions, they have different types of costs and benefits. Building a new network will have specific costs, but the benefits are intangible as they are not related directly to customer sales.

Organisations typically support a portfolio of projects like this – some of them help to build the infrastructure. They develop the ability of the organisation to perform effectively and efficiently, but viewed in isolation deliver no tangible benefits. Nonetheless, shareholders will need reassurance that the investment is sound.

A simple approach is to categorise certain types of projects as 'enablers', making no attempt to determine benefits as they are hard to quantify in isolation. Instead managers justify them on the basis that they cannot implement other specified projects without the prior implementation of the enabler project. It makes sense to accept the proposal if its costs, added to those of the projects it enables, are covered by the benefits of the latter. The portfolio, or programme, of projects has a positive business case, being a balance of enabler and enabled projects.

Ross and Beath (2002) describe a more detailed approach to viewing IS investments across the organisation and suggest four categories of IS investment that make up the 'framework for IT investment' shown in Figure 5.1.

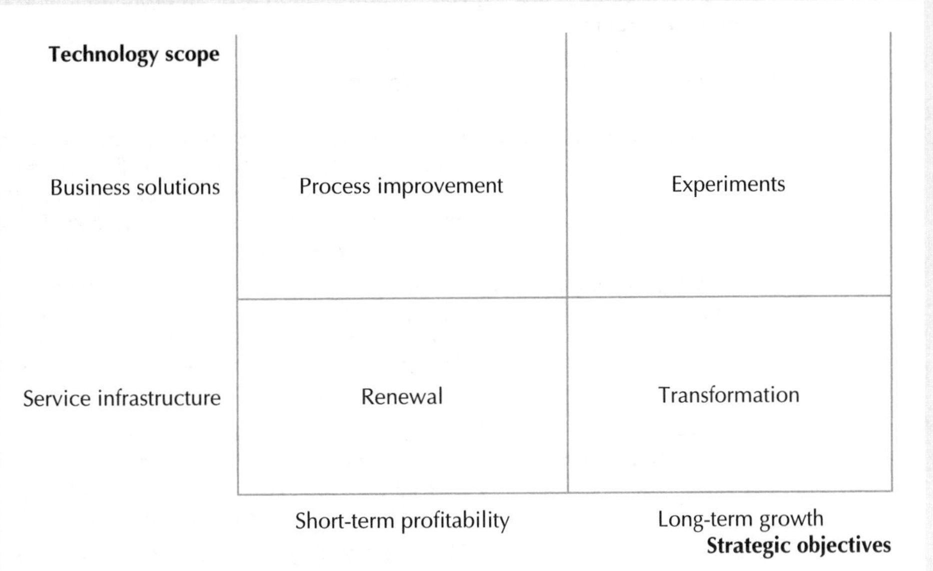

Technology scope

	Short-term profitability	Long-term growth
Business solutions	Process improvement	Experiments
Service infrastructure	Renewal	Transformation

Strategic objectives

Figure 5.1 **A framework for IT investment**
Source: Laudon and Laudon (2004), p. 53.

By balancing short- and long-term projects on the Strategy scale, and infrastructural and business solutions on the Scope scale, organisations can achieve an effective mix of IS investments.

Summary

- Often, IS projects cannot be justified on a formal–rational basis in isolation, but must be viewed in the context of the other IS investments taking place at that time.
- Some IS projects must be justified on the basis of the benefits received from other projects that they 'enable'.
- Organisations often must achieve an effective mix of different IS investments – short- and long-term, infrastructural and business-specific.

5.5 Problems of formal–rational evaluation

Formal–rational techniques depend on the assumption that the costs incurred in purchasing the system, and the benefits obtained from it, can be identified and accurately estimated. This applies to both the values and their timing. This assumption is rarely met in the fast-changing world of information systems. Technology changes during the course of the project – and will continue to do so during the expected life of the system. This plays havoc with the approach.

Table 5.2 Reasons often given for information system projects failing to meet investment appraisal targets

Reason	Description
Overemphasis on purchase costs	When planning an IT investment, the most obvious costs are those related directly to the purchase of the necessary equipment and software. However, studies of existing systems show that these initial purchase costs are only a part, and often the lesser part, of the overall system costs.
Over-ambitious rates of return	In setting rates of return in DCF calculations, figures of 12 per cent and even 15 per cent are not uncommon. However, studies of the real cost of capital upon which these return rates should be based (e.g. Kaplan, 1986) indicate that a figure of 8.5 per cent per annum is a much more realistic target.
Underestimation of implementation time and costs	The project is not finished when the system is purchased or built. It then has to be rolled out to the operational areas of the organisation and start delivering the anticipated benefits. The time and costs incurred in this implementation stage are frequently misunderstood.
Poor communication with users and customers	Misunderstandings over the functions and uses of a new system add to costs. Alienating staff can make them reluctant to use the system. Both of these problems are caused by a lack of effective communication with staff. Further problems can be incurred when customers have not been kept informed and experience problems when they use the new system for the first time.
Unrealistic benefit predictions	Enthusiastic project managers overestimate the expected benefits. Careful analysis of the likelihood of achieving them can reveal significant overstatements.
Unexpected demand levels	When introducing a new system that customers access directly, such as a call centre or a website, it is difficult to anticipate early demand. Providing too much capacity is as costly as providing too little and losing business.
Not learning from past experiences	Most organisations fail to learn from their experiences with previous projects and so repeat mistakes. Formal post-implementation reviews are not popular with busy project teams, but can bring huge learning benefits.

Table 5.2 lists the commonly quoted reasons for information system projects failing to meet their investment appraisal targets. These testify to the complexities surrounding such projects and limiting the ability of the formal–rational techniques to predict adequately the value of a project.

A common error in formal–rational investment appraisal is to overemphasise the costs, which tend to be easier to quantify, and underemphasise the benefits, which are less certain and harder to justify. This inevitably has a detrimental effect on the attractiveness of the project. It is also common for decisions to be biased towards those IS projects whose benefits are easy to identify, such as cost reduction through automation. This limits the success chances of revenue-generating projects and can lead to the late adoption of critical infrastructure investments. Research by Bensaou and Earl (1998) shows this to be a cultural factor, not a force of nature – see the box below.

Research Summary — **Western and Japanese approaches to investment**

A study by Bensaou and Earl (1998) of the differences between western and Japanese IS investment decision-making revealed an important difference in approach:

> In Japanese corporations, IT [sic] projects are not assessed primarily by financial metrics; audits and formal approval for investments are rare. Instead, because operational performance goals drive most investments, the traditional metric is performance improvement, not value for money. (p. 123)

This was not an excuse for poorly defined benefit values. The Japanese companies in the study had very firm views on the performance improvements that were expected from a new system, and accurately tracked these before and after implementation.

Many of the benefits of information systems are qualitative in nature and do not lend themselves easily to the strictly quantitative approach of the formal–rational techniques. There is nothing new about this. In her study of twenty companies implementing CAD/CAM systems, Currie (1989) found that managers were routinely fabricating cost–benefit cases to pass formal–rational appraisal hurdles in order to gain the qualitative benefits which they knew were essential for the success of their departments. She later found that 85 per cent of managers believe that qualitative benefits are as important as the financial ones, but only 53 per cent attempt to quantify them because of their vague nature (Currie, 1995). Ignoring such intangible benefits, as Kaplan (1986) noted, is a common folly.

Activity 5.2 Evaluating a personal IS

Think of a computer-based information system you use regularly, e.g. the computer you use at work or your Internet connection at home.

- List all of the items of cost incurred in operating this system.
- List the benefits you gain from using it.
- How easy would it be to quantify these costs and benefits?
- If you had to justify keeping the system on a purely monetary basis, would you find it easy to do so?

Any evaluation process requires us to consider the size and timing of costs and benefits. Formal–rational techniques do this, but the depth to which information systems integrate themselves within organisations, and the impact of human factors, require a holistic, organisation-wide view of the costs and benefits. As we argue throughout this book, information systems integrate themselves deeply into an organisation. They affect not just the processes to which they are applied, but the whole job design of the users and resources, plus the broader spectrum of stakeholders such as support staff, customers, suppliers, managers, investors and so on. They are central to the strategic direction of the organisation, they cross divisional, brand and geographic boundaries, they affect the culture and staff behaviours, they alter the distribution of power. The organisation changes alongside the new information system, which should also be reflected in the appraisal process. Section 5.6 presents some ideas on how to handle this problem.

■ Summary

- ■ The quantitative approach of traditional formal–rational evaluation techniques does not fit well with the complexity of information system projects.
- ■ Information systems integrate themselves deeply into organisations. Their value therefore requires consideration of a wide range of factors beyond the system itself.

5.6 Wider criteria for evaluating IS

Given the difficulties we have described with formal–rational methods for evaluating IS proposals, it is no surprise that people have attempted to address the need for an evaluation method that takes account of a wider set of factors. For example, Doherty et al. (2003) list a set of measures for information systems success as shown in Table 5.3, only one of which covers the costs and benefits.

Saarinen (1996) describes a four-dimensional model of IS success measurement, illustrated in Figure 5.2. The first dimension, Development Process, considers the success of the development of the system. This incorporates adherence to the allocated budget (costs) and time schedule, and the efficient use of development resources. The second dimension, Use Process, covers the effectiveness and efficiency of service delivery to the users of the system. Together, these define the process success of the system and relate to the costs of both build and ownership.

The third dimension described by Saarinen, Quality of the IS Product, relates to system factors such as reliability, accuracy, robustness, usability and flexibility to change. The fourth dimension, Impact of the IS on the Organisation, covers the

Table 5.3 **Measures for system success**

Measure	Description
Systems quality	Reliability, features and functions, response time
Information quality	Clarity, completeness, usefulness and accuracy of information provided
Information use	Regularity of use, number of enquiries, duration of use, frequency of report requests
User satisfaction	Overall satisfaction, enjoyment, no difference between information needed and received, software satisfaction
Individual impact	Problem identification, correctness of decision, decision effectiveness, time taken to take decision, improved individual productivity
Organisational impact	Contribution to achieving goals, cost–benefit ratio, return on investment, service effectiveness

Source: Doherty et al. (2003).

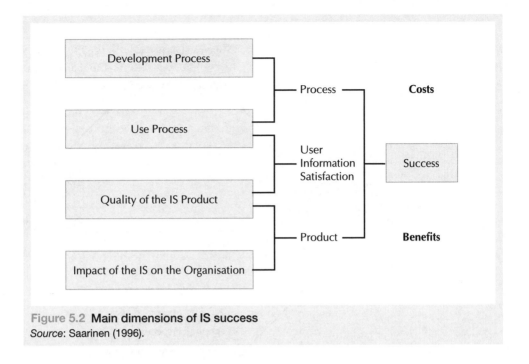

Figure 5.2 Main dimensions of IS success
Source: Saarinen (1996).

extent to which the system contributes to cost savings, productivity improvements, increased market share, competitive advantage, etc. (i.e. the benefits). Together, these latter two dimensions define the success of the system as a product.

Strassman (1999) goes further by saying that there is no relation between a company's investment in IT and its profitability. The benefits of an effective system come from improvements in competitive advantage, strategic positioning and management style and quality – which merely investing in IT does not deliver. The benefits come from reshaping the organisational factors, not from spending on IT. A company that spends wisely – even if sparsely – on IT and makes the appropriate organisational changes will see its performance enhanced. A company that spends indiscriminately on IT will see its performance diminished, because IT will merely amplify its poor business practices.

Many companies have used the Balanced Scorecard technique (Kaplan and Norton, 1992) to measure performance against strategic objectives. This technique seeks to develop an organisation-wide view of performance based on an appropriate balance of four measures: financial, internal effectiveness, customers and innovation/learning.

Kaplan and Norton developed the technique to offer an alternative to the formal–rational techniques, for much the same reasons as we have discussed above. They wanted to offer a way of viewing information systems in a broader organisational and human perspective. Figure 5.3 shows the four elements of the scorecard.

Financial measures will obviously still be important, and a favourable impact of the new system on these measures will be critical. This is the area that has traditionally been given most attention in organisations and is most supported by the traditional formal–rational approach, so requires least explanation here. The

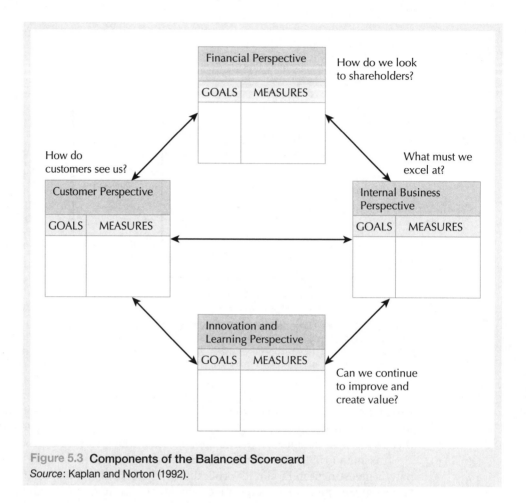

Figure 5.3 Components of the Balanced Scorecard
Source: Kaplan and Norton (1992).

important lesson from the Balanced Scorecard approach is that concentrating solely on financial measures can lead to a dangerously short-term perspective.

Customer measures will drive the organisation towards the way it wishes to be perceived by its customers. They can include such specific goals as time taken to fulfil orders, customer satisfaction levels and market share. Information systems can do all of these things, but their benefits are hard to quantify. The formal–rational method would therefore be biased against such projects, to the detriment of the company.

Internal effectiveness measures define what the organisation must do internally to compete effectively. They can include productivity levels, error rates, safety records and staff skills. A new information system could be expected to impact on all these factors and so its value to the organisation should be assessed from all these perspectives.

Innovation/learning measures are intended to drive the organisation towards continuous improvement and the creation of ever greater value to customers and shareholders. These refer to such measures as percentage of revenue from new products and/or markets, research and development achievements, and improvements in operating efficiencies. Many of these measures are strongly influenced by the ways in which information systems improve performance and expand opportunities in organisations.

The example in the box below illustrates the use of the method.

MIS in Practice **The Balanced Scorecard at WHC**

Wayton Haulage Contractors Ltd (WHC) was considering implementing an Internet-based tracking and customer communication system. This system would create a website linked to a database of orders, items in transit, drivers, vehicles and customers. Head-office staff could access the database through a browser, entering new information and tracking progress with the movement of goods. Drivers could access the system through truck-mounted mobile network devices to enter progress with deliveries and to pick up new instructions. Customers could access information on progress with their deliveries through a secure extranet link.

To evaluate the system, WHC senior management applied the costs and benefits of the system to the measures in their existing Balanced Scorecard to ensure that a holistic view was taken, linked to their overall strategy.

Financial measures were considered first. Formal–rational techniques were applied to measure the rate of return on investment that could be achieved. This required some estimation of future costs and benefits that WHC knew could change due to the unpredictable nature of such initiatives. Nonetheless the measures suggested adequate financial performance.

Next, the WHC management thought about their customers. Theirs is a cut-throat market, with tight margins and low customer loyalty. Providing leading-edge, convenient service based on reliability and timeliness was a key strategic goal. The new system would provide customers with a convenient means of tracking the progress of their deliveries, leading to higher satisfaction and retention rates.

From an internal effectiveness perspective, the new system would have several advantages. Responding to customer enquiries traditionally took up a great deal of staff time, and giving customers access to their own information seemed like an ideal way of reducing back-office processing costs and lead times. Further efficiencies could be expected from improved utilisation of drivers and vehicles through coordinated job allocation processes.

Finally, WHC management recognised that the system would provide them with opportunities to understand their work patterns and customer requirements better by providing a means of tracking trends and outcomes. Their ability to innovate and learn from the system was therefore assured.

Using the four elements of the Balanced Scorecard, WHC was able to take a holistic and strategic view of the new system. This went much further than financial measures, which required an element of guesswork, and ensured that the value of the system was considered from a relevant set of organisational perspectives.

Summary

- To overcome the limitations of formal–rational evaluation, several alternative methodologies for measuring the value of information system have been developed.

- The Balanced Scorecard in particular relates IS to strategy, by considering the effects on customers, internal processes and learning, as well as on financial performance.

5.7 Organising for IS evaluation

Having reviewed some of the methods for evaluating information systems proposals, this final section considers the place of evaluation within the organisational structure. This links closely to the broader discussion of IS structure in Chapter 7. The significance is perhaps emphasised by later developments in the Chapter Case.

CHAPTER CASE: PART 2

Evaluating IS at a utilities company: continued

The earlier part of the case described how the company had introduced non-traditional evaluation methods. Success was mixed, and analysis identified these reactions.

The accountants and senior managers viewed the inherent subjectivity of intangible benefits with suspicion and so rejected many outputs from the new methods that incorporated more intangible factors. Stakeholder groups tended to have subjective, informal views and hidden political agendas that influenced their judgement on certain topics. Many methodological changes lacked a champion at a sufficiently senior level to counter objections and to maintain support. Typically, a new method achieved patchy recognition at best and application became a mixture of old and new across different stakeholder areas.

The most successful new method focused on traditional financial elements, and owed its success less to its superiority than to the political influence of its owners – the finance department. It was apparent that proposed new methods did more than challenge the validity of the existing one. They also challenged the traditional roles of the stakeholder groups. So, accountants may have perceived their influence as being usurped, while business managers may have been uncomfortable with new unfamiliar types of accountability.

Due to the large size of the organisation, and the complex nature of its decision-making processes, it was often unclear who should make a particular decision and where accountability lay. During the period of analysis, the company was performing successfully in the market. This may have led staff to be unenthusiastic about the new appraisal methods that were designed to improve performance.

Nevertheless, it was clear that the company had benefited from recognising the importance of IS as a strategic element. The experiment had helped to move it away from exclusive reliance on the formal–rational approach to IS evaluation, and towards a more entrepreneurial style.

Source: Based on Serafeimidis and Smithson (2000).

CASE QUESTIONS 5.2

In view of the ideas in this chapter, evaluate in general terms the value of the non-financial methods which the company introduced.

Why do you think they were not widely accepted?

What effects may that have had on the value the company has gained from its investments in information systems?

▦ Central project evaluation teams – a structural solution?

Project sponsors and owners are poor judges of the value of their project. They naturally have a biased preference and are often familiar with only a single area of the business. These factors can lead to sub-optimal investment decisions if the individual project teams are left to fight it out for board funding.

One way of addressing these problems is to establish a central project evaluation team (CPET). Ideally, such a team will be made up of a selection of experienced project managers from different areas of the organisation, with a variety of skills, including marketing, economics, finance and IT. Their role would be to take an objective view of projects and assess their value using a standard approach based on the Balanced Scorecard or something similar. By putting every proposal requiring significant funding through the same assessment, but one more broadly based than the formal–rational approach, boards can be presented with a better set of options.

Another role for the CPET would be to carry out post-implementation reviews of the projects which have been previously approved. This is done very rarely, yet the omission prevents valuable learning. By measuring the actual costs and benefits (broadly defined) of a new system the team can learn useful lessons for future assessments.

However, the CPET approach will have disadvantages for the analysis of IS projects:

▦ the lack of local awareness and knowledge will detract from the team's ability to understand the less tangible aspects of a project's value;

▦ the systemic approach to evaluation could be viewed as 'bureaucratic' – slow and inflexible;

▦ a central team is less likely to react quickly to changes in the marketplace.

MIS in Practice   Budget ownership – a plea for business control

IT purchasing policy at Northern Rock Building Society incorporates an unusual stratagem – business units that have proposed an installation are made financially responsible for the projects. 'The onus is on the business side to justify expenditure,' says Neil Wilkinson, strategic development manager. 'This has produced greater cohesion between IT and business managers. We work closely together and it is in the business managers' interests to justify the process.'

Source: Financial Times IT, July/August 1999.

In many organisations the IS department owns the budget for system developments. Business divisions lobby IS to win part of the budget for their project. The weakness of this approach is that IS departments are not responsible for the revenues of the organisation. This responsibility lies with the business divisions who own the value chains from which revenues flow. For IT budgets to be applied effectively, business areas need to be able to purchase requirements from whichever source, and at whatever price, supports their business.

The CPET may work best where:

▦ projects are related to a well-established system;

▦ organisations are more formal and risk-averse;

▦ environments are stable.

Localised business budget control may work best where:

- projects are related to new types of opportunity;
- organisations are flatter with more decentralised autonomy;
- environments are dynamic and uncertain.

Summary

- To manage the costs and benefits of IS effectively, the organisation structure must be aligned to support the needs of the business areas in a technically aware manner.
- Central project evaluation teams have some advantages, but many disadvantages, for the evaluation of IS initiatives.
- Business areas will always claim budget ownership and view the technology departments as suppliers, potentially competing with outside suppliers.

Conclusions

This chapter has discussed the problems of using the traditional formal–rational techniques (rate of return on investment, payback period and so on) for evaluating information systems. The extent to which such systems integrate themselves in organisations, and the complex human interactions involved, require a more holistic approach to be taken that goes beyond simple financial measures.

The costs and benefits of information systems are in themselves complex in nature and require skilled judgement of many indirect and intangible factors. The common approach of ignoring factors that do not easily translate into definite quantities has led to the rejection of many valuable projects, and the acceptance of many poor ones.

In many cases, the costs and benefits of IS projects cannot be viewed in isolation, and an organisation-wide view of short- and long-term benefits accruing from all IS investments is needed.

Ideally, a company will evaluate its information systems taking account of organisational factors impacted by the each system. Some methods of doing this have been presented, such as the Balanced Scorecard, which is a way of encouraging consideration of the broader range of organisational, human and strategic factors that information systems will inevitably influence. Finally, the importance of ensuring that the organisation structure is aligned to support quality IS decision-making has been discussed.

CHAPTER QUESTIONS

1. What are the attractions of using formal–rational evaluation techniques for information system project proposals?

2. What political influences might there be within an organisation that sustain the use of formal–rational evaluation techniques?

3. Discuss the difficulties which a department manager might have in justifying expenditure on a new computer system to senior management. What might they do to overcome these difficulties?

4. As senior IT manager in a large organisation, you know that you have to invest in the basic IT platform and supporting infrastructure to keep supplying businesses with the systems they need. However, there are significant costs and no direct benefits from this investment. How will you justify it to the senior management?

5. What aspects of an organisation structure hinder the quality of information system decisions?

Further reading

Kaplan, R.S. and Norton, D.P. (1996) *The Balanced Scorecard: Translating Strategy into Action*, Harvard Business School Press, Boston. The scope of the Balanced Scorecard approach has only been touched upon in this chapter. There are many good practical examples of its application in this book which will help you to make use of it in evaluating IS projects.

References

Baker, B. (1995) 'The role of feedback in assessing information systems planning effetiveness', *Journal of Strategic Information Systems*, **4**(1), 61–80.

Bannister, F. and Remenyi, D. (2000) 'Acts of faith: instinct, value and IT investment decisions', *Journal of Information Technology*, **15**, 231–41.

Bensaou, M. and Earl, M. (1998) 'The right mind set for managing information technology', *Harvard Business Review*, **78**(5), 119–28.

Brynjolfsson, E. and Hitt, L.M. (2000) 'Beyond computation: information technology, organizational transformation and business performance', *Journal of Economic Perspectives*, **19**(4), 23–48.

Clemons, E.K. (1991) 'Evaluation of strategic investments in information technology', *Communications of the ACM*, **34**(1), 23–6.

Currie, W. (1989) 'The art of justifying new technology to top management', *Omega*, **17**(5), 409–18.

Currie, W. (1995) *Management Strategy for IT: An International Perspective*, Pitman, London.

Doherty, N.F., King, M. and Al-Mushayt, O. (2003) 'The impact of inadequacies in the treatment of organisational issues on information systems development projects', *Information and Management*, **41**, 49–62.

Farbey, B., Land, F. and Targett, D. (1993) *How to Assess your IT Investment: A Study of Methods and Practice*, Butterworth-Heinemann, Oxford.

Farbey, B., Land, F. and Targett, D. (eds) (1995) *Hard Money – Soft Outcomes: Evaluating and Managing the IT Investment*, Alfred Waller, Henley-on-Thames.

Gregory, A.J. and Jackson, M.C. (1992) 'Evaluation methodologies: a system for use', *Journal of Operational Research*, **43**(1), 19–28.

Hawgood, J. and Land, F. (1988) 'A multivalent approach to information systems assessment', in N. Bjorn-Anderson and G.B. Davis (eds), *Information Systems Assessment: Issues and Challenges*, North-Holland, Amsterdam, pp. 103–24.

Hirschheim, R. and Smithson, S. (1987) 'Information systems evaluation: myth and reality', in R. Galliers (ed.), *Information Analysis: Selected Readings*, Addison-Wesley, Sydney, pp. 367–80.

Johnson, J. (1995) 'Chaos: the dollar drain of IT project failures', *Application Development Trends*, **2**(1), 41–7.

Kaplan, R.S. (1986) 'Must CIM be justified by faith alone?', *Harvard Business Review*, **64**(2), 87–95.

Kaplan, R.S. and Norton, D.P. (1992) 'The Balanced Scorecard: measures that drive performance', *Harvard Business Review*, **70**(1), 71–9.

Laudon, K.C. and Laudon, J.P. (2004) *Management Information Systems: Organization and Technology in the Networked Enterprise*, Prentice Hall, Englewood Cliffs, NJ.

Peters, G. (1994) 'Evaluating your computer investment strategy', in L. Willcocks (ed.), *Information Management: The Evaluation of Information Systems Investment*, Chapman & Hall, London, pp. 99–112.

Powell, P. (1992) 'Information technology evaluation: is it different?', *Journal of Operational Research*, **43**(1), 29–42.

Ross, J.W. and Beath, C.M. (2002) 'New Approaches to IT Investment', *MIT Sloan Management Review*, **43**(2), 51–9.

Saarinen, T. (1996) 'An expanded instrument for evaluating information system success', *Information and Management*, **31**, 103–18.

Serafeimidis, V. and Smithson, S. (2000) 'Information systems evaluation in practice: a case study of organizational change', *Journal of Information Technology*, **15**, 93–105.

Strassman, P.A. (1999) *Information Productivity*, The Information Economics Press, New Canaan, Conn.

Willcocks, L. (1994) 'Introduction: of capital importance', in L. Willcocks (ed.), *Information Management: The Evaluation of Information Systems Investment*, Chapman & Hall, London, pp. 1–27.

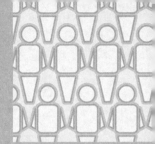

PART 3

Organisation

In a review of research into the relationship between IS and organisations, Eason (2001) noted that a common theme was the diversity of the effects observed:

> *For every study which found increases in job satisfaction there was a study which found increases in job dissatisfaction. In an international study of the effects on power we found every possible outcome . . . centralization, decentralization, lateral transfer across departments and no impact at all.* (p. 323)

He attributed this diversity to the fact that computers are flexible technologies that enable change, but do not determine its form. This depends on the specific application, the objectives that the promoters hope to achieve (such as lower costs or a more distinctive service), and how users respond. As Eason points out, the 'many stakeholders at the receiving end of a new system will be active in responding to the technical system to avoid negative consequences for themselves and if possible achieve benefits' (p. 324).

In consequence, predictions about the effects of IS are likely to be wrong, as they ignore 'very powerful agencies in the organisation which shape the outcomes' (p. 324). This analysis implies that those implementing systems have perhaps more choice than they imagine about the form of the organisation as well as the form of the technology. This Part illustrates the range of organisational options and the processes that shape their evolution. This will enable readers to take an informed and critical view of proposals.

A related theme in IS research is that people typically manage projects with a technical or (sometimes) a business focus, rather than an organisational one. This is despite the clear and accumulating evidence that applications which accompany technical innovation with appropriate organisational innovation are more successful than those which attend only to technical factors (Brynjolfsson and Hitt, 2000). Those promoting IS projects are more likely to benefit the organisation, its members and their own careers if they are able to combine organisational and technological changes in a way that enhances human satisfaction and performance.

Chapter 6 deals with three elements of the organisational context of IS: culture, structure and power. Chapter 7 deals with one aspect of structure, namely the place of the information function itself within the organisation. It outlines options such as centralised, decentralised, federal or outsourced provision, and the benefits and costs of each. Chapter 8 examines the interaction between information systems and people – especially in their roles as users, retail customers or members of the public.

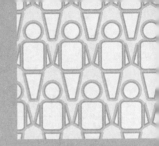

CHAPTER 6

Cultural, structural and political aspects of information systems

Learning objectives

By the end of your work on this topic you should be able to:

- Anticipate how the culture of an organisation or department will affect how staff react to proposals for new IS hardware or software

- Consider whether an information system is achieving the right balance between central and local control of activities

- Suggest questions to consider in deciding how an IS-based venture should relate to the existing organisation

- Assess systematically how an organisation is using IS to alter its relationship with customers and other organisations

- Examine the relationship between organisational power and information systems

- Use the ideas to evaluate potential changes in culture, structure and power linked to an information systems project

Kwik-Fit

Kwik-Fit is a motor repair chain with branches throughout the UK and in several European countries. Tom Farmer founded the company in 1971 and it grew rapidly through acquisition and internal growth. The core business is the drive-in, 'while-you-wait', fitting of replacement parts such as tyres, exhausts and batteries. Customers visit roadside depots, staffed by a manager and a team of fitters.

Each transaction creates an administrative burden – notably to account for the revenue and to replenish stocks. In the early years the company used a manual administrative system. Staff kept paper records of transactions, receipts and stocks in boxes and files. There was a very small central management team based in Edinburgh, led by Farmer. He firmly believed in keeping the number of administrative staff as low as possible. Even when the company had almost 500 depots in the UK, they employed only about 90 administrative staff at head office. They supported depot managers on matters such as sales analysis, finance and stock control.

By 1982 the company was experiencing severe administrative problems. It had bought two similar businesses since 1979, increasing the number of depots from 50 to 180. The acquired companies still operated almost as separate entities. The problems of merging the companies into a single business proved more difficult than expected: 'We had an administrative structure that was good for 50 units, but not for 180 units. The whole structure began to creak.' At the time the depot managers, though part of a national chain, still retained significant local autonomy. They decided when to reorder stock and how much to buy, and had some discretion on which suppliers to use. Although the company had an official price list, in practice the managers had considerable freedom to vary prices, especially through discounting.

Senior management decided that the only way forward was to automate the whole system, using electronic point-of-sale (EPOS) equipment in each depot, supported by a central computing facility. The board set the objectives: to remove the administrative burden from depot managers; to centralise administration on one site; to allow painless expansion; and to improve stock control.

The company installed the system in 1982, based on robust EPOS machines in each depot used by managers and fitters. The machine held prices and descriptions of all items in the inventory. The keyboard was clear and easy to use, as each key showed a system function such as 'cash sale' or 'stock delivery'. Pressing a key led the user through the process. During the day the terminal performed administrative tasks in the depot, essentially recording all the transactions that occurred. For a few minutes each night it linked to the mainframe computer at head office. The system transferred all the depot transactions to the mainframe and processed the data into management reports. It also sent replenishment orders to suppliers. At the same time, the mainframe sent information back to update the terminal in the depot – for example, new prices.

This system has evolved significantly since its introduction, as has the structure of the organisation. The chapter will introduce several themes that relate to management actions at Kwik-Fit, such as the balance between central and local control, and the positioning of a new IS-based line of business.

Source: Based on Boddy and Gunson (1996).

Introduction

Chapter 3 showed how managers can use the power of computer-based IS to improve the strategic position of the enterprise. They also need to consider if the present organisation within which people work is consistent with their strategy, or whether it too needs to evolve. Deciding, for example, to launch an online service also requires a decision about the form of organisation through which to deliver it. This is a highly uncertain area of management as there are conflicting views about the kind of organisation to have and how it affects performance. The existing organisation will have an impact on whether people see a technological opportunity, and whether that develops into a new strategy. There is a close and continuing interaction between IS, strategy and organisation.

People frequently ignore organisational issues, despite evidence that they affect the outcomes of an information system. Studies by Voss (1988) and Symon and Clegg (1991) showed that advanced manufacturing systems require complementary changes in organisation, but that few companies made changes on the scale required. These qualitative studies have received convincing support from the econometric work of Brynjolfsson and Hitt (2000).

This chapter examines this relationship between organisations and information systems. Powerful forces within the organisation influence the outcomes of IS investment whether or not those promoting the scheme consciously attempt to exert influence. Awareness of these forces will enable those involved with an IS project to make more informed choices about how to anticipate and respond to them.

The Chapter Case is about a company that has used IS to good effect from its early days. EPOS systems were used to grow the original business, and have been responsible for several structural changes.

The chapter first outlines how perceptions of the prevailing culture in a unit colour the way people view a new information system. A second theme is that IS enables managers to alter the balance between central and local control – the dilemma is whether to use the technology to control staff more closely or to support local autonomy with better information. If their view of IS developments encourages managers to launch new products or services, do they integrate them within the existing busines or create a separate operation? We then consider the increasingly fluid links between organisations as information systems make it possible to radically change relationships within a supply chain. Finally, we examine the relationship between information systems and the exercise of power within and between organisations.

The aim of this chapter is to indicate the range of organisational choices available, to illustrate the interaction between information systems and their cultural, structural and political context, and to offer tools with which to analyse those links.

6.1 Cultural influences on information systems

Studying information systems from the perspective of organisational culture can increase our understanding of what IS mean to people and why people respond in the way they do. When culture first came to prominence in books and courses on management, writers such as Deal and Kennedy (1982) argued that effective organisations had strong, distinct and, above all, unified cultures. Sometimes referred to as the 'social glue' that binds an organisation, cultures develop as members work together to deal with problems. In doing so they establish shared beliefs about their world and espouse common values about their organisation:

■ **Beliefs** relate to what the members of a culture observe about their world, how they believe it works and what are the main cause and effect relationships – for example success depends on rapid and flexible response to demand or on following well-defined and orderly procedures.

■ **Values** relate to the ideals that members of the culture regard as worth striving for and what people should aim to achieve – for example you can trust people to act responsibly and with self-control or you need to monitor them closely.

The beliefs and values that prevail within an organisation, or a part of it, help to shape the choices that people make about the way the organisation develops. Culture acts as a filter through which members perceive and interpret their environment.

The relevance of this to information systems is that how people react to an IS development will be influenced by how they interpret the proposal in relation to their view of the prevailing culture. A study by Pliskin et al. (1993) showed a wide gap between the actual culture in an organisation and the culture which an IS vendor presumed to exist. The company had a central headquarters group and several geographically separate plants – each of which had a relatively high degree of autonomy. In particular, the plants had a culture whose members believed that informal interpersonal relationships worked well, and valued that management approach. Senior management engaged a consulting firm to implement a computerised employee evaluation system, whose design made several assumptions about the culture in the plants. It depended, for example, on instituting a formal and structured process of employee evaluation. This clashed with the culture of autonomy. Several similar examples led the authors to conclude that the differences between the culture presumed by the consulting firm and the actual culture at the company were so dramatic that they led to the failure of the project.

Current studies of culture emphasise their diversity and suggest examining subcultures within an organisation, rather than a single culture. Martin (2002) identifies three perspectives in cultural research – integration, differentiation and fragmentation – which Table 6.1 summarises.

Those who take an integration perspective look for consistency in how people respond to organisational issues, and for consensus around established policies. They will expect people to support management proposals for, say, an information system and may regard opposition to a project as due to misunderstanding or poor communication. Those who take the differentiation perspective acknowledge the likelihood of conflict between business units or functional groups, based on distinctive interests and views of the world. These may be expressed in conflicting views

Table 6.1 **Three perspectives on organisational culture**

Cultural perspective	Focus	Metaphor
Integration	Consistency between aspects of culture, consensus, clarity	A monolith that most people see as being the same, from whatever angle
Differentiation	Inconsistency between subcultures in different parts of the organisation	Islands of clarity in a sea of ambiguity
Fragmentation	Ambiguity – people interpret aspects of culture in an uncertain way, depending on the issue	An audience in which each member responds to an issue uniquely, in a transient combination with others

Source: Based on Martin (2002).

about the benefits or otherwise of an information system as people interpret its likely effects from the perspective of their subculture. A fragmentation perspective sees organisations as being in a state of flux, with people expressing different views in shifting alliances with others as they interpret and reinterpret events and policies around them. This ambiguous position may reflect, and perhaps exacerbate, confusion over the intentions of new policies, especially among people far from the centre who receive little information.

Research Summary   Multiple-cultures

Although we are unaware of empirical work directly testing this model in relation to IS projects, a study by Ogbonna and Harris (1998) found substantial support for the model in a study of strategy in a retail business. Senior managers adopted an integration perspective, stressing the value of everyone pulling together and working to make the established policies work. Managers in the retail stores corresponded to the differentiation perspective, as a major part of their job was to reconcile the conflicting expectations of senior managers and the shopfloor staff. The latter expressed views close to a fragmentation position, being confused about shifting policies and uncertain about their roles – changes were being made more quickly than they could learn to deal with them.

Source: Ogbonna and Harris (1998).

One way in which subcultures differ is in their view of information in general, and an information system in particular. Do they see information as:

- belonging to individuals, or to the organisation?
- a means of control, or a source of creativity?
- something you protect and hoard, or something you share?
- more valuable if it is hard and quantitative, or if it is soft and qualitative?

People in subcultures differ in the information they require and how they obtain and process it. This will affect how satisfied they are with an information system and how they view a new one. They will welcome a system that fits the culture and resist one that conflicts with it.

The competing values model illuminates why people in different subcultures may vary in how they react to IS projects. Quinn et al. (2003) propose that organisations have inherent tensions along two dimensions – order or flexibility on one axis, and external or internal focus on the other. The resulting four cultural types (shown in Figure 6.1) express 'competing values' about how people should manage organisations.

Open systems (external, flexibility)

This represents an open systems view, in which people recognise that the external environment is significant, seeing it a vital source of ideas, energy and resources. They also see it as complex and turbulent, requiring entrepreneurial, visionary leadership and responsive behaviour. Key motivating factors are growth, stimulation, creativity and variety. Examples are: start-up firms, business development units – organic, flexible operations.

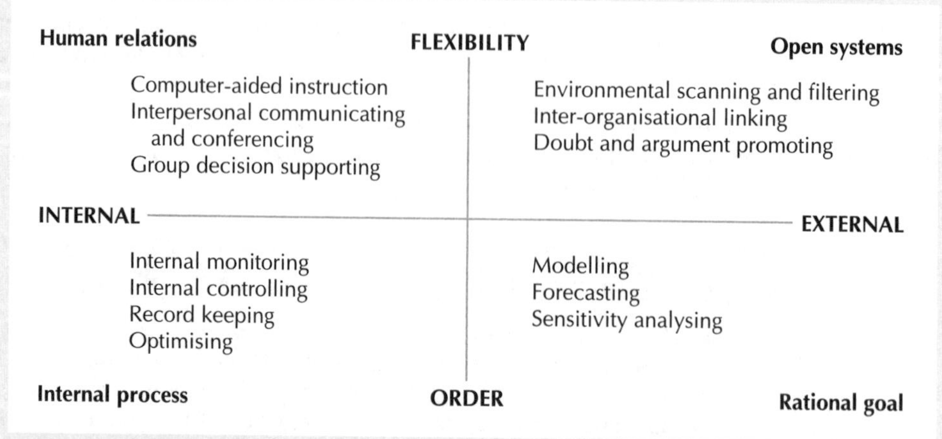

Human relations	FLEXIBILITY	Open systems
Computer-aided instruction Interpersonal communicating and conferencing Group decision supporting		Environmental scanning and filtering Inter-organisational linking Doubt and argument promoting
INTERNAL		**EXTERNAL**
Internal monitoring Internal controlling Record keeping Optimising		Modelling Forecasting Sensitivity analysing
Internal process	**ORDER**	**Rational goal**

Figure 6.1 Information systems associated with cultural types
Source: Based on Cooper (1994) and Quinn et al. (2003).

Rational goal (external, order)

Members see the unit as being a rational, efficiency-seeking operation. They define effectiveness in terms of production or economic goals that meet familiar and stable external requirements. Managers create structures to deal efficiently with this stable outside world. Leadership tends to be directive, goal-oriented and functional. Motivating factors include competition and achieving targets. Examples are: large, established production or service activities (sales departments?) – mechanistic, rule-driven.

Internal process (internal, order)

Here members pay little attention to the external world and focus instead on internal issues. Their goal is to make the unit efficient, stable and controlled. Goals are known, tasks repetitive and methods stress specialisation, rules, procedures. Leaders tend to be conservative and cautious, emphasising technical issues. Key motivating factors include security, stability and order. Examples are: established IT or finance departments – suspicious of change.

Human relations (internal, flexibility)

People emphasise the value of informal, interpersonal relations rather than formal structures. They place high value on maintaining the organisation and the well-being of its members, and define effectiveness in terms of developing people and their commitment. Leaders tend to be participative, considerate and supportive. Motivating factors tend to be attachment, cohesiveness and membership. Examples are: professional service firms, some internal support functions.

Intuitively we can sense that people with these different cultural values will react differently to many things, including proposed information systems. For example, people in an internal process culture will welcome systems that give more control and promote order and predictability. They will be critical of systems that increase the flow of new ideas and external information, threatening established methods.

Cooper (1994) tested this idea among the IS community. He specified ten IS applications that would be likely to support (and so be accepted by) one of the cultural types. He presented the model shown in Figure 6.1 to members of the IS community, asking them to rank the extent to which each system was likely to support the focus of each cultural type. Their conclusions, with one exception, agreed with the author's prediction.

This confirmed that people associate certain IS applications more closely with one culture than with others and that the cultural context is likely to affect how people respond to information systems. One of the authors of this book presented the model to staff from a large European bank and invited them to identify which of the four cultural descriptions best represented their part of the organisation. Two cultures were well-represented – open systems (mainly people from the bank's business development unit, charged with finding and building new markets) and internal process (mainly people from the IT department, charged with running the bank's well-established computer systems that processed vast amounts of routine business very efficiently). He invited the two groups to react to a proposed Internet banking scheme. Those in the open systems culture welcomed it, as it would be consistent with, and supportive of, their culture. Those in the internal process culture were deeply uneasy, believing that the proposal would disrupt their well-established and effective operating systems.

Research Summary **Culture affects use of IS**

In a study reported more fully in Chapter 8, Boonstra et al. (2004) studied the low rate of acceptance by general practitioners (GPs) in the Netherlands of an electronic prescription system (EPS). Some GPs accepted the new system (which was intended to reduce the cost of prescriptions) quite readily, but many did not. A research team concluded that a major factor in this variability was the culture of the different practices.

Interviews using the Competing Values model enabled the researchers to assign each GP to one of the cultural types. Those who expressed the values of the rational goal culture – efficiency, standards, etc. – accepted the EPS as consistent with that culture. Those who expressed the values of the human relations culture – individuality, informality, an interpersonal relationship – rejected EPS, as they interpreted it as an attack on that culture. More broadly, they interpreted the motives of the ministry trying to promote EPS as an attempt to undermine the professional autonomy of GPs, which for many has been, and remains, an important feature of their position.

Source: Boonstra et al. (2004).

These examples support the idea that if people interpret a proposed system as being consistent with their culture they are likely to accept it with enthusiasm and commitment. If there is a mismatch between the culture and the proposed system, they will resist it.

Summary

- People may interpret the culture of their organisation not as something unified and integrated, but as one in which there are several subcultures.

- One dimension or manifestation of a culture is how its members see information.

Activity 6.1 Research on culture

If you have the opportunity in an assignment or project, you could test the Competing Values model by interviewing people in several departments about their reaction to an IS. Try to find out:

- *What the IS was, what it was intended to achieve and what is the current status?*

- *What people in (say) three different departments think of it – support, oppose, mixed?*

- *What is the culture in the respective departments? Investigate this by giving them a copy of the descriptions of the four cultural types and asking them which description best represents their department.*

- *Consider if their replies and comments seem to relate to the culture of the department.*

- If people interpret an IS application as supporting their current culture they are likely to accept it; if they believe it will threaten their culture they are likely to reject it.

6.2 IS can support central or local decision-making

One aspect of an organisation's structure is the extent to which decisions are made by people at different levels in the hierarchy.

- Centralisation is when those at the top make most decisions, with those at middle and lower levels following the policies thus established;

- Decentralisation is when a relatively large number of decisions are made by those working at middle and lower levels.

Each has advantages and disadvantages. Centralisation enables people to respond consistently to change and avoid duplicating resources, but they may be unresponsive to local conditions. Decentralisation avoids this problem, but brings with it the risk that people in different parts of the company follow different practices, thus confusing customers.

The relevance to IS is that computer-based systems can support either approach. Early writers on the topic took a relatively deterministic position, predicting, for example, that IS would lead to more centralisation (Leavitt and Whisler, 1958), while others predicted the opposite – that it would promote decentralisation (Burlinghame, 1961). For convenience, Figure 6.2 adapts Figure 1.6 which illustrated the three perspectives. Figure 6.2(a) illustrates the deterministic relationship. Another view is to reverse the causal relationship and to argue that organisation structures, and indeed the form of technology, depend on organisational requirements. Thus Robey (1981) proposed that organisation structure was not influenced by IS alone, but that both were influenced by more fundamental factors of size, type of business and environmental uncertainty – see Figure 6.2(b).

A third possibility is that the relationship is hard to predict as it emerges from a continuing process of social interactions, shown in Figure 6.2(c). People who are

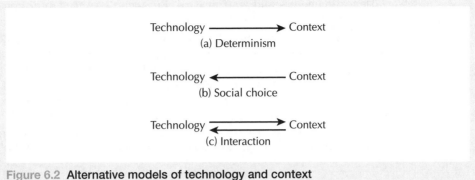

Figure 6.2 Alternative models of technology and context

able to influence the change may try to use IS to increase the control of the centre over local decisions and that may indeed be the result. Alternatively those at lower levels may interpret this as an unwanted interference with their authority, interests and local conditions. They may try to counter the proposals and resist centralisation. The outcomes will depend on the ability of the respective groups to argue their case and to adapt the way people use the system during and after implementation.

The box describes the initial direction at Kwik-Fit.

Kwik-Fit: Towards more central control

At the time of the change the company had five geographical divisions. Day-to-day control was in the hands of a management board between the main board and the divisions. One insider described it as: 'a very flat structure, inasmuch as if we wanted to change something tomorrow we could do it – we have not got a hierarchy that people have to go through'. Under the manual system, the depot managers had had to perform many administrative tasks. These included checking stock, raising purchase orders, dealing with suppliers and managing cash receipts. Equally, area managers had to check that managers were running the depots properly. This became progressively more difficult as the business grew – with the paper-based system it was almost impossible to check on stock levels or discounts given by the depots.

This changed dramatically when the company installed an EPOS system. Staff at HQ now received all details of a depot's sales activity of the previous day and could immediately question any unauthorised discounting – which ceased very rapidly. In these and many other ways the system enabled the company to become much more tightly controlled from the centre. The founder had always wanted a tightly run business, but the growth of the business exceeded its communication capacity. The EPOS system helped the centre to catch up. Managers at head office now received much more information about performance across the company. For example, the sales manager could review the following day the performance of any depot:

The systems have ensured that we have information to monitor what we are about – every morning I have a daily update. It tells me for the company as a whole, through our major product categories, what we sold across the depots, their value and the margin we generated. And we could have an individual depot if we wanted to. It gives us prices, margins and all the necessary monitoring elements. All this information goes to the manager as well, because they need to know how they are doing.

Source: Based on Boddy and Gunson (1996).

Depot managers and staff at Kwik-Fit accepted the tighter central controls, as they were consistent with what had always been a relatively centralised company. The IT system did not introduce the idea of centralisation, but made it easier to apply the well-understood management practices. The IT system was also designed to bring several tangible benefits to depot managers and staff, which also helped them to accept it. In other cases people have opposed attempts to centralise decisions through an information system – as Markus's (1983) classic study on resistance to a centralising system clearly demonstrates (see p. 165).

Managers can also use the capacity of information systems to support decentralisation, and the box below describes a later development at Kwik-Fit.

Kwik-Fit: Towards more divisional control

In 1992 senior management changed the emphasis of their control as they installed a new generation of more powerful equipment. The aim was to keep management close to the changing needs of the business. The board gave the five geographical divisions greater autonomy, and the divisional directors now had full responsibility for the profitability of their division. Speaking in 1992, a senior manager explained:

There was a large degree of autonomy within divisions, but there were a number of things they had to refer to the centre for approval. We have now decided that we do not really want to have a central core of people servicing these divisions. We would rather have the divisions as autonomous units.

To support this organisational change, the company adjusted the computer systems to make them operate semi-independently for each of the divisions. It split the purchase ledgers, for example, into multi-company operations. It partitioned the database so that each division could access its data, but senior management were able to see the totality of the business. One of the new divisional directors noted how this worked:

We process the invoices for all the purchases our depots make. Head office would previously have dealt with that on behalf of the depots, but now the supplier invoices the division here. We do all our invoice matching, our own electronic checking. Head office still produces the cheques and the payments electronically – but we initiate it. We only depend on head office for two things – marketing and advertising, and central computer services.

He pointed out that the information to enable close monitoring of the depots had been already in place – but that someone managing 75 depots could do it better than someone managing 400. Divisionalisation allowed them to make better use of the information provided by the information system. The divisional managers could now use this information, and their local knowledge, to manage their part of the business in a relatively decentralised way.

Source: Based on Boddy and Gunson (1996).

Powerful computer systems allow management to rethink how they balance central and local control. Malone (1997) believed that the falling cost of communication would alter this judgement. When communication costs are high, most decisions, for the lack of any alternative, are made by relatively independent local decision-makers. As communication costs fall, managers can choose (for operational or political reasons) to bring more of the information together for use at the centre. As communication costs fall further, managers have the new option of passing more information to local staff and empowering them to make more decisions themselves.

CASE QUESTIONS 6.1

Summarise how (and why) Kwik-Fit shifted the balance between central and local control.

What role have information systems played in helping or hindering those changes?

Does this account support or contradict Malone's theory?

The box below contains an example of another company, Oticon, that used IS to eliminate a conventional hierarchy.

MIS in Practice   Oticon – using information systems to change the hierarchy

Oticon, a high-technology Danish hearing-aid company, is an example of a company that took a radical approach to its design, with IS at the centre. In 1994 the company was one of the five largest producers of hearing aids, exporting 90 per cent of its production. Changes in customer demands threatened its position during the 1980s and, after a period of financial losses, the board appointed a new chief executive, Lars Kolind. Kolind took a radical approach to the problem and sought to replace an existing organisation with one that was innovative, flexible and learning. To do this he:

- eliminated traditional departments – people now worked on projects, moving between them as the flow of work changed;
- created a project organisation – senior management appoint project leaders, who then advertise electronically for staff from within the company to join them;
- increased staff mobility – people occupy several positions, on different projects;
- removed private desks – and replaced them by mobile trolleys, the core of which was a mobile PC. These gave staff access to databases and other tools, and they wheeled them to meetings;
- eliminated paper – all documents were scanned and stored electronically. Anyone with the relevant authority could access the data. Results of meetings are stored electronically and can be used by people on other related projects.

By using IT, with radical structural changes, 'Oticon is able to bring a full range of resources to bear on a problem much more quickly than can their competitors'.

Source: Based on Bjorn-Anderson and Turner (1994).

However, a recent study provides evidence of increasing central control. Finnegan and Longaigh (2002) studied the use of IS in 15 subsidiaries of pan-national organisations located in Ireland, concluding that redesigned and standardised business processes were increasing the power of headquarters.

IT has facilitated more direct monitoring of day-to-day operations, while communication technology has vastly improved responsiveness to queries.

This has enabled headquarters to take responsibility for many operations that were previously left to subsidiaries. (p. 159)

We conclude from this contrasting evidence that in some circumstances people believe a relatively centralised structure is appropriate and in others they believe the opposite. Managers in successful organisations will have tried to develop a structure and information system that is appropriate to the conditions. If they see new IS applications becoming available that will further support their established approach (whether centralised or decentralised) they will promote them. If other players accept management's diagnosis of the conditions they will accept the information system (as happened at Kwik-Fit).

However, if managers seek to impose a system that others see as unsuitable for the conditions, they may experience a different reaction. At Oticon, where managers used IS to help change an established structure, they had to convince others players that the change was essential. Many were comfortable with the stable, hierarchical system – and were unconvinced about the radical change being proposed. Similarly, people in local units may dislike senior managers' attempts to use IS to impose a more centrally dominated structure.

Summary

- Managers can use computer-based IS to increase central control.
- They can also use it to increase the ability of local units to make operational and sometimes strategic decisions.
- If people believe the established balance of control is suitable they are likely to accept an IS that reinforces that balance and oppose one that weakens it.
- Managers can also use IS to change the established balance, but changing both IS and structure will be a more challenging task than changing either on its own.
- The balance reflects how people interpret perfomance demands on the organisation and the interests of powerful players.

6.3 Structures to support IS-enabled ventures

Information systems give people the opportunity to develop new lines of business – and the challenge of deciding how to organise them. Should the new operation be integrated with the current business or established as a separate operation? We show contrasting approaches to the issue, and conclude with an analytical tool.

Some companies have created new businesses that operate separately from the parent group. The Daily Mail group of companies initially created a separate business to develop online publishing, and several banks have created online banking services with a separate name from the parent (Egg, for example, is owned by the Prudential Insurance Company). Others have taken a different route – online banking offered by The Royal Bank of Scotland is visibly part of the established group. In retailing, Tesco and John Lewis offer online services through the physical stores, while others, among them Sainsbury's and Ocado, have built separate distribution facilities for the online business.

Kwik-Fit: The new business

As managers in the company came to understand the potential of the system, they identified ways of developing the business in new directions. EPOS provided the base for activities that managers believed would not have been feasible otherwise. The most visible of these is Kwik-Fit Insurance Services (KFIS), established in 1995. Earlier developments had resulted in the company having a robust point-of-sale system, which among other things collected information about each customer, including their telephone number. This, and the strong Kwik-Fit brand name, were the basis for KFIS.

The distinctive feature of the business is that it uses the customer database created by EPOS in the depots. The head-office mainframe passes the daily transaction data created by the EPOS system to KFIS the following day. KFIS staff telephone each customer, enquire about the service they received at the depot and ask if they would like a free insurance quotation. If so, staff ask for their renewal date and enter this into an electronic diary. Shortly before the renewal date staff call again to give the customer an insurance quotation. The company claims to be the only major insurance company operating with this business model.

At first Kwik-Fit created the new business with an autonomous management structure. Staff were rapidly recruited to work in a new call centre, separate from head office. It built the business quickly, installed advanced technology and established business processes for handling calls, applications and claims.

Initially the new business was structured as a separate venture, with good information systems. As management later acknowledged, however, they paid little attention to how that structure would affect the management of staff. There were difficulties over recruiting, training and motivating staff, which in turn led to some service problems. The Kwik-Fit board quickly realised that if customers were in any way dissatisfied with KFIS, this could damage the main brand. They therefore changed the way the subsidiary operated, and put a new management team in place. Several aspects of the Kwik-Fit culture were transferred to KFIS. As a senior manager pointed out:

Our current obsession with customer satisfaction is not an accident – that's happened because of Kwik-Fit . . . Kwik-Fit make sure that we look after customers in the way that Kwik-Fit would like them to be looked after. We had some senior managers from Kwik-Fit to help us get the satisfaction up, by working on all our systems, processes and people to see where the weak links were.

KFIS also employed a quality manager, who introduced several new control mechanisms. These changes brought a much tighter Kwik-Fit culture to the new venture, which appeared, in late 2003, to be working well.

Source: Based on Boddy and Gunson (1996) and interviews with KFIS management.

Gulati and Garino (2000) offer a model that helps to evaluate the options. They studied three retail companies that had developed online ventures and observed the choices the companies had made about relating the new venture to the old:

- Spin-off?
- Strategic partnership?
- Joint venture?
- In-house division?

The authors concluded that the appropriate choice would depend on how managers interpreted the answers to questions about the brand, the management and operation of the new venture, and about whether staff sought a financial stake.

Table 6.2 **Questions on separating or integrating an Internet venture**

Separation	Questions	Integration
	Brand	
	Does the brand extend naturally to the Internet?	Yes
Yes	Will we target a different customer segment or offer a different product mix?	
Yes	Will we need to price differently online?	
	Management	
	Do current executives have the skills and experience needed to pursue the Internet channel?	Yes
	Are they willing to judge the Internet initiatives by different performance criteria?	Yes
Yes	Will there be major channel conflict?	
Yes	Does the Internet fundamentally threaten the existing business model?	
	Operations	
	Do our distribution systems translate well to the Internet?	Yes
	Do our information systems provide a solid foundation on which to build?	Yes
	Does either system constitute a significant competitive advantage?	Yes
	Equity	
Yes	Are we having trouble attracting and retaining talented executives for the Internet division?	
Yes	Do we need outside capital to fund the venture?	
Yes	Is a certain supplier, distributor or other partner key to the venture's success?	

Source: Gulati and Garino (2000).

To illustrate the approach, Table 6.2 shows the suggested questions under each theme.

The authors advised that depending on the balance of answers to these and similar questions, managers would get an insight into the decision to integrate or separate the venture. Note that the answers depend on judgement and interpretation, and will often point in different directions – so while they provide a way of structuring the decision, they may still leave it ambiguous and uncertain.

Summary

- Using the power of computer-based information systems for new business ventures raises major structural questions for managers.

- They need to decide whether to run the Internet venture as a separate enterprise or to integrate it with the existing business.

- One empirically based model suggests managers analyse this decision by considering the dimensions of brand, management, operations and equity.

CASE QUESTIONS 6.2

Review the last section of the Chapter Case (Kwik-Fit: 4 – The New Business).

Use the Gulati and Garino questions to analyse whether KFIS should have been more clearly separated, or more closely integrated, with the established business.

What additional questions would you add to the Gulati and Garino list?

6.4 IS enables new structures

Products and services are the outcome of a chain of activities linking internal processes to those in customers and suppliers – a value-adding chain that may stretch across continents and oceans. IS developments make it possible (though not easy) to transform the organisational structure through which people manage successive steps in the supply chain.

A comparatively simple example is the way in which Kwik-Fit used the EPOS system to smooth transactions with their suppliers, enabling staff at different parts of the supply chain to use common, accurate information. The system enables staff to locate stock quickly and automatically sends information electronically to suppliers about what has been used. Suppliers then deliver stock directly to the depots to sustain agreed inventory levels and receive payment electronically. A subsequent development allowed an automatic link to the Banks Automated Clearing System (BACS). The software in the depot terminals was modified to capture and validate credit card numbers. The transaction details were collated centrally and transmitted automatically to BACS – removing another administrative load from the depots.

IS makes it much easier for firms to coordinate activities in physically separate locations. This means that companies have much greater freedom over:

- the way they deal with customers (face to face or remotely);
- whether they own the resources they use (it may be easier to contract with other organisations to provide what they need); and
- how they manage knowledge (perhaps using expertise in other organisations as well as their own).

Some writers use the term 'virtual organisation' to express the idea that IS makes it possible for firms to deliver goods and services with very little in the way of a physical presence. The development of Linux, outlined in the box below, is one example.

However, with a few rare exceptions, all organisations have both some physical facilities and some degree of physical separation within their value chain. Venkatraman and Henderson (1998) offer a useful and practical perspective on the topic in proposing that the virtual organisation is not so much a state as a process. Organisations differ in the degree to which they are 'virtual' rather than being either one or the other. The authors suggest that 'virtualness' is a characteristic of any organisation, based on its position along three vectors – customer interaction, asset configuration and knowledge leverage (see Figure 6.3). This idea allows us to consider how IS developments enable long-established organisations to introduce a greater degree of physical separation in their activities.

MIS in Practice   Developing Linux

The familiar story of how the Linux software system developed illustrates a new approach to organisation structure. Linus Torvalds, who developed the initial version, made it available on the Internet and invited other software developers to download it freely to test and modify it. It gradually attracted enthusiastic software developers, until the Linux community involved thousands of developers around the world, all sharing their work. Within a few years this informal group, working through the Internet, created a highly successful piece of software used by many corporate IT departments.

The community (and other 'open source' communities) have evolved mechanisms and processes to ensure order, despite the potential for chaos. These include:

- high intrinsic motivation and self-management among developers, ensuring they deliver high quality work and appropriate social behaviour. Receiving payment for contributing to a software project is important, but so also is the development and maintenance of reputation;

- membership is fluid, but managed. Development teams typically have a core community, with additional members brought in for particular tasks;

- control is exercised through a few simple rules, designed to ensure appropriate conduct and fair play;

- self-governance is achieved formally through discussion and voting among community members, and informally through social control by other members.

Source: Markus *et al.* (2000).

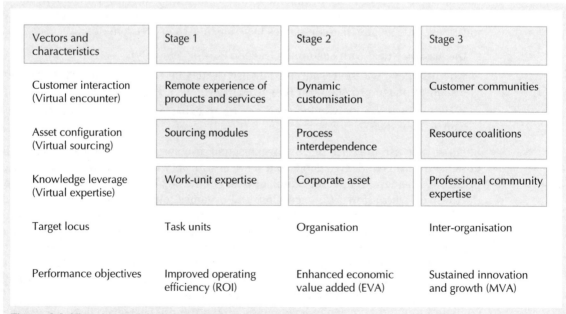

Vectors and characteristics	Stage 1	Stage 2	Stage 3
Customer interaction (Virtual encounter)	Remote experience of products and services	Dynamic customisation	Customer communities
Asset configuration (Virtual sourcing)	Sourcing modules	Process interdependence	Resource coalitions
Knowledge leverage (Virtual expertise)	Work-unit expertise	Corporate asset	Professional community expertise
Target locus	Task units	Organisation	Inter-organisation
Performance objectives	Improved operating efficiency (ROI)	Enhanced economic value added (EVA)	Sustained innovation and growth (MVA)

Figure 6.3 Virtual organising: three vectors and three stages
Source: Venkatraman and Henderson (1998).

Customer interaction

Here Venkatraman and Henderson consider how IS makes it easier for customers to experience products and services remotely and perhaps engage in some dynamic customisation. Fundamentally this is no more than an extension of mail-order catalogues, which enabled physical retail stores to give customers some 'feel' for the products available without being physically present. IS, especially when linked with television, clearly offers many more possibilities for customers to view alternatives, select their options and conduct the transaction electronically.

Asset configuration

Here the focus is on the extent to which a firm coordinates resources and activities within a network – it does not depend only on assets it physically controls. Again, this extends established practice, as firms have always depended on suppliers for things they preferred not to make themselves. IS makes it possible for firms to do much more of this, and to manage it more actively, than was possible with manual systems. The Internet allows access to a wider range of possible suppliers and customers, and can also be used to manage the relationships much more closely. The technology, and wider economic developments, are also encouraging managers to outsource some of their business processes to other organisations.

Sun Microsystems, for example, has a corporate arrangement with three transport companies to manage its logistics – including not only transportation but also warehousing, pre-assembly work and final delivery. In more extreme cases, Venkatraman and Henderson envisage companies not as collections of physical assets, but as coalitions of resources. The competitive advantage comes from managing the resources, physically present in other companies on the network, in the most imaginative and productive ways.

Knowledge leverage

This means gaining access to wider sources of expertise, including that in other organisations. IS allows staff in a work unit to have access to information generated elsewhere – staff in a call centre can access data about customer histories and spending patterns so that they can discuss a transaction more confidently. Groupware tools enable teams to share information more widely. A second level of development is when the firm shares information across the organisation as a whole – again by groupware or similar systems. A third level is when an organisation actively draws on expertise beyond its boundaries – in professional communities, or from customers and suppliers. Internet developments make the rapid sourcing of such expertise technically possible.

Andal-Ancion et al. (2003) also deal with this issue, although they do not express the issue in terms of progressing through the stages suggested by Venkatraman and

---

Activity 6.2 Linking theory and practice

Use the Venkatraman and Henderson model to assess the position of an organisation (such as your college or university) as a virtual organisation. Gather evidence to show which stage it has reached now on each of the three vectors (customers, assets and knowledge), and what plans there are, if any, to move to a 'more virtual' position.

Henderson. Instead they suggest that managers need to decide what kind of relationship they want to have with other organisations. They set out the options:

■ **Disintermediation**. A company uses the capacity of information systems to eliminate intermediaries (such as distributors) between itself and its customers or suppliers. Example: easyJet only sells tickets over the Internet, eliminating the travel agent as an intermediary;

■ **Remediation**. A company uses IS to enable it to work more closely with intermediaries in close, long-term relationships that add value to its service. Example: Sainsbury (a UK supermarket chain) sells electricity under its own brand by (invisibly) using the expertise of a power company (Scottish Power) to deliver energy to customers;

■ **Network-based mediation**. Companies use IS to build a network of alliances and partnerships, which they use in fluid and variable ways in response to changing supplier offers and customer needs. Example: Sun Microsystems (a leading IT company) develops an extensive network of partners with manufacturing and logistics expertise, allowing the company to focus on product development and design, instead of manufacture.

In all cases the new arrangements are supported by sophisticated information systems – and the choice for managers is which kind of relationship will best suit their business. Andal-Ancion et al. offer a model helping managers analyse this

---

MIS in Practice   Internet procurement at IBM

IBM's Internet procurement project is an example of network-based mediation, in the sense that the company used the Internet to radically change the way it managed the supply of goods and services from worldwide suppliers. Traditionally, IBM buyers printed a purchase order from their PC and faxed it to the supplier. The supplier's staff reviewed the requirement, and wrote their acceptance or other comments on the printed order. They faxed this back to IBM, where staff checked it and keyed it into the system. This enabled a buyer to see whether the material required would be available. This procedure was slow, labour-intensive and open to error, as was the invoicing process.

The company decided to create an Internet-based system. The procedure now is that when a buyer releases an order from the IBM order system it goes electronically to the supplier. They reply by keying their commitment (if they choose to do so) to deliver on a certain date, or other response, into a field on the original purchase order, and return it electronically into the IBM system. If the buyer observes a potential delivery problem, they discuss that with the supplier.

The system eliminated much administrative work from the transaction, and brought major benefits to both sides. But a major management problem was that some suppliers were less ready than others for the change. A procurement manager commented:

Many suppliers told us they were more ready for EDI than they were. When our team met them it was very clear that the supplier's processes were not ready. They underestimated the activity involved in becoming an electronic company. They needed to change both their IS system and other parts of the organisation – and this was a much bigger task than many had expected.

Source: Information provided by the company.

choice and based on ten 'business drivers'. These include factors such as the characteristics of the product (whether it can be delivered electronically or not), the scope
for aggregation (whether products from the separate organisations can be combined
to add value) and missing competences (which IS can enable them to draw from
other organisations).

Andal-Ancion et al. recommend identifying which drivers are most relevant
to businesses and using that interpretation to help evaluate possibilities for transforming the organisation. They also stress that whatever that evaluation suggests,
there will still be a substantial task of organisational change to manage within the
company, and possibly with suppliers and customers as well.

CASE QUESTIONS 6.3

*How many examples of the new forms of relationships suggested by Andal-Ancion et al. can you
observe in the Kwik-Fit case?*

*What new opportunities may the company be able to consider by using one or more of these new
forms?*

▨ Summary

- ▨ Computer-based IS increasingly support the flow of data and information across
  company boundaries.

- ▨ This makes it easier to separate the physical aspects of a business and to perform
  them in geographically separate places.

- ▨ Managers therefore have more options over how they manage customers, assets
  and knowledge.

- ▨ They also have more options over their relations with other organisations as they
  can choose between disintermediation, remediation or network-based approaches.

- ▨ Implementing such systems is a major challenge, as other business partners may
  also need to make significant organisational changes.

6.5 The political aspects of information systems

The prevailing distribution of power within an organisation has considerable, if
often hidden, influence on the direction of an IS project. Power is essential to get
things done in organisations, including the achievement of personal goals and
rewards. Those with power want to retain it, while those with less power may seek
opportunities to increase it. People can use information systems to threaten or
strengthen the existing distribution of power, so we need some tools to analyse the
links between IS and power. People use power to get things done, and seek to protect or increase their capacity to do so:

- ▨ power is the capacity of individuals to exert their will over others;
- ▨ that capacity comes from five bases of power: coercion, reward, administrative
  expertise, technical expertise and referent.

Bases of power

Building on early work by French and Raven (1959), Hales (1993) showed that a person's power is not just a personal characteristic, but follows from their position in the organisation. The five sources of power (each of which can have both a personal and an organisational aspect) are outlined below.

- **Coercive**. This is the authority to give instructions with the threat of sanctions or punishment available to back them up. Managers with this power can use it to instruct development staff about priorities or to instruct users to use (or not use) a new system.

- **Reward**. This is the ability to use the financial and other resources of the organisation to bestow status or rewards on others in return for their support. Managers with large budgets and links into valuable networks of contacts have power. They can commit some of their resources to others in return for the support they need – for example to persuade a manager in another department to support their IS project or to commit staff to work on the design.

- **Administrative expertise**. This is the power that the holder of a position has to create organisation policies which bolster their influence. They may use their position to decide which IS projects go ahead, what their objectives are or who will be on the project team – which in itself will shape the direction of the project.

MIS in Practice   The flowering of feudalism

'Knowledge is power' has become such a managerial cliché that many at the top of big companies tend to forget that the principle can work both ways. Those lower down the management hierarchy also have an interest in husbanding information – and the power that goes with it. According to a survey of large European companies by the management consulting arm of KPMG, an accounting firm, the vast majority have found it impossible to establish pan-European management information systems for the simple reason that middle-ranking managers in different countries do not want those at headquarters to know what they are up to.

By 1993, few companies had succeeded in taking the first step by collecting information on their own far-flung European operations in a uniform way. After interviewing the chief executives or financial officers of 153 large European companies, KPMG found that only 8 per cent of them had established common information systems across their European subsidiaries. And this was not because of glitches with computers. 'Technically, of course, anything is possible with information systems these days,' observed the boss of a Danish tobacco firm. 'It is not the technical aspect that we find daunting; it's the time and energy we have to spend explaining it to people and persuading them to accept it.'

When they try to introduce the computers and procedures to gather such information, reported Alistair Stewart, who conducted the survey, European firms meet 'Ghandi-like' resistance from their subsidiaries. European HQs may be sending mixed signals to subsidiary managers: preaching autonomy and responsibility while trying to computerise all aspects of their business so that staff at headquarters can monitor their every move. 'People are reluctant to share their information,' complained the head of one French company, which manufactures industrial equipment. 'Managers in particular seem to think it gives them extra power.' Clever chaps.

Source: Based on 'The flowering of feudalism', *The Economist*, 27 February 1993.

- **Technical expertise**. As well as an individual's personal expertise, power can also arise if a person holds a position that gives them access to information so that they are aware of what is happening and of emerging threats or opportunities. They can use their position, and the contacts that go with it, to build their image as a competent person and to influence the direction of an IS project.

- **Referent**. This refers to situations where managers can use their position to influence others by showing that what they propose is consistent with the accepted values and culture of the organisation. They invoke wider values in support of their proposal or of their opposition to a proposal.

Power and IS

The relevance of this to information systems is that people compete for access to, or control over, information and the power that goes with it – as the 'flowering of feudalism' feature indicates.

If people are concerned about their power within the organisation, one of the criteria they will use to evaluate an information system is its likely effect on their power. Will it increase it, reduce it or have no effect? They are likely to promote and

---

Research Summary — Golden Triangle Corporation

Golden Triangle Corporation grew from a merger between a chemical company and two energy companies. The structure consisted of a headquarters staff group, including corporate accounting, and four operating divisions. The divisions had a relatively high degree of autonomy over marketing and investment decisions, reflecting the diverse businesses they conducted. Traditionally, the divisional accountants collected and stored transaction data however they saw fit, but reported summary data to corporate accountants in a standardised form.

The corporate accounting department proposed the creation of a financial information system. A taskforce from corporate accounting analysed the need for such a system, and recommended the purchase of a financial accounting package. This would enable a single corporate database to replace the divisional databases.

The system collected, summarised and distributed financial data. Divisional accountants entered their transactions into the system, and the IS automatically summarised the data into reports (e.g. monthly profit and loss statements) for corporate accountants and for the relevant division. The first division went into the system in January 1975.

In October 1975, an accountant from the division wrote that: 'Except for providing more detailed information, the IS has not been beneficial to us.' In October 1977, he wrote: 'After two years and seven months my opinion has not changed. Even worse, it seems to have become a system that is running people rather than people utilising the system.' Other divisional users shared his views. One division kept on using its old accounting methods after it started using the IS, even though this required time and effort. Some divisional accountants admitted to 'data juggling' to circumvent the system.

The corporate accountants welcomed the system enthusiastically. It automatically performed tedious tasks of calculation and reporting that they had formerly done by hand. Corporate accountants could not account for the resistance of divisional staff members. One said: 'I can't understand why the divisions don't like the IS. There are so many benefits.'

Source: Based on Markus (1983).

favour IS applications that enhance their power, and resist those that threaten it – as Markus (1983) showed in her classic study (see Research Summary above) .

More recently, Knights and Murray (1994) showed how managers at Pensco, an insurance company, used their respective power to try to shape the services provided by an IS project. Dysfunctional conflicts between them appeared to result in a system that was more expensive and less useful than the promoters had expected. Webster (1995) showed how major companies in the automobile and retail industries had used their power over suppliers to enforce the use of inter-organisational information systems. Power is also essential during the implementation of systems, a theme we explore in Chapter 9.

▨ Summary

- ▪ People in organisations value the power that ensures their capacity to influence others.
- ▪ Power comes from both personal and positional sources of coercion, reward, administrative and technical expertise, and referent.
- ▪ Each of these sources can be strengthened or weakened by an information system.
- ▪ One factor in how people react to an information system is its likely effect on their power.
- ▪ If they see an IS as a means of enhancing their power they will use their existing power to support the project, and vice versa.

Conclusions

We have examined the interaction between three aspects of organisation – culture, structure and power – and information systems. The Chapter Case has also illustrated the way in which these elements not only interact but also evolve as conditions and interpretations change. Kwik-Fit management varied their approach to suit different phases of development – initially centralising, then decentralising to support more autonomous divisions. They later had to cope with the dilemma of how to structure the new insurance business – an issue that other companies also face, especially established ones setting up an Internet venture.

As the issues are dealt with, we see an interaction between technology, strategy and other elements of the context. The Chapter Case shows how the original business grew rapidly, encouraging management to install the first EPOS system, bringing order and routine to administration. As they realised the power of the information being received, they responded by acquiring more enhanced systems and used them to extend the strategic scope of the business. That in turn led to an interaction with new structural forms.

Information systems open up choices for managers over how they adapt the organisation – whether to adapt the culture or the information system, how much centralisation to aim for, the degree of integration between traditional and IS-based businesses. While managers can analyse these dilemmas using rational analyses such as those suggested in the chapter, they do so within their cultural contexts. This will affect how they and others interpret events, how receptive people are to change and whether the change supports or challenges the distribution of power.

At least as important as the choices in any one area is whether the sequence of changes complement each other, so building a coherent response to external events. That is also true of how they organise the IS function itself, which we examine in the next chapter.

CHAPTER QUESTIONS

1. What are the implications for management wishing to implement a company-wide IS if they find that major departments occupy different positions in Figure 6.2?

2. Evaluate Malone's theory about the evolution of centralised and decentralised organisations, in the light of your experience and/or other evidence.

3. Suppose your university is considering offering an online learning programme. Use the Gulati and Garino model to develop an appropriate set of questions that would help the university to decide whether to integrate the online venture with traditional courses or launch it as a separate venture.

4. What are likely to be the main difficulties facing a company that wants to create an extranet to link it to all of its suppliers?

5. Use the Andal-Ancion et al. model to gather and compare examples of organisations changing their relationships with other organisations or customers.

6. Have you any personal examples of political interests affecting how managers reacted to a proposed IS?

Further reading

Jasperson, J., Carte, T.A., Saunders, C.S., Butler, B.S., Croes, H.J.P. and Zheng, W. (2002) 'Power and information technology research: a metatriangulation review', *MIS Quarterly*, **26**(4), 397–459. Highlights different theoretical perspectives on the topic and has a comprehensive list of sources. More than you will ever want to know about power and information systems, but useful as a source.

Sampler, J.L. (1996) 'Exploring the relationship between information technology and organizational structure', in M.J. Earl (ed.), *Information Management: The Organizational Dimension*, Oxford University Press, Oxford. A fuller and well-referenced account of the literature on IT and structure.

References

Andal-Ancion, A., Cartwright, P.A. and Yip, G.S. (2003) 'The digital transformation of traditional business', *MIT Sloan Management Review*, **44**(4), 34–41.

Bjorn-Anderson, N. and Turner, J.A. (1994) 'Creating the twenty-first century organization: the metamorphosis of Oticon', in R. Baskerville, S. Smithson, O. Ngwenyama and J. DeGross (eds), *Transforming Organisations with Information Technology*, North-Holland, Amsterdam.

Boddy, D. and Gunson, N. (1996) *Organizations in the Network Age*, Routledge, London.

Boonstra, A., Boddy, D. and Fischbacher, M. (2004) 'The limited acceptance by general practitioners of an electronic prescription system: reasons and practical implications', *New Technology, Work and Employment*, **19**(2), 128–44.

Brynjolfsson, E. and Hitt, L.M. (2000) 'Beyond computation: information technology, organizational transformation and business performance', *Journal of Economic Perspectives*, **19**(4), 23–48.

Burlinghame, J.F. (1961) 'Information technology and decentralization', *Harvard Business Review*, **39**(6), 121–6.

Cooper, R. (1994) 'The inertial impact of culture on IT implementation', *Information and Management*, **27**(1), 17–31.

Deal, T.E. and Kennedy, A.A. (1982) *Corporate Culture: The Rites and Rituals of Corporate Life*, Addison-Wesley, Reading, Mass.

Eason, K. (2001) 'Changing perspectives on the organisational consequences of information technology', *Behaviour and Information Technology*, **20**(5), 323–8.

Finnegan, P. and Longaigh, S.N. (2002) 'Examining the effects of information technology on control and coordination relationships: an exploratory study in subsidiaries of pan-national corporations', *Journal of Information Technology*, **17**, 149–63.

French, J. and Raven, B. (1959) 'The bases of social power', in D. Cartwright (ed.) *Studies in Social Power*, Institute for Social Research, Ann Arbor, Mich.

Gulati, R. and Garino, J. (2000) 'Get the right mix for bricks and clicks', *Harvard Business Review*, **78**(3), 107–14.

Hales, C. (1993) *Managing Through Organization*, Routledge, London.

Knights, D. and Murray, F. (1994) *Managers Divided: Organizational Politics and Information Technology Management*, Wiley, Chichester.

Leavitt, H.J. and Whisler, T.L. (1958) 'Management in the 1980s', *Harvard Business Review*, **36**(6), 41–8.

Malone, T.W. (1997) 'Is empowerment just a fad? Control, decision making and IT', *Sloan Management Review*, **38**(2), 23–35.

Markus, M.L. (1983) 'Power, politics and MIS implementation', *Communications of the ACM*, **26**(6), 430–434.

Markus, M.L., Manville, B. and Agres, C.E. (2000) 'What makes a virtual organization work?', *MIT Sloan Management Review*, **42**(1), 13–26.

Martin, J. (2002) *Organizational Culture: Mapping the Terrain*, Sage, London.

Ogbonna, E. and Harris, L.C. (1998) 'Organizational culture: it's not what you think . . .', *Journal of General Management*, **23**(3), 35–48.

Pliskin, N., Romm, T., Lee, A.S. and Weber, Y. (1993) 'Presumed versus actual organisational culture: managerial implications for implementation of information systems', *The Computer Journal*, **36**(2), 143–52.

Quinn, R.E., Faerman, S.R., Thompson, M.P. and McGrath, M.R. (2003) *Becoming a Master Manager*, 3rd edition, Wiley, Chichester.

Robey, D. (1981) 'Computer information systems and organization structure', *Communications of the ACM*, **24**(10), 679–87.

Symon, G. and Clegg, C.W. (1991) 'A study of the implementation of CADCAM', *Journal of Occupational Psychology*, **64**(4), 273–90.

Venkatraman, N. and Henderson, J.C. (1998) 'Real strategies for virtual organizing', *MIT Sloan Management Review*, **40**(1), 33–48.

Voss, C.A. (1988) 'Success and failure in advanced manufacturing technology', *International Journal of Technology Management*, **3**(1), 285–97.

Webster, J. (1995) 'Networks of collaboration or conflict? Electronic data interchange and power in the supply chain', *Journal of Strategic Information Systems*, **4**(1), 31–42.

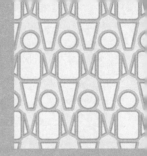

CHAPTER 7

Organising and positioning information system activities

Learning objectives

By the end of your work on this topic you should be able to:

- Contribute to well-considered decisions about IS strategy, acquisition and operation

- Deal with the managerial dilemmas raised by IS management

- Assess alternative ways to position IS activities

- Conduct an informed discussion about whether to outsource IS

- Outline staff issues relating to IS provision

- Assess different ways of controlling IS activities and relate these to wider strategy

The Antonius Medical Centre

Frank Verhage has just begun work as interim head of the information services department at the Antonius Medical Centre. At a meeting with the board of directors he outlines the problems in the field of information systems and computing that he has already observed. These include:

- distrust and disinterest among medical staff (especially professors) towards hospital-wide information systems;

- an information services department with a heavy technology focus. These IT experts see their main task as keeping the old hospital-wide patients' information system working. Helping the medical staff to support their work with modern information systems is a low priority for IT staff, who are not user-centred.

- many local systems (e.g. with patient records or with planning tasks) are rather amateur and not integrated with the hospital-wide system;

- lack of good and focused information for managers.

The board had hired Frank Verhage to manage a major change in information services, as the situation is no longer acceptable. Managers need more focused and reliable information. Doctors and other medical personnel need adequate IS support. Systems need to be integrated and the IS staff need to become more customer-oriented. The former IS manager took early retirement and the board want major changes in the coming year.

Information services was originally part of the finance department as this was the first area to use computers. Some years later it became a separate support division, but was still focused towards administrative tasks. There are now 30 employees in information services, most with a technical background (computing, programming, mathematics, etc.). They see their main responsibility as managing and maintaining existing applications. These include systems for:

- patient records – stores data about patients, including treatments and their cost;

- finance – calculates the cost of treatment, sends invoices and records payments;

- personnel – pays salaries and produces related management information.

These applications run on a mini-computer networked to 800 terminals and PCs around the hospital. The software and hardware are old and need a lot of maintenance, which takes up a large amount of IS staff time. They have neither the capacity nor the expertise to meet requests for new and improved applications. An internal audit stated that 'there is a high degree of dissatisfaction about the centrally provided information and automation services. The complaints cover nearly the whole field of IS services.' The (now retired) head of the department had said: 'I am willing to improve this situation, but it will require a significantly higher budget which has to be agreed by the directors.'

The directors are uneasy about the current use of IS. They clearly need more information to help them run the hospital. Financial reports lack the information they need for planning. Simple questions about the number of patients, cost of treatments, or costs per patient are difficult to answer. They often cannot answer questions from government and insurance companies – who then doubt the reliability of other information. The directors depend on the IS department, so to improve matters they asked the previous head to retire and brought in Frank Verhage.

Verhage observed many operational problems. For example, patients complained that tests were sometimes repeated by different doctors because they did not have each other's data. It was not always clear what medicines doctors had given to them and there was no information on the comparative success of treatments. Doctors complained that the central patient file was unreliable. Some refused to cooperate with the central information systems, preferring to use their own computer- or paper-based files. Several now use their own budgets to buy computers (sometimes connected in small local networks) for administrative tasks within their department. Others use computers to support their medical work – for example for diagnosis or to record treatment given. Because many doctors have taken these initiatives independently, the hospital now has many incompatible software packages for these functions.

The board of directors agrees with Frank Verhage's analysis of the problems. Mr Andoni,

the CEO, says: 'We have the same feeling about the problems we face. We hired you to identify the problems, to analyse them and to come up with a plan to deal with them. Between now and this time next year, we expect a strongly improved, up-to-date and promising situation.' Frank Verhage, an experienced IS manager and consultant, feels he faces an uncomfortable challenge.

The chapter will offer several ideas that are relevant to the hospital, such as how to organise information services, how to divide the budget and how to manage the inevitable differences between constituencies.

Introduction

As information systems grow in significance, so too does the question of how to provide them. Chapter 3 examined how information technology can support competitiveness and how to align information systems with broader strategy. That depends on how managers position their IS function and who is responsible for delivering IS services. There is always competition for the IS budget. How should managers divide this among units? How can the company ensure that IS professionals understand business needs and customers? Equally, how can they ensure that non-IS professionals understand the business implications of information systems? Managers now debate how they should organise Internet and e-commerce activities.

The Chapter Case is about a hospital that has major information system problems. IS staff focus exclusively on technology, operations and maintenance. Senior managers lack insight into emerging IS issues. This combination has led to a situation where the systems support operational rather than strategic purposes. The systems are unreliable, provide poor information and frustrate their users.

The chapter first outlines alternative ways to position IS activities within the organisation. Outsourcing is a further option and we examine the dilemmas around this. Then we look at how managers can divide and control the IS budget among competing units. The final topic is the complexity of the culture gaps between three constituencies: IS management, user management and general management. The aim of the chapter is to show the alternative ways of providing computer-based information systems, and the dilemmas within these options.

7.1 Alternative ways to structure IS activities

How do managers organise their information systems? Sometimes rationally, but also reflecting historical and contemporary factors. Centralised organisations will tend to centralise information systems. Decentralised organisations will usually give responsibility for IS to the business units, to cope with the variety of systems required. Established IS managers in either type of business will try to maintain oversight of IS activities. They will resist attempts to decentralise or outsource the service. Managers of local units will try to increase their control over IS resources.

There is no right answer. We can only indicate the alternative IS architectures and some of the factors that influence the choice. By 'IS architecture' we mean the way in which the IS assets (hardware, software, telecommunications) are deployed and connected and the ways they interact with each other (Oz, 2002). Positioning IS architectures in ways that do not fit the culture or structure will cause tensions. Markus and Robey (1983) refer to this as 'organisational invalidity', when the use of IS does not fit with the organisational properties. Noble and Newman (1993) showed that an integrated system did not work as expected in a culture that valued departmental autonomy.

We set out the alternatives as pure forms, though in practice companies often combine them to reflect local features or political situations.

Concentrating IS activities in one user department

In the early days of computing, the IS functions were often part of the functional department that made most use of them. Figure 7.1 represents this. This works well when interest and use are mainly in one area as it enables people to build experience and expertise. The difficulty arises when this position is only a legacy of an initial pattern and ignores recent developments. As other departments begin to make fuller use of computer-based systems they depend too much on the resources, willingness and ability of the 'responsible' department. The Chapter Case is an example of this.

Centralising IS activities

In this arrangement, a central IS unit is responsible for most computing activities (Figure 7.2). When a user department requires a new or enhanced system, it applies for it through the IS department. The IS department prioritises requests, using guidelines agreed with senior management, and then delivers and supports the services.

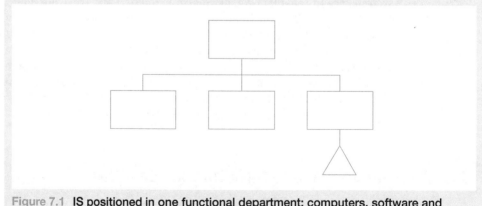

Figure 7.1   **IS positioned in one functional department: computers, software and data directed to one specific functional department**

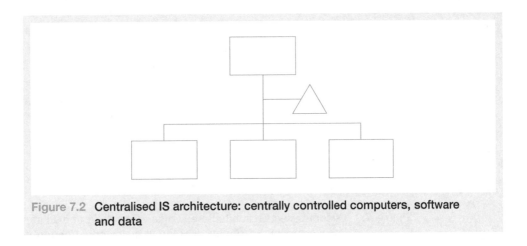

Figure 7.2 Centralised IS architecture: centrally controlled computers, software and data

Changing IS organisation at a water company

The water company has various functional departments. IS was previously part of the finance department, but in 1998 management decided to centralise it. The main reason was that this would make it easier for the IS department to provide an equal service to the functional departments. It would also promote centralised decisions about IS investment. This would be consistent with a recent decision to implement a company-wide enterprise resource planning (ERP) system. This covered most processes of the company in an integrated way. Management believed that the only way to implement, operate and maintain such a company-wide system was through a centralised unit.

The example in the box shows that systems integration, accessibility and concentrated expertise are major advantages of a centralised IS function. It allows people to focus on corporate rather than local needs. A disadvantage is that the centralised department can be inflexible and remote from the business and may appear technologically arrogant to users. Departments have different information needs; with centralised systems, all receive a common service so that few are fully satisfied. The Chapter Case is an example of a central department that has lost touch with its users. Technical staff may emphasise technical excellence rather than business value. The centralised model fits best with organisations that make other decisions centrally, that work in a stable environment and where there is little communication between units.

Decentralising IS activities

When IS is decentralised the organisational units become responsible for their systems – including development, acquisition, operations and maintenance. Figure 7.3 represents this. This is only possible when there is little interdependence between units, and so little need for communication between them. Specialists from the (former) central IS department now work in the business units.

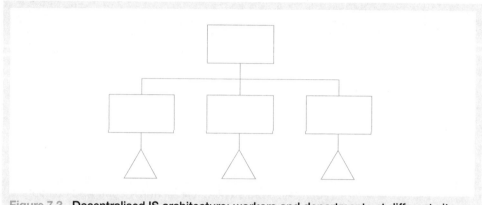

Figure 7.3 **Decentralised IS architecture: workers and departments at different sites use information resources directed to their work or department**

MIS in Practice   **Examples of decentralised IS**

Atag is a company with more than 30 divisions. The divisions operate in different countries and in relatively unrelated businesses. All are free to organise their IS in the way they think is best.

Unilever, a worldwide operating company in food and healthcare, has many different business units and a variety of brand names and products. It organises its IS activities at a business-unit level. The business units only have to agree on harmonised reporting structures to the top level.

GUS, a mail-order company, disbanded its corporate e-commerce unit in September 2000 and placed this responsibility with the separate business units.

Davenport (1994) made a distinction between 'information globalism which seeks to create meanings that apply to an entire organisation, and information particularism, in which individuals and small groups define information that makes sense to them'. To summarise the contrasts:

Globalism	Particularism
Corporate needs	Local needs
Strategic focus	Customer focus
Future operating flexibility	Current operating flexibility
Corporate value for money	Budgetary responsibility and authority

Source: Based on Davenport (1994).

In a decentralised setting, the business units are in control of IT and make their own decisions in this field. If managers see the advantages of decentralisation but also the disadvantages of full independence, they may choose the federal model.

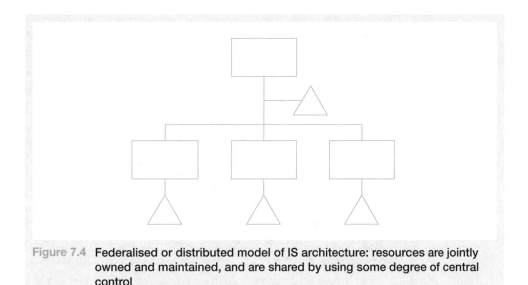

Figure 7.4 **Federalised or distributed model of IS architecture: resources are jointly owned and maintained, and are shared by using some degree of central control**

Federalising IS activities and distributed information systems

Some companies choose to decentralise IS tasks such as specification and administration, while maintaining central control over others such as data standards and hardware compatibility. A centralised department can determine information strategy for the organisation and administer the corporate system and database. The decentralised departments can develop and manage local IS within those corporate guidelines. A distributed IS architecture means that departments have some independence in developing and using IS without losing the benefits of centralised control over data and communications. Figure 7.4 shows this model.

MIS in Practice   **A tax and customs administration**

A tax and customs administration has five divisions based on the class of the taxpayers. Systems definition, data entry and customer contact activities take place at divisional level. Systems development, data management and operations take place centrally.

In adopting the federal model, companies have to determine which IS activities to centralise, which to decentralise and which to outsource. This often leads to a dynamic situation where activities move from one level to another. Other terms for the federal model are 'distributed' and 'cooperative' (Fiedler and Grover, 1996). This model fits best in organisations with a high interdependence, a high need to share data, a turbulent environment and decentralised decisions.

The models mentioned above are ways of dealing with companies' IS resources. People who take a rational view of things believe that managers select a model that is best suited to their unique circumstances (Fiedler and Grover, 1996). They may aspire to this, but history and other subjective considerations will also influence events:

- Using the Internet for e-commerce suggests a centralised or business unit approach to IS, to ensure that systems can connect with those of other organisations. Such a change is impossible in situations of anarchy or feudalism.

- Implementing an ERP system can lead to monarchy or technocratic utopianism – a more centralised, standardised and integrated management structure (Davenport, 1998; Langenwalter, 2000). That may not be right for the business at that time.

Activity 7.1 Positioning IS activity

Identify, for an organisation you know, which of the models (Figures 7.1–7.4) best describes the positioning of its IS activities.

- *What are the most important reasons for organising that way? Use the factors in the models to prepare your answer.*

This chapter identifies a number of possible reasons for positioning IS activities in a certain way. These include the need to share data as well as a range of organisational factors.

- *Try to assess which of these reasons best explain the pattern in that organisation.*

The Antonius Medical Centre: Decentralising some IS

The directors decided to decentralise certain IS responsibilities to divisions. The board expected them to make their own IS plans within the limitations of the hospital's technical infrastructure. They should design, implement, operate and maintain their own systems. New IS staff had to operate as internal consultants, helping the divisions with their plans. The IS department also had to evaluate these plans in terms of costs, strategic alignment and possible integration with other plans or systems. The IS staff and the divisional managers recognised the conflicting nature of this double role of assessor and adviser. Divisions had formal IS responsibilities but it took time to educate people to take these responsibilities seriously. Divisional managers felt that the new control function of the IS department conflicted with the responsibilities of divisions. It showed the ambiguity of decentralisation.

Another question was how to implement this decentralising policy. The hospital needed integrated systems and a central body to manage, operate and control them. It also needed local systems to support local operations that linked with the wider system, but organising that would be extremely difficult. Some division managers complained that they did not have the means

(finance and expertise) to do so, but most appreciated the basic idea.

As well as the hospital-wide system, many local systems ran on PCs or local networks:

- an operations planning system in a surgery;
- a system which supported certain kinds of operation; and
- systems which stored medical data about a doctor's patients.

More than 40 of these systems were used by groups of more than five people and many more were used by smaller groups or individuals. It was hard to meet maintenance standards with these systems as they were often built by amateurs. They lacked documentation, were of questionable quality and used inconsistent data; they were called 'freakware'.

Since the divisions were now independent it was difficult to oblige people to make these systems compatible with other systems or of higher quality. Their existence, seen as low-quality by the IS department but highly valued by individual users, was perceived as one of the hospital's biggest problems in the field of information policy.

Research Summary   Information management policy

Davenport et al. (1992) see the positioning of IS activities from a political point of view. They suggest that all these types of positioning are actually power battles between various parties with specific interests. They distinguish five approaches to managing information politics, which vary from all power at the top to anarchy (see Figure 7.5).

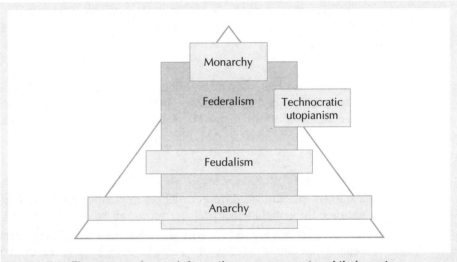

Figure 7.5 **Five approaches to information management and their centre of control**

- **Technocratic utopianism.** A heavily technical approach to information management, stressing categorisation and modelling of an organisation's full information assets, with heavy reliance on emerging technologies. This approach will often lead to centralised IT activities, where IT experts are most powerful.

- **Monarchy.** Defining information categories and reporting structures by the firm's leaders, who may or may not share the information willingly after collecting it. This is again close to the centralised model, where senior management is in charge rather than IT experts.

- **Feudalism.** The management of information by individual business units or functions, which define their own information needs and report only limited information to the overall corporation. This is quite close to the federalised model with an emphasis on decentralisation.

- **Federalism.** An approach to information management based on consensus and negotiation on the organisation's key information elements and reporting structures. This approach is very close to the feudal model, as mentioned above.

- **Anarchy.** The absence of any overall information management policy, leaving individuals and user departments to obtain and manage their own information. This will often lead to the decentralised model.

Source: Davenport et al. (1992).

CASE QUESTIONS 7.1

What are the possible reasons for the problems which the hospital has in organising its information services – such as cultural or structural factors? Use the model in Figure 7.5 to help organise your answer.

How did the hospital organise its IS function before and after the change? Use the Davenport et al. model from the Research Summary to analyse this.

What are alternative ways to organise this? Relate your answer to the models as discussed in this chapter. Discuss each alternative, using the text of this chapter, and provide suggestions to the management of this hospital.

Chapter Case has shown the dilemmas with respect to the positioning and IS responsibilities faced by managers. It also shows a mixture of anarchy, federalism and technocratic utopianism. The following section explores the in-house or outsourcing dilemma.

Summary

- Management can use different models in positioning IS activities in their organisations; these include centralised, decentralised and federalised models.
- Each model has its own features, advantages and disadvantages. The pattern depends on factors such as the stage in using IS, and the structure and culture of the organisation.

7.2 Outsourcing or in-house?

To try to overcome the centralisation–decentralisation problem, some organisations have concentrated part of their IS expertise in a resource pool. Business units or departments can hire this as required. Figure 7.6 illustrates this 'resource pool' approach.

MIS in Practice   Example of a resource pool

Achmea (*www.achmea.nl*), a Dutch insurance company, has many business units and brand names, following a series of mergers and acquisitions. The business units concentrate on certain groups of insurance and related products, such as social insurance, life insurance, banking activities and health insurance. Every unit has its own IS department. The company recently began an integration policy to concentrate resources and know-how. It will also promote data-sharing about customers. Management created a company-wide IS organisation – 'Achmea Active' – which every business unit can hire. This operates as a resource pool. It works with service-level agreements and charges market prices for its services. Business units are also free to buy services from other providers.

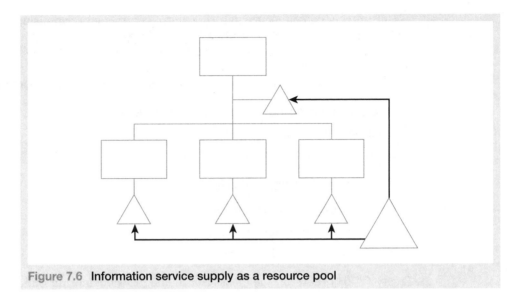

Figure 7.6 Information service supply as a resource pool

Resource pools concentrate expertise, while business units decide whether to use them. The approach raises questions such as (McFarlan and Nolan, 1995):

■ Can other organisations hire the resource pool?
■ Can business units hire expertise from other providers?

Such arrangements are often an introduction to the (partial) outsourcing of IS.

The idea behind outsourcing is that it allows management to concentrate on the core activities of the business. It also allows companies with fluctuating IS needs to pay only for what they use. Other reasons are to keep up with technological changes and to overcome the problems of hiring good IS staff. Figure 7.7 represents an organisation that outsources IS.

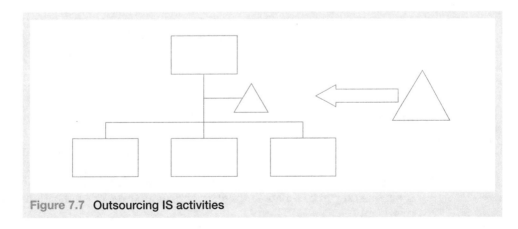

Figure 7.7 Outsourcing IS activities

Outsourcing can either mean a short-term contractual relationship with a service firm to develop a specific application or a long-term relationship in which the service firm takes over all of an organisation's IS functions. We focus on the latter, in which outsourcing includes application development, software, hardware and telecommunications purchasing and maintenance. The advantages can include:

- access to highly qualified know-how and consulting;
- lower personnel and fixed costs;
- greater attention to core business.

On the other hand, outsourcing carries major risks:

- loss of control, and greater dependency on the service company;
- loss of experienced employees;
- paying too much for the service.

Lacity (2001) therefore suggests that managers considering outsourcing should ask:

1. Are the systems (being outsourced) truly not strategic?
2. Are we certain that our IS requirements will not change?
3. Even if a system is a commodity, can it be broken off?
4. Could the IT department provide this more efficiently than an outside provider?
5. Do we have the knowledge to outsource an unfamiliar or emerging technology?
6. What pitfalls should we expect when negotiating the contract?
7. Can we design a contract that minimises risks and maximises control and flexibility?
8. What in-house staff do we need to negotiate strong contracts?
9. What in-house staff do we need to ensure we get the most out of our contracts?
10. What in-house staff do we need to enable us to exploit change?

Outsourcing of information systems management will be encouraged by the advent of companies known as application service providers (ASPs) (Hirschheim and Bandula, 2003). These enable customers to use IS applications they need over the Internet. The applications are installed at the ASPs' locations, along with the databases and other files that the application processes for the client. Employees access these over the Internet. Companies such as Peoplesoft (Booker, 2000) and Microsoft (Ricadela, 2000) are investing heavily to make their software available on the Internet. *Business Week* carried a report about the Talbert Medical Group with 110 doctors in Costa Mesa, California (see box below).

As the Internet gets faster, more reliable and more secure, many people expect more companies will outsource their computer operations to more ASPs. This may lead to so-called 'web-services architecture', which means that companies rent the functions they need – data storage, processing power or applications – from service providers.

MIS in Practice   ASP at Talbert Medical

It was a techie version of a heart transplant. When the doctors of Talbert Medical Group spun their practice out from a bankrupt physician-management company last year, CIO Al Herak faced a daunting task: to build the computer underpinnings for the new company in just three months. It would normally take at least a year. If he couldn't pull it off by the time the bankrupt outfit closed its doors on 1 August, Talbert's 110 doctors would be helpless – unable to schedule appointments or track records, potentially forcing their patients to look elsewhere for care. If botched, this manoeuver might have wrecked the partnership. Instead, Talbert is in the pink of health – on track to do $80 million in business this year. And Herak is a hero. He got the job done cheaper, faster and better than he had ever thought possible. How?

He turned to TriZetto Group Inc. in Newport Beach, Calif., a new breed of tech company that houses computing gear at its own facilities and dishes out software to customers such as Talbert over the Internet: no fuss, no muss – and fast. Herak doesn't have to spend upwards of $1 million on computer systems and then more every year to keep them running. Instead, he pays a monthly fee of some $100,000 – the same way he pays a utility bill. 'We're just saving money, and if it goes down, I just make a phone call and say, "It's your stuff, you work it out",' says Herak. 'I love it.'

Source: 'Technology on tap', *Business Week*, 19 June 2000.

Example: A bank can process loans in the traditional way or by web services architecture. In the former the process is usually supported by a very complicated application maintained by an individual bank. With web services architecture, the bank connects with the most appropriate institution for such transactions. Different suppliers offer various bank modules and the bank can shift among providers, using one service for (say) risk analysis of loans to restaurants and another for loans to hospitals (Hagel and Brown, 2001).

However, IS outsourcing is not an isolated decision, as other activities (such as manufacturing, R&D, finance) can also be outsourced. Two extreme positions are:

- All activities are carried out in-house. The company even tries to buy suppliers and customers in order to control the value chain completely. This can lead to powerful conglomerates and hierarchically managed and controlled bureaucracies.
- All non-managerial activities are performed by others. The company buys services from specialised companies for almost all its activities – purchasing, manufacturing, marketing and so on. This is close to the concept of the networked organisation. The organisation becomes lean, flexible – and dependent on its partners.

Most companies are positioned somewhere between these two extremes. This raises the question of which activities are performed by the company and which by other companies (Applegate et al., 2003). The Internet raises new strategic considerations on this issue (Gilley and Rasheed, 2000).

The following example illustrates how Cemex, a Mexican multinational, moved through these phases of organising IS. The example shows that organisational and technological changes also impact on the IT department. IS directors become relationship managers, maintaining relations among senior management, users and service providers.

Activity 7.2 Research on the IS function

Take a familiar company and describe how it has organised the IS function.

■ *What advantages and disadvantages do people in the organisation see in that structure?*

■ *What alternative forms might be realistic for the company?*

■ *Has it considered using ASPs, or outsourcing its IS requirements?*

MIS in Practice Cemex – global growth through information capabilities

Cemex is an example of an agile, efficient, e-business pioneer. It is rapidly spreading across the globe, and its aim is not necessarily to get bigger than its competitors, only to stay more profitable. The Mexican company also owes its success to what is known as 'the Cemex way'. This corporate philosophy involves wholeheartedly embracing new technology and imposing tightly controlled standards worldwide, for both its technology and in-house management techniques. Cemex's ability to apply this philosophy rests on a continuous mix of modest beginnings, good timing and the technology fetish of the company's chief executive, Lorenzo Zambrano, now reckoned to be Mexico's second-richest man. 'I could say that I had a vision,' says the jolly, 58-year-old Mr Zambrano, 'but it doesn't really work that way'.

The company, founded in 1906, grew domestically and diversified into mining, hotels and petrochemicals. In 1987 Zambrano hired Gelacio Iniguez to develop Cemex's information technology. At the end of the 1980s, it set up a satellite network so that it could transmit all the internal data to its headquarters in Monterrey, Mexico's dusty northern business capital. Cemex deployed this system, Cemexnet, to allow data and voice transmission among the eleven production facilities in Mexico. More valuable than reduced headcount, though, was the data that the automation produced. Mr Zambrano could check sales figures or kiln temperatures on the network. Gradually, computerisation spread throughout the group. Cemex has never had a big mainframe, relying instead on distributed, interconnected systems that share information across the company. These allow top managers to see what is going on, but they also give lower-level employees some access – enough to allow 'a healthy degree of competition between the different units', says Hector Medina, Mr Zambrano's number two.

With the arrival of the Internet, the transparency spread outside the company, pro-voking some complaints from within that it was making too much information public. Cemex is now pushing the information culture even further, putting computers with Internet access into its employee's homes. Connectivity has also transformed many of the company's internal processes – most notably the delivery of ready-mixed concrete. Getting mixer trucks from the plants to the building sites at the right time, with cement needing to be poured within 90 minutes of mixing, is always a logistical hell. But by put-ting a computer and a global-positioning system receiver in every truck, and combining their positions with the output at the plants and the order from the customers, Cemex has been able to produce a system that not only calculates which truck should go where, but also enables despatchers to redirect the trucks en route.

That has reduced the 'window of time' for delivery from 3 hours to under 20 minutes, even with the chaotic traffic and the last-minute cancellation of orders that are typical of Mexico City. It has enabled each truck to meet many more orders per day. Cemex also developed practices to collect and process customer feedback. Truck drivers surveyed customers upon delivery and the information was entered into online customer files. Based on this information, the order-taker would be able to apologise when a dissatisfied customer called.

The goal of Cemex is to become fully web-based, with all its employees having access to their own files, the company's data and outside information through a single, personalised portal. Operations will be centralised through the Internet, even though the management teams themselves may be spread around the globe. Corporate finance is already run in this way, and procurement, sales, distribution and supplier and customer relations are also intended to become as Internet-based as possible. The objective of this programme is to share the company's best practices around the world.

Source: Based on e-strategy brief (*The Economist*, 16 June 2003), IMD case study on Cemex (GM 1081, 2002) and *www.cemex.com*.

Activity 7.3 Cemex

Analyse the Cemex example by describing the successive ways of using and structuring information systems. Use the models in Figures 7.2–7.8 to illustrate the changes.

- *How does Cemex deal with outsourcing?*
- *How does this change the characteristics and core competences of the firm?*

Summary

- Outsourcing IS services can range from small services to the complete function.
- The advantages will vary between organisations and with circumstances.
- Lacity (2001) suggests some questions for those considering outsourcing.
- IS outsourcing may be considered as part of an overall strategy of the organisation towards outsourcing of processes or services.
- Application service providers are a further possibile way of securing IS services.

7.3 Charging for IS activities

Another organisational issue is how to divide the costs of information systems. This relates to how management responds to questions such as:

- Should IS be a business within a business or managed as a service centre?
- Should IS be an expense or an investment, and what are the consequences of each?

- Should IS be charged at cost prices or at market prices?
- Should business units be able to use external IS providers?

In response to such questions, companies have devised four ways to control and charge for IS activities:

- **Service centre**. Users do not pay for IS resources. The service is 'free'. Non-financial goals are more important than financial ones and IS does not have to earn revenue or recover costs.
- **Cost centre**. Here the costs of services are allocated to users through charge-out. Users are as responsible for cost consciousness and financial accountability as the specialists. IS investments are intended to reflect cost–benefit analysis, but are not necessarily funded by cost recovery.
- **Profit centre**. IS services are charged at 'cost-plus' or market prices. The IS department operates as a business unit. Managers expect it to earn a return on the investment made.
- **Hybrid centre**. Users pay for some services and some receive a central subsidy. Innovative and turnaround activities are managed loosely, while routine core activities are managed tightly. The IS function has clear financial and non-financial goals.

The way organisations deal with these questions depends on factors such as:

- stage of use of IS: many organisations will grow from a service centre to a profit centre and from a profit centre to a hybrid centre;
- structure of the organisation: decentralised organisations tend to profit/cost-centre structures and centralised organisations tend to cost/hybrid-centre structures;
- culture, power and people issues: charging for IT services is a more formal approach, while offering them free is better suited to small and informal organisations;
- financial resources: charging IT services is often a reaction to growing IT expenses;
- technology choices: company-wide technologies such as corporate databases and corporate networks will often be seen as overhead costs that should be divided in an arbitrary way to user departments. Technologies used by specific departments are charged more easily. See Figure 7.8.

Earl (1992) sets out the advantages and disadvantages of each approach, and Table 7.1 summarises these.

Summary

- Management has to decide which part of the IS resource should support existing operations and to acquire and maintain operational systems.
- Depending on the organisational properties mentioned this may lead to the provision of IS activities as a service centre, a cost centre, a profit centre or a hybrid centre.

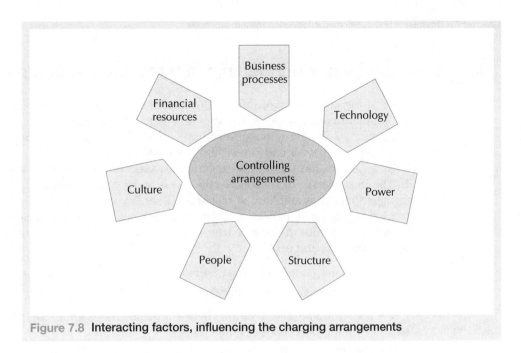

Figure 7.8 Interacting factors, influencing the charging arrangements

Table 7.1 Advantages and disadvantages of four ways of managing the cost of IS

Advantages	Disadvantages
Service centres	
Stimulates usage and experimentation	Can create uneconomic requests
Suited to first stages of assimilation	Can protect IS from accountability
Avoids accounting complexities	Requires good funding decisions
Avoids organisational conflicts	May dilute organisational learning
Fits turnaround and support activities	Inappropriate for strategic and factory activities
Can fit centralised IS unit	Rarely fits decentralised IS organisation
Cost centres	
Encourages reasoned use requests	Can be a deterrent to IS use
Creates control of IS	Can focus on costs, not on benefits
Suits later stages of assimilation	Can cause arguments
Satisfies desires for charge-out	Many accounting choices
Fits cost-centre organisations	Often unsatisfactory in practice
Relatively simple accounting	Disliked in profit-centre organisations
Profit centres	
IS function has to control costs	IS function can cut costs and service
IS function has to market itself	IS function may go external
IS–user partnership can be forged	Users may act as short-term traders
IS activities may become innovative	IS function may become too entrepreneurial
Hybrid centres	
Can manage IS loosely or tightly	Can be confusing
Suits later stages of assimilation	May be misfit with host management controls
Suits different assimilation stages for different technologies	Can cause internal conflicts
Fits turnaround and strategic activities	Needs strong direction
Facilitates central push in decentralised context	Can be complex accounting

7.4 Managing IS as a partnership of three interest groups

Much of the complexity of information systems management stems from managing the conflicting cultures of three groups – general management, users and IS staff (see Figure 7.9). Many observers have recognised that a cultural gap develops between these players that can severely damage relations.

These groups have different expectations, tasks and responsibilities in relation to IS. The IS staff have to respond to the needs and requirements of users within management guidelines and limited resources. Users expect a high level of IS support to do what management expects of them. Management have to decide about IS strategy in coordination with the other parties. This all takes place in a dynamic environment, causing tensions and problems:

- IS staff do not understand what users and managers do and need;
- Users and managers do not understand what IS staff do and need.

It is not surprising that relations between these groups are tense, and Figure 7.10 lists how each group perceives the others.

The challenge for management is to deal with these potential problems and to contribute to a more productive organisational arrangement. Some possible measures are shown in the following sections.

To improve good communications between the parties

Examples:

- An IS manager on the board (CIO – Chief Information Officer) can help to place IS challenges and problems on the agenda at the highest level;
- A steering group including representatives from the three groups mentioned can improve communications and understanding between these groups.

To improve understanding in IS matters

Examples:

- Education programmes, information meetings and distribution of internal or external publications on IS can improve understanding between the three parties.

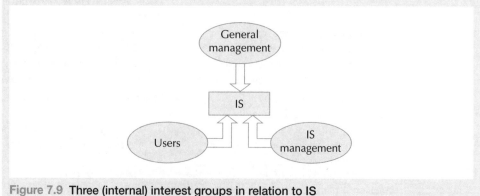

Figure 7.9 Three (internal) interest groups in relation to IS

Line managers' failings	Users' failings	IS staff failings
No clear business plan available	No clear expression of needs and expectations of IS	Inability to match information systems to business needs
Inability to spot strategic uses of IS	Focus only on operational support, no strategic vision	Preoccupation with the technicalities of IS
Failure to communicate requirements to systems staff	Lack of appreciation of technical complexities	Lack of understanding of business environment
Lack of appreciation of technical complexities	No contribution to planning and policy of IS	Failure to market business successes of information systems
Insistence on cost justifying all investments		

Figure 7.10 **Perceived failings from other parties' perspectives**

Line managers need to know enough about IS to view it as a crucial factor in strategic and operational business planning. They must be in a position to manage IS as a normal part of their business management responsibilities.

■ Systems staff must be educated in such a way that they become committed supporters of line-management IS initiatives. Many of them still have to make a determined effort to shake off their traditional image, which is often perceived by line managers as alien and obstructive. Education in this field is most successful when it is organisation-specific and action-related, and it should be a continuous process, not a one-off 'awareness' course.

To position the IS function at an appropriate place in the organisation

As suggested earlier, a structural solution may also help – such as positioning IS in such a way that business units are themselves responsible for IS. The federal model may improve communications and put responsibilities at the right level of the organisation.

Activity 7.4 Interest groups

This section suggests that IS should be managed as a partnership of three interest groups who should balance each other. Discuss and describe what will go wrong when:

■ *IS staff are in charge and make the main decisions on systems without considering the management's or the users' point of view;*

■ *Users and user departments are in charge and make the main decisions with respect to IS without considering the IS and the managerial perspective;*

■ *Managers make the main IS decisions without consultation or the participation of IS staff and users.*

Table 7.2 **Suggested characteristics of hybrid managers**

Characteristic	Description
Business knowledge	Knowledge of the organisation's goals, providing a global view
Organisation-specific knowledge	Culture, structure, processes, key people and their motivation
IS knowledge and experience	Managing IS applications in the business; awareness of potential applications; knowledge of sources of expertise
Interpersonal skills	Able to influence top management; can develop cooperative relations with many people inside and outside the organisation; develop teamworking; sensitive to personal needs; can motivate subordinates, specialists and peers
Communication skills	Listening skills, informal communication skills, responsive
Cognitive capabilities	Above-average intelligence; moderately analytical; strongly intuitive; good problem-solving skills
Personality traits and behaviour	People-oriented; change focus; outgoing; commitment and integrity; energy and enthusiasm

Source: Based on Skyrme and Earl (1990), p. 3.

A solution proposed by Skyrme and Earl (1990) has been the development of hybrid managers. It is envisaged that such people will combine three skills: business literacy, technical competence and organisational astuteness. The idea is that managers with this (extremely rare) combination of skills will be able to guide senior managers towards uses of information systems that are appropriate for the business. Table 7.2 summarises the ideal characteristics of hybrid managers.

Summary

- It is a management challenge to create optimal working conditions among business units, users and IS experts in order to make the best use of information systems.
- Some writers have encouraged people to develop the skills of hybrid managers, able to bridge the cultural gaps between the three communities.

Conclusions

In this chapter we have examined the issues companies face in organising and positioning their increasingly influential information systems activities. We outlined a range of structural choices, covering functional, centralised, decentralised and federal arrangements. There is also the more radical option of outsourcing. Whichever is chosen, there is the question of how to share the costs.

The Chapter Case shows the interaction between the setting in which the management is operating and the information systems they provide. A fragmented organisation with many independent units inevitably ends up with many separate systems, tailored more or less to suit individual or local needs. Attempts to change that system to one that is more integrated across the whole organisation may seem very sensible to the outsider. The difficulty is that it is not just a technical matter: introducing a centralised information system into a decentralised culture is bound to raise tensions.

That change can occur even in very traditional organisations, as was illustrated by the tax administration Chapter Case (Chapter 4) and by many other examples throughout this book. The skill appears to lie in managing the partnership between the various parties with an interest in the system, and in building their support during implementation. These are topics to which we turn in Chapters 9 and 10.

CHAPTER QUESTIONS

1. List some IS activities and decide who should do them (e.g. managers, users, IS staff, customers, suppliers, ASP, outsourcing companies). Explain your opinion.

2. Give examples of (a) an integrated and secure system and (b) an open and accessible IS. Explain when integration and security are the top priority, and when openness and accessibility are the top priority.

3. Many organisations implement ERP systems. Can you relate ERP with:

   - the centralisation versus decentralisation issue;
   - the in-house versus outsource issue;
   - the rationalistic versus participative issue.

4. Under what circumstances would you advise a company not to outsource IS?

5. An organisation wants to promote the use of the Internet for internal and external transactions and for sharing of information. At the moment few staff use this kind of service. Would you advise the service-centre approach, the cost-centre approach, the profit-centre approach or the hybrid-centre approach? Explain your choice.

6. An organisation uses a groupware system. Managers want to evaluate this system and ask three groups (management, users and IS staff) to define evaluation questions. Provide six questions (two from each group) to illustrate the perspective of each group.

Further reading

Applegate, L.M., McFarlan, F.W. and McKenney, J.L. (2003) *Corporate Information Systems Management: Text and Cases*, Irwin, Chicago. Extensive text on strategic and managerial issues of IS management, including the decentralisation–centralisation dilemma and various aspects of outsourcing.

Ghoshal, S. and Gratton, L. (2002) 'Integrating the enterprise', *MIT Sloan Management Review*, **44**(1), 31–8. This article emphasises the need for horizontal integration in companies which can be realised in four ways: (1) *Operational* through standardised technological infrastructure, (2) *Intellectual* through shared knowledge base, (3) *Social* through collective bonds of performance and (4) *Emotional* through shared identity and meaning.

Hagel, J. and Brown, J.S. (2001) 'Your next IT strategy', *Harvard Business Review*, **79**(10), 105–13. Introduces the idea of shared services, application service provision and web services architectures.

Willcocks, L.P. and Lacity, M.C. (1998) *Strategic Sourcing of Information Systems: Perspectives and Practices*, Wiley, Chichester. Discusses the positioning of IS services, including the outsourcing dilemma.

References

Applegate, L.M., Austin, R.D., McFarlan, F.W. (2003) *Corporate Information Strategy and Management: Text and Cases*, McGraw-Hill/Irwin, Boston.

Booker, E. (2000) 'Peoplesoft as application service provider', *InternetWeek*, **805**, 20 March, 19.

Davenport, T.H. (1994) 'Saving IT's soul: human-centered information management', *Harvard Business Review*, **72**(2), 119–33.

Davenport, T.H. (1998) 'Putting the enterprise into the enterprise system', *Harvard Business Review*, **76**(4), 121–32.

Davenport, T.H., Eccles, R.G. and Prusak, L. (1992) 'Information politics', *MIT Sloan Management Review*, **34**(1), 53–66.

Earl, M.J. (1992) *Management Strategies for Information Technology*, Prentice Hall, Hemel Hempstead.

Fiedler, K.D. and Grover, V. (1996) 'An empirically derived taxonomy of information technology structure and its relationship to organizational structure', *Journal of Management Information Systems*, **13**(1), 9–35.

Gilley, K.M. and Rasheed, A. (2000) Making more by doing less: an analysis of outsourcing and its effects on firm performance, *Journal of Management*, **26**(4), 763–90.

Hagel, J. and Brown, J.S. (2001) 'Your next IT strategy', *Harvard Business Review*, **79**(10), 105–13.

Hirschheim, R. and Bandula, J. (2003) 'Determinants of ASP choice: an integrated perspective', *European Journal of Information Systems*, **12**(3), 210–24.

Lacity, M.C. (2001) *Global Information Technology Outsourcing: In Search of Business Advantage*, Wiley, Chichester.

Langenwalter, G.A. (2000) *Enterprise Resource Planning and Beyond: Integrating Your Entire Organization*, St Lucie Press, Boca Raton, Fla.

McFarlan, F.W. and Nolan, R.L. (1995) 'How to manage an IT outsourcing alliance', *MIT Sloan Management Review*, **36**(2), 9–24.

Markus, M.L. and Robey, D. (1983) 'The organizational validity of management information systems', *Human Relations*, **36**(3), 203–26.

Noble, F. and Newman, M. (1993) 'Integrated system, autonomous departments: organizational validity and system change in a university', *Journal of Management Studies*, **30**(2), 195–219.

Oz, E. (2002), *Management Information Systems*, Thomson, Boston.

Ricadela, A. (2000) 'Microsoft takes stake in application service provider', *Information Week*, **778**, 145.

Skyrme, D.J. and Earl, M.J. (1990) *Hybrid Managers: What Should You Do?*, British Computer Society, London.

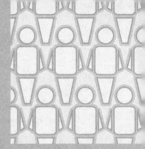

CHAPTER 8

People and information systems

Learning objectives

By the end of your work on this topic you should be able to:

- Explain the nature and significance of an interpretive approach to IS

- Describe the discipline and contribution of human–computer interaction

- Summarise the variables in the technology acceptance model and the conclusions of empirical work using the model

- Use the work design model to analyse the actual or possible effects on motivation of an IS

- Explain the contextual factors that affect the value of computer-based systems to support distributed working

- Outline the idea behind the socio-technical approach to system design

- Evaluate proposed IS projects from these perspectives and make plans accordingly

Radical change in an ambulance service

The organisation transports patients to and from hospitals – either for routine treatment at a clinic or as a result of an accident or other medical emergency. The (routine) Patient Transport Service (PTS) accounts for 85 per cent of patients carried; the rest are accident and emergency (A&E) cases.

The service is visible and politically sensitive – media and politicians highlight cases of delay and failure. Hospitals and doctors for whom it provides a service are setting tighter quality standards. All expect it to provide a cost-effective service.

PTS work involves ambulance crews transporting patients between their homes and clinics within a hospital. The service had developed flexible manual procedures for receiving transport requests, planning efficient routes for vehicles and for rescheduling vehicles as demand changed during the day. Control assistants received requests over the telephone, wrote the information on a form and passed it to a control officer. He or she allocated an ambulance to the work using their knowledge of their area, wrote or typed a schedule and issued it to the crew. A&E work involves crews carrying patients requiring urgent treatment between hospitals or from the scene of an incident. Control assistants and officers followed much the same procedure as for PTS work, though in much more urgent and stressful circumstances.

Although the manual procedures were flexible, they were labour-intensive. To reduce costs, the service had closed many controls centres and transferred the work to those remaining. The service had also invested heavily in computer systems, including a route planning system for the PTS and a command and control system for the A&E work.

The route planning system helped staff plan the PTS routes of the vehicles more efficiently. Staff receiving orders keyed them into a computer, which stored them until the day before the appointment. It then sorted them by area and allocated them to an available ambulance crew. The list was then printed, checked for feasibility by the control officer and issued to the crew.

The A&E command and control system contains complete geographical information about the area. When staff receive a telephone call they key details directly into the computer, following a menu displayed on-screen. Using continually updated knowledge of the location and status of ambulances, the system automatically identifies the best vehicle to deal with that case.

One issue is whether staff in the control room should use that information in deciding which vehicle to deploy or whether it should be sent directly from the computer to a screen in the cab. That decision will reflect managers' assumptions about their staff, and how best to link their skills and experience with the power of the information system.

Source: Based on a case in Boddy and Gunson (1996).

Introduction

The widening use of computer-based information systems touches people in many roles. As users, customers, individuals, technical specialists, managers or project sponsors they experience information systems and may shape their form. A comprehensive view of IS means being alert to the interactions between the system and the people who engage with it. In this chapter we focus on people as individuals, in contrast to Chapter 6 where the focus is the organisation. We present ideas about human capabilities, needs and motivation – ideas which help us to understand how people interact with information systems.

IS projects develop when people with sufficient influence in an organisation come to believe that the potential benefits (however measured) of an enhanced system will exceed the costs (however measured). The benefits may relate to the strategic possibilities of new products or markets, or of dealing more effectively with the forces of competition. Or they may reflect a desire by those at the centre to exercise more surveillance and control over a geographically dispersed set of operations. In others cases, promoters aim for more innovation and flexibility to meet customer expectations.

Sophisticated computer-based information systems can support all these innovations, but people remain essential to most organisational processes. Organisations do nothing: people do things. While modern information systems are necessary for economic performance, they depend on people and procedures (Figure 1.3 p. 11). A delivery system that needs to respond quickly and imaginatively to customer preferences needs well-informed, motivated people. Such people develop knowledge and skills, which information systems can support and complement, but rarely replace.

Information systems eliminate people from many routine data transfer operations and many specific processes operate automatically. But completely automated activities are only part of the customer-service process, and jobs that are lost in these areas are often more than offset by more people doing higher value work elsewhere in the business. There are also examples of companies that have used information systems in ways that ignored the skills and knowledge of staff. Buchanan and Boddy (1983), Frenkel et al. (1998) and Lloyd and Newell (1998) all report cases in which employees have experienced less satisfying and motivating work after their employer introduced a new information system. The companies either ignored the human aspects of the system or used the new technology to impose inappropriate controls. These proved self-defeating and almost certainly ensured that the companies received less return on their investment than they could have done.

Such negative effects are not the result of technology, but of the way people managed it and the assumptions they made about human capabilities. These issues no longer affect only employees. Many information systems enable customers to interact directly with an organisation; others deliver public services directly to individuals. So the range of people and interests involved with information systems is increasing in number and variety.

The Chapter Case illustrates the widening role of IS as it concerns the introduction of increasingly sophisticated systems into a traditional, labour-intensive public service. These systems enabled people to work more effectively, and the Case is an example of how people generally welcome advanced systems if they are carefully designed and implemented.

The chapter begins by tracing how people interpret their context, and how this shapes the meanings they attach to a system. It then presents three approaches to understanding and managing people in relation to information systems: Human–computer interaction, the technology acceptance model and theories of human needs. This leads to a comparison of underlying management policies of seeking control or commitment and a discussion of managing distributed working arrangements. The chapter concludes by considering how the system design process can satisfy both human and technical requirements, introducing the ideas of socio-technical design and user-centred design methods.

8.1 An interpretive perspective

Most people are not passive recipients of information systems, but active players who shape their use and their effects. As people sponsor, design, adapt or use an information system they observe and interpret their context and try to shape that context to meet their needs. People view a proposed or actual IS not as an objective reality, but within a historical and contemporary context. They promote, or react to, an IS project to support their objectives, based on their interpretation of the existing context. They act to change that context – by proposing a new system or process – which others then interpret in the light of *their* objectives. The players use their power (also an element of context) to influence decisions and how to implement them. If they believe that a proposed system is likely to enhance their power, or is consistent with accepted cultural values, they will form a favourable attitude towards it and act accordingly. The evolving outcomes arising from these interactions may or may not support the originally stated objectives of those promoting the change.

Taking this perspective means paying particular attention 'to the context of the information system, and to the process whereby the information system influences, and is influenced by, this context' (Walsham, 1993, pp. 4–5). Studying context means identifying elements, such as those identified in Figure 1.5 (p. 16), and recognising that people will be interpreting these from different perspectives. Walsham (1993) also observed that 'a more subtle set of contexts for an information system are the various social structures which are present in the minds of the human participants involved with the system, including designers, users and any of those involved with the system' (p. 5). This implies that people not only observe the physical aspects of the system and its relation to organisational strategy, but also the likely effects on social structures – such as relations between departments, between centre and local, and on personal networks. They will consider how best to influence events in a way that meets their interests, using the sources of power and influence available to them.

As they do so, they interpret elements of the context to give meaning to events, perhaps through questions such as 'why are they proposing that system rather than another one?' or 'what may that do to the position of our department?' As they attempt to develop or adapt the system they try to create or reinforce meaning – 'if we use this system it will show that we are a modern, efficient business' or 'that will undermine the way our customers expect us to work'.

The interpretive perspective also draws attention to the continuously shifting nature of the context. People draw on aspects of the context (such as new technology becoming available) and their perceived authority (an aspect of power) to propose and develop an information system. Some players may make similar interpretations and support and develop the project; others may see things differently and propose changes or abandonment. Both will use apparently rational and objective arguments to back their case. The evolving system will reflect the relative ability of each party to influence the actions of other players – it will reflect the multiple realities which coexist in the minds of those involved in the project. Being willing to recognise multiple realities affects how people develop information systems. It affects, for example, whether promoters recognise critics as having equally legitimate views of the world that they need to take into account or dismiss them as symptoms of a communication problem.

■ Summary

■ How people respond to an information system reflects their interpretation of the system and its context – including the social system of which they are part.

■ They favour applications that support their interests and disfavour those which threaten them.

■ They interpret a system and its context as a source of meaning – a way of understanding what the change implies for them and the organisation.

8.2 Human–computer interaction

The discipline of human–computer interaction (HCI) tries to understand both the human user and the computer system, and to make the interaction between the two more satisfying and productive. In this it is dealing with two highly complex systems: the computer and the human user. Analysts aim to understand how users function, the tasks they perform and how best to create a computer-based system that supports users. 'The aim is to create computer applications that will make users more efficient than if they performed their tasks with an equivalent manual system' (Faulkner, 1998, p. 2). This involves users, their tasks and the environment in which they work.

People interpret the outside world through their five senses – vision, hearing, taste, smell and touch. The most important of these (for those without serious eye defects) is vision – which depends on the brightness and colour of the light entering the eye. This should influence the layout of screens, as the combination of brightness and colour will influence whether the people find the display (of an internal system or a customer-centred website) visually pleasing or not. People find screens with too many colours confusing and prefer them to be sparse and uncluttered, with menu choices arranged in a way that makes sense. Touch is also important, especially in the design of keyboards.

People designing information systems inevitably make assumptions about human memory as their designs represent what they expect users to remember when working with the system. Experiments on memory provide many relevant pointers to designers. For example the work by Miller (1956) on short-term memory showed that the typical capacity of a person's short-term memory is 7 plus or minus 2 chunks of information. Chunking means grouping information in a way that makes sense to the individual – a nine-figure number is hard to remember, but becomes easier if divided into three chunks each with three digits. Most people would find a password with 15 digits (combining letters and numbers) unacceptable.

Another HCI issue is to understand the task that an information system is intended to support. This is done by the process of task analysis – breaking the whole job into its component parts, by asking questions such as:

■ What does the performer of the task do?

■ What information is used for each task?

■ What affects task performance?

■ What are the good features of the present system? (to retain if possible)

■ What are the bad features? (to eliminate if possible).

A task analysis should produce a clear picture of what the activity is intended to achieve; it must then be converted into a new, or more likely enhanced, computer-based form. That leads to a consideration of the interface between the human and the computer.

The interface between people and the information system mediates between the two and has a major effect on how users perceive the system. It shapes the mental model people form of the system they are working with, and enables them to predict what the system will do. Faulkner (1998) proposes five principles of interface design:

- naturalness – it should seem to be the natural way to perform the task and reflect the natural language for the task involved;

- consistency – it should be consistent in its requirements for input and should have consistent mechanisms for the user to make demands on the system. The language and position of messages should as far as possible be the same throughout;

- relevance – the interface should not ask for redundant material; on-screen information should be short and relevant (a problem for users of online banking systems is the volume of 'small print' that industry regulators require the banks to post on their sites);

- supportiveness – the interface should provide adequate information to allow the user to perform the task;

- flexibility – users have different requirements, skills and preferences. While meeting these is an ideal, doing so may run counter to the ideal of consistency. Too much personal flexibility will also make it harder for people within an organisation to share information.

HCI draws on many other disciplines, including ergonomics, which takes account of the physical aspects of work. Practitioners study how systems can best be designed to suit the physical and mental processes of users. Examples include:

- how the layout and brightness of screens affects eye-strain;
- comparing the physical workload required by different input devices;
- the effect of the height of visual display units on fatigue among users; or
- the effects on productivity of different work–rest schedules.

As managers respond to competitive pressures by increasing performance expectations they risk endangering employees' physical and psychological health. Ergonomic studies help to identify the risks involved, and encourage designers to produce systems that are compatible with the physical attributes of staff using them.

The scope of HCI work is expanding as rapidly as the scope of information systems – especially as local and national governments begin to use IS to deliver a widening range of services and benefits. As computers have moved from being pieces of scientific equipment to becoming tools for enhancing organisational productivity and widely accessible parts of community life, so the scope of HCI has widened. In a communication-intensive society users 'are not only the computer-literate, skilled, able-bodied workers driven by performance-oriented motives . . . but could include the young and the elderly, residential users, as well as those with disability' (Stephanides, 2001, p. 6).

■ Summary

■ Practitioners of human–computer interaction aim to make the interaction of people and computers more satisfying and productive.

■ They observe the physical and mental capabilities of users, and encourage system designers to take account of them.

■ They can be expressed in the design of the interface, which should be natural, consistent, relevant, supportive and flexible.

■ HCI concerns are extending as people extend IS to new applications (especially in providing public services) as this widens, and varies, the constituency of users.

8.3 Technology acceptance model

Davis (1989, 1993) developed the technology acceptance model (TAM) which predicts that whether or not people accept and use an IS depends on two distinct variables: perceived usefulness (PU) and perceived ease of use (PEU). He defined PU as 'the degree to which a person believes that using a particular system would enhance his or her job performance'. Since people usually receive rewards that reflect in some way their job performance, it is plausible to assume that the more they think a system will help them achieve valued rewards, the more likely they are to use it. PEU is 'the degree to which a person believes that using a system would be free of effort' (Davis, 1989, p. 320). Users have to allocate effort between alternative demands, so are more likely to accept a system that they believe will be easy to use. Davis predicted that these variables would influence users' attitudes (negative or positive) towards an information system, as shown in Figure 8.1.

Davis's studies showed that relationship between PU and usage was much stronger than that between PEU and usage. People are more likely to welcome a useful system than one that is easy to use. They are likely to cope with a system that

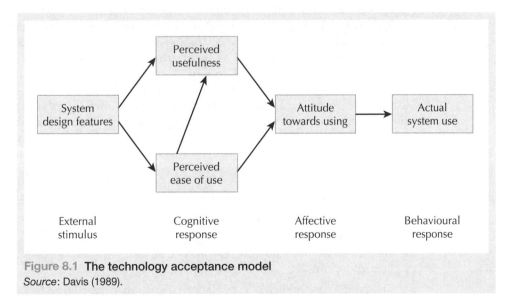

Figure 8.1 The technology acceptance model
Source: Davis (1989).

Research Summary   Technology acceptance model

Davis (1989) provides valuable detail on the way he developed and tested the scales used in the research. PU and PEU were each measured by 6 items, which respondents were asked to rate on this 7-point scale:

| Likely | | | | | | Unlikely |
| extremely | quite | slightly | neither | slightly | quite | extremely |

(Usefulness – PU)
Using (the system) in my job would enable me to accomplish tasks more quickly
Using (the system) would improve my job performance
Using (the system) would increase my productivity
Using (the system) would enhance my effectiveness on the job
Using (the system) would make it easier to do my job
I would find (the system) useful in my job

(Ease of use – PEU)
Learning to operate (the system) would be easy for me
My interaction with the system would be clear and understandable
I would find it easy to get (the system) to do what I want it to do
I would find (the system) flexible to interact with
It would be easy for me to become skilful at using (the system)
I would find (the system) easy to use

Source: Davis (1989), p. 340.

---

is difficult to use if it provides them with valuable information, but unlikely to use one whose only virtue is that it is easy to use. There are clear implications here for those planning to promote an information system.

Later studies have validated and sometimes extended the model, including those by Igbaria (1993), Straub et al. (1997), Sheppard et al. (1998) and Horton et al. (2001). The latter work, for example, used the model to explain the extent to which people in two organisations used their respective intranets.

The model has also been used to predict the behaviour of customers – for example Shih (2004) applied it to the likelihood of a person being willing to shop online. Using measures such as 'I feel that most websites allow information to be easily accessed online' (PEU) and 'Trading on the Internet will save me time' (PU), the survey found that these variables had the predicted effect on consumer attitudes towards e-shopping. The results also showed that customers varied in their reactions. Those who stressed the importance of information quality prefer to shop online, but those who were more concerned with service quality were less willing to do so.

Summary

- The technology acceptance model attempts to predict whether people will accept an information system.

- Empirical studies indicate that perceived usefulness has more effect than perceived ease of use.

- The model can predict IS acceptance by customers as well as by Internet users.

Research Summary | An electronic prescription system

To control the cost of drugs prescribed by general practitioners, the Netherlands Ministry of Health decided to implement an electronic prescription system (EPS). A study had shown that, for similar cases, prescription costs varied by up to 40 per cent, depending on the quantity and brand prescribed. It calculated that if all GPs made more consistent and cost-efficient prescriptions, drug costs would fall by 20 per cent. The Ministry (and other bodies) therefore invested heavily to develop and promote the EPS.

The doctor types in the patient number and a code representing the diagnosis. The EPS then uses a list of available drugs and the patient's medical record to recommend a therapy, including any drugs. The EPS can print the prescription and e-mail this directly to the pharmacist if the patient wishes. GPs are autonomous, self-employed professionals and they reacted to the system in different ways – some used it in full, some partially and some not at all. Only 12 per cent of all GPs used the system as intended, so the cost of prescription drugs did not fall to any worthwhile extent.

To gain some insight into GPs' attitudes to the system researchers interviewed designers and managers at the Ministry and 36 GPs about their attitudes to EPS. They identified five influential factors:

- the system itself – its ease of use, etc.;
- finance – the costs associated with using the system;
- the system as part of the consultation process – did it help, or interrupt, this?
- culture – GPs' values, and how they saw their role in relation to patients;
- policy environment – perceived government plans to control healthcare more closely.

The conclusion was that while the factors in the Technology Acceptance Model (PEU and PU) were relevant to some GPs, they did not have a significant influence on the majority. One unexpected factor was the way the system affected the consultation process. The study also identified the effects of culture and the policy environment on GPs' decisions to accept or reject the system. Those with a traditional, personal culture tended to reject the system, whereas those who saw themselves as running professional and efficient practices welcomed what they perceived as the ability of the EPS to support that culture.

GPs had different opinions on each of these factors, and these contrasting perceptions appeared to have had a significant influence on acceptance. They held strongly contrasting views on each of the factors identified. This is consistent with the theory that people have different values and interests, and that these will inform the meaning they attach to a system.

Source: Based on Boonstra *et al*. (2004).

8.4 Theories of human needs

Human–computer interaction approaches and the technology acceptance model attempt to understand how people relate to information systems by analysing certain human needs. These can give valuable insights, but additional insights can be gained from considering a broader set of human needs and motivation.

Employment is essentially an exchange relationship. Staff affected by a new information system will assess whether the effort they put into adapting to the new

Figure 8.2 The cycle of motivation
Source: A.A. Huczynski and D.A. Buchanan, 2003, *Organizational Behaviour: An Introductory Text*, 5th Edition, Financial Times, Prentice Hall.

system is matched by rewards which they value. It is up to project sponsors or managers to create conditions in which those affected see an IS project as being in their interests and so be willing to make the effort. Understanding individual motivation is the basis for this. People are willing to do things if they feel they are acting in their best interests and achieving their personal goals. Those implementing information systems need to find ways of identifying these interests and help people to satisfy them.

Motivation is a decision process through which an individual chooses desired outcomes, and sets in motion behaviour that will help achieve those outcomes. Figure 8.2 shows this.

Psychologists disagree over 'needs' as they are complex and changing. Yet people managing a project need some practical guidelines – a theory of motivation that is understandable and practical, even if it lacks sophistication. Many readers will be aware of the range of motivational theories and the factors that affect commitment. The work of writers such as Hackman and Oldham, Herzberg and McGregor are highly relevant to IS projects (for a review, see Boddy, 2005).

A key idea in such theories is the distinction between extrinsic and intrinsic rewards. Extrinsic rewards are those that are outside the job and separate from the performance of the task such as pay, security and promotion possibilities. Intrinsic rewards are those that people receive from the performance of the task itself – the use of skills, a sense of achievement, work that is in itself satisfying to do. Recall that a central element in Frederick Taylor's doctrine of scientific management was the careful design of the 'one best way' of doing a piece of manual work. This was typically arrived at by analysing carefully how people normally did the job. Experts then identified the most efficient set of tasks, usually by breaking the task down into many small parts that people could learn quickly. Jobs of this sort are boring to many people, and often lead to dissatisfaction, absenteeism and carelessness.

As the limitations of mechanistic designs became clear, researchers began to seek ways of making jobs more interesting and challenging – in the belief that this would tap into other sources of motivation. The idea was that staff would work more productively if management offered intrinsic as well as extrinsic rewards. A series of research projects appeared to support this approach and led to the work design model.

The work design model

The work design model extended the work of earlier motivation theorists by proposing that managers could change specific job characteristics to meet human needs more closely – especially the intrinsic rewards inherent in the work itself. Advocates proposed that this would motivate employees and promote job satisfaction. Managers have choices – they can consider how the design of the proposed system could affect working practices and how to shape these choices to enhance user needs and motivations. Richard Hackman and Greg Oldham (1980) developed a widely quoted model (see Boddy, 2005, or Buchanan and Huczynski, 2004).

Central to the model are five core job dimensions which the model predicts contribute to the motivational potential of a job:

- **Skill variety**. The extent to which a job makes use of a range of skills and experience.

- **Task identity**. Whether a job involves a relatively complete and whole operation.

- **Task significance**. How much the job matters to others, or to the wider society.

- **Autonomy**. How much freedom a person has in deciding how to do their work.

- **Feedback**. The extent to which a person receives feedback on performance.

The model also shows how management (or staff) can increase the motivational effects of a job by using one or more of five implementing concepts:

- **Combine tasks**. Combine work so people use more skills and complete more of the whole task.

- **Form natural workgroups**. Perform a complete operation.

- **Establish customer relations**. Educate staff in what their customers expect.

- **Vertical loading**. Workers take on some responsibilities of supervisors.

- **Open feedback channels**. Ensure people receive feedback on performance.

Figure 8.3 summarises the model.

This model was developed in the context of work on established, regular tasks but the principles are likely to apply to IS projects. These are creating something new, so may offer opportunities to arrange the tasks in a way that enhances motivation. The project is an opportunity to consider if the system can be designed in such a way as to enhance the skills people use or improve the feedback they get. Conversely, people can be alert to the possibility of (perhaps unintentionally) limiting, for example, task significance or autonomy. Alongside appropriate extrinsic rewards, the intrinsic aspects of the job will affect staff motivation.

The theory can be linked to practice by considering how to apply the implementing concepts in a design activity. Project managers may be unable to do much directly about extrinsic rewards as these depend on wider policies. They may be able to influence intrinsic rewards, by using the work design model. Table 8.1 summarises some options for using the implementing concepts to increase the motivation of a job affected by an information system.

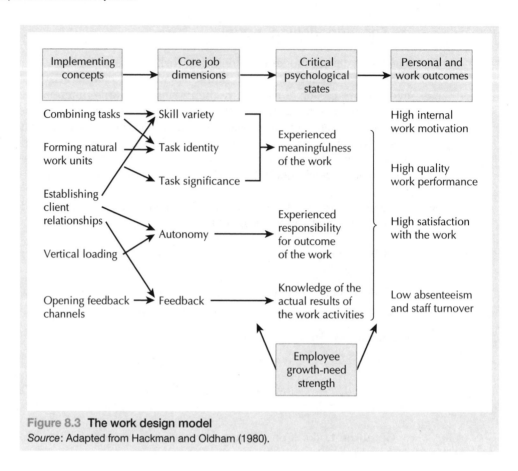

Figure 8.3 The work design model
Source: Adapted from Hackman and Oldham (1980).

Table 8.1 The work design model and information systems design

Implementing concept	Possible use in designing IS
Combining tasks	Use the information system to combine several processes into a single task so that staff use more skills and complete more of the whole task. See Chapter 4 on process redesign.
Form natural work groups	Give team responsibility for a significant part of the task, and ensure the information system provides information to the team.
Establish customer relations	Use technology to provide staff with more or better information about the customer they are dealing with. Link staff to specific customers, with awareness of customer needs.
Vertical loading	As the system takes over routine tasks, give staff more responsibility, supported by the information system, for scheduling, planning, budgeting, client liaison, etc.
Opening feedback channels	Use the power of the system to pass on information from customers. Ensure positive as well as negative messages. Encourage more internal review and evaluation of performance.

Review the ambulance case and then consider how information systems will have affected the work of the control room assistants.

What features of HCI could apply in this situation?

Use the technology acceptance model to consider how the design of the system may have affected PU and PEU.

Use the work design model (especially the 'implementing concepts') to suggest opportunities for redesigning their work as the system came in.

Activity 8.1 Using the work design model

Review an IS with which you are familiar and consider how it will have affected the work of those involved. Use the 'implementing concepts' within the work design model to suggest opportunities for redesigning their work.

Summary

- Theories of human needs identify intrinsic as well as extrinsic motivational factors.
- The work design model provides a tool for analysing the intrinsic motivation of jobs.
- The theory can be used to assess motivational effects as people design the human aspects of information systems.

8.5 Using IS for commitment or control?

As managers promote and develop information systems they have a choice about how they relate them to staff. They can either use the systems to increase control over staff, by closer surveillance and monitoring of performance, or they can use them to support self-control and commitment among staff. This section gives examples of both approaches.

Examples of the changes which computer-based information systems bring to individuals' work are all around us. When customers make a purchase through a website, the roles of staff change. They spend less time discussing options and handling the routine aspects of the transaction, such as payment and delivery requirements. They can then spend more time on tasks that develop the business. The director of global e-commerce at IT group Cap Gemini has said that:

> *These changes in staff responsibilities mean that different types of skills are needed and rewarded. There is more need for creative qualities, and a tendency to define staff roles less, resulting in a fundamental change in a company's culture. (Financial Times, 1 September 1999)*

Loot, a UK classified advertising website, has benefited from allowing staff to innovate and bring in new ideas.

Our approach has been 'don't outspend the competition, outsmart them', and it takes people to do that . . . Despite the technical nature of the industry, never has an industry depended so much on the intellect and skill of its employees. We encourage staff to be creative . . . as continuous innovation is critical to succeeding in new media. We have learnt to erase as much of our hierarchy as we possibly can, as creative people thrive in such an environment.

(*Financial Times*, 1 September 1999)

MIS in Practice   Changing work in a call centre project

Reviewing his experience of call centres, a leading UK call centre consultant, Mike Colman, provided an example of the benefits from changing working arrangements:

It's also a time to think about the work people do. A couple of companies had a field sales force, and before we started the call centre, I thought it would be useful to collect some benchmark data. When they put the call centre in place, they found the call centre agents were selling far more than any of the salesmen. So they did some very basic things. They still wanted salesmen, but wanted to direct them to the things they should be doing, like building strategic partnerships and moving the business on. They could leave the selling to the call centre to maintain the relationship and exploit the database.

The call centre people were looking ahead, and starting to use cross-selling and up-selling. That again is relationship selling, because you have all the information about the customer in front of you, it tells the customers that you know about them. The technology re-establishes and supports the personal link, and it is the people that transmit that relationship position, the human link.

Source: Personal communication.

Activity 8.2 Call centre work

Review the above account of the views of an experienced call centre consultant.

■ *Which of the implementing concepts from Table 8.1 does it mention?*

There is a difference between systems that replace and those that complement human skills (Buchanan and Boddy, 1983). Most people welcome the delegation to the machine of boring, repetitive, error-prone tasks. Where people see that an IT system can perform these more effectively than they could themselves, they usually react positively (Clegg et al., 1997). This is most likely to happen when people interpret the situation as being one in which they will still have a job and that they will be able to do more interesting work.

We deal with about 200,000 invoices every year, which all had to be keyed in, matched, filed, stored. [With e-procurement] we will have fewer key entry staff. We used to have five, there are now three. They are applying for other jobs in the plant. It's a good illustration of the way EDI is taking people away from the transactional tasks to ones where they can add value.

Source: An IBM finance manager, on the company's e-procurement system in 2000.

What people do not welcome is the delegation to the machine of significant or valued skills and experience. Nor do they welcome losing their employment if they are replaced by the machine. If they remain in the job performing only residual tasks, they become psychologically distant from the task. They are likely to lose interest and commitment, and so add little value.

In contrast, 'complementarity' refers to a situation in which the technology supports or enhances the value of an existing skill. Staff receive better or faster information that allows them to apply their skills more productively to the right target. This helps both performance and commitment. Giving staff information about the inner workings of the process they are managing enables them to act more confidently. They can see the effects of their efforts and develop a deeper understanding of the process. They know how things work and can use their knowledge to suggest improvements. Staff have more information and are able to combine this with their knowledge of the operating processes. They can contribute imaginatively to higher-value work and can probably respond to change quickly and effectively, without needing to consult their manager. This in turn may enable the managers themselves to enhance their role. Figure 8.4 shows the possibilities.

As an example, we can return to the ambulance case. The next box gives the comments of a control manager some two years after installing the systems.

Two messages come from this example. The first is that there is choice in the way people design work around IS. In the ambulance case these choices included:

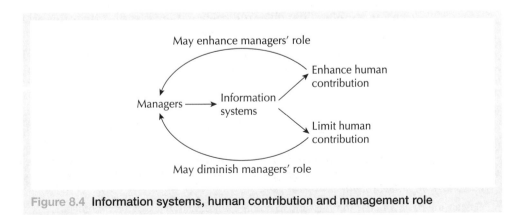

Figure 8.4 **Information systems, human contribution and management role**

The ambulance service: Complementing skills

We have a monthly meeting of all the control managers, and they can ask for cosmetic changes to the way data appears on-screen. The basic system has not changed but we have made some changes in how we use it. We used to tell the crew how to action the run: what we do now is put all the patients in a geographic area onto a log sheet, with their appointment times. We have devolved responsibility to the crew members to decide how best they should schedule that journey to meet the patients' appointments.

How they pick them up is up to them – they also take breaks to suit the overall schedule: we do not schedule them. Initially we told them in much more detail, manually intervening with the computer data. But it was very labour-intensive, and we did not see the traffic jams. We hand out the work in the morning, and we only want to hear if the crews are having operational problems.

The planning officer's role has developed into a liaison role with the hospitals. Building up a relationship with them, because there has to be some come and go. The person in the planning department becomes a crucial personality, not just a worker. Someone coming into the job now could take two years to build up those working relationships. The machine does the routine bits. At first the planning officer did that: now we have pushed it down.

The command and control system identifies the patient by urgency, and recommends the most suitable resource. I stress 'recommends' – the essential point is that the controller makes the decision as to who goes. The system only recommends the deployment – we do not want the computer deciding. We will keep in the human element. The decision of the control officer goes through the screen. I am convinced that we would have needed more staff without the system. It is user-friendly because we insisted that the software writers made it so. It mirrored very closely the old paper system, and it has been very successful. It is now extremely quick to deploy ambulances.

Source: A control manager.

- designing the command and control system to recommend rather than prescribe the vehicle to go to an incident – people had the final say;
- designing the command and control system so that it closely matched the existing paper system – this had worked effectively, staff were familiar with it and transition to the new system was correspondingly easy;
- in the Patient Transport Service, devolving responsibility to the crew to decide the route to follow in collecting their patients, rather than the original method of having the system prescribe the route;
- using the machine and control assistants for routine work, and the control officer to improve links with hospitals and community – adding value to the service.

CASE QUESTIONS 8.2

Review the ambulance case to identify points at which it mentions specific management actions that contribute to the conclusions in the previous paragraph. Comment on how these may have encouraged users to accept the system.

Review the Kwik-Fit case in Chapter 6 to identify any similar management practices.

The second message is that these choices reflected a clear view of the nature of the work and an acknowledgement of the skills of those doing it. Using the technology to remove routine tasks enhanced work. Retaining human control of decisions that staff themselves could make enhanced it further.

Even more gains are possible if information shows staff links between processes, or allows them to see the wider picture. If people understand the links between processes, and can see their current state, they can act intelligently according to the latest plan or event. Providing timely and accurate information to staff complements their skill and supports responsible action. Lloyd and Newell (1998) reported an example of a database system that failed to complement staff knowledge. It was installed in a division of a pharmaceutical company (referred to as Pharma), and used by the 70 sales representatives. As the box shows, the database was inaccurate and failed to acknowledge the accumulated staff experience. The incentive system nevertheless required staff to use the system, even when they knew that this would lower performance.

Research Summary   A database that ignored experience

The representatives visited doctors, nurses and pharmacists and encouraged them to prescribe Pharma products. They were relatively well educated, and 40 per cent had been with the company for more than seven years. They covered a defined territory and had developed their own target lists, based on their knowledge of doctors and their prescribing practices.

In 1996, management installed on the reps' laptop computers a marketing database of the most fruitful sales prospects in each rep's area. They expected staff to call on these prospects at a specified frequency and to ignore doctors not on the list.

Staff were keen to use new technology to support their work; but they complained about the poor quality of the database, as management themselves later acknowledged. A market research company had compiled the database and staff believed it was inaccurate. They could not change more than 10 per cent of the entries in any year. Moreover,

> The computer system linked to the database meant that the reps' performance was being assessed on the basis of calls which could not be made because the targets were no longer in the territory, were not interested in [the product] or never saw reps. The system would only accept data about recognised target customers. (p. 112)

The reps claimed the database information did not reflect their knowledge and experience. Staff turnover rose sharply, staff did not meet sales targets and the number of calls declined.

Source: Based on Lloyd and Newell (1998).

The box below provides a direct contrast to the Pharma case. The company has several plants, including some in the United States, and makes high-quality chemicals for the semiconductor industry. The parent company decided in 1998 to introduce an ERP system, mainly to improve financial control of the group. The manufacturing manager of the UK plant saw that the system had much greater potential and has enthusiastically adopted the system to help manage the whole of the manufacturing process. Of particular interest here, he has used the opportunity to change the role of production operators. The box records part of an interview.

Most of the operators have never travelled – now they are travelling. A culture change has happened that says the power and the information are no longer in the management team. The people who are driving the business process and producing the management reports are the people on the machines. They have not generally been looked on as the people who have that knowledge. The whole ERP process is pushing that. They can see the information directly on the screen by their machine. The system generates information for each process rather than in a global form. That means the people down there running the process have more information than management has got. I have asked them to structure the reports and tell me every week what's happening. They order materials directly – they know what they've used, and what is in the production plan.

If we then bolster that by having them travel to other plants to see how they work, you are driving a whole improvement process on the spine of ERP. Then you see the things that are possible. That whole bar-coding team, of which three are manufacturing operatives, will be going to [Company X] to see their bar-coding system. They would never have had that opportunity before, and probably no one else other than myself will see it. They will come back and probably spend £100k on implementing a bar-coding system. A whole change of management style.

Source: Interview with Chem-Tec manufacturing manager.

Managers can use information systems to reduce the human contribution (as in Pharma). Activities previously done by people are embodied in the system or become highly structured. Staff do the task by following highly specified on-screen scripts or prompts. While this enables a business to handle routine transactions quickly, consistently and cheaply, it also carries the danger that staff will see it as an attempt to impose tighter control.

Information systems make it possible to monitor staff and operational performance very closely. The issues arise much more widely. Wherever staff use an IT system for their operational work, or where they need to record specified stages through the computer, it is possible to monitor, track and compare performance. The management issue is how to use this technical capacity. Some managers will choose to use it to monitor tightly, in the belief that this will enable them to control and then enhance performance. Others will be more wary, conscious that staff may resent this and see it as intrusive and showing a lack of trust. It also reduces the autonomy which people experience in the job. As Watad and DiSanzo (2000) observed in another context (that of telecommuting), 'business managers need to change their focus of control from attendance monitoring to managing for results' (p. 96).

Summary

- There is some scope for choice in the way work is designed as IS are introduced.
- Companies have benefited from using IS to eliminate routine work, thus cutting duplication, errors and costs.
- They have also benefited from using IS to complement the skills of their staff, and obtain more value from the tasks performed.

■ Managers also use IS to monitor and control staff more closely – which may be counter to staff needs for greater autonomy and self-control.

8.6 Managing distributed work

Many organisations use developments in computing and information technologies to change where and when work is done – with many implications for the people doing the work. Practice takes many forms but a broad division is between 'individualised' and 'collective' forms. The former (often called telecommuting, or teleworking) refers to practices in which companies provide the technical facilities that enable people to work with more independence of time and place than conventional work-spaces allow. The latter occurs when a company uses the power of technology to redistribute tasks between locations, within which people work in conventional ways.

■ Individual remote working

Technical developments have made it increasingly possible for people to work away from the conventional central office space, and to do so at times and intervals that vary individually. Although the technologies to enable this are widely available, tele-working is still a minority activity. Belanger and Collins (1998) reviewed 58 selected studies of distributed work arrangements, to identify the factors which affect the outcomes.

They defined three forms of distributed working, in which people:

■ do not have a permanent work location on company premises – they work in a building regularly but do not have a designated personal space, or 'hotelling' where staff book space when they need it;

■ work at sites intentionally located near their home – sometimes called 'satellite' or 'neighbourhood' work centres, they are mainly in response to employee demands to avoid long journeys to work;

■ work at least part of the time at home – supported by computers and telecom-munications equipment, this is known as 'telecommuting' or 'teleworking'.

Figure 8.5 illustrates the model, and we explain each factor briefly.

Individual characteristics

If managers decide to implement teleworking, they need to establish who will move to this system, since it will not suit those, for example, who require the stimulation of colleagues, or the control of a structured work environment. The authors identified two individual characteristics important for distributed work:

1. Objectives: it is attractive to people who want to reduce costs (mainly travel) and increase control over their work schedule (often with family commitments).

2. Skills: it is most suited to people with computer skills and who are self-sufficient, self-disciplined and good communicators.

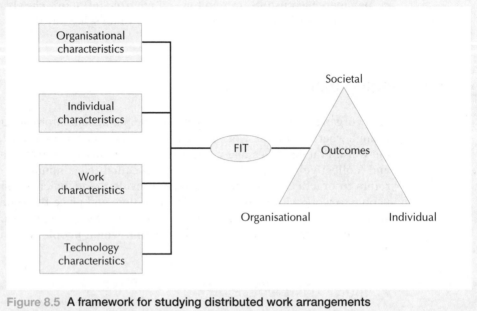

Figure 8.5 A framework for studying distributed work arrangements
Source: Belanger and Collins (1998).

Work characteristics

Whether work can be done remotely follows from its interdependence with other people or units. A common typology of interdependence is:

1. Pooled: each worker contributes to the product, but has little communication with others.
2. Sequential: one-way flow between workers, like an assembly line.
3. Reciprocal: information flows to and from all those involved in the task.
4. Team: similar to reciprocal, but with the flow taking place more quickly.

Tasks with reciprocal or team interdependence imply intense and rapid communications, which would be hard to provide in a distributed environment, even with good information systems. Tasks with pooled or sequential interdependence may be more suited to remote working patterns.

Organisational characteristics

The authors identified three organisational aspects affecting distributed work:

1. Goals: companies hope to save costs through lower building costs and perhaps through lower staff costs – though they incur substantial set-up costs.
2. Culture: staff working at a distance may not develop the beliefs and values held by those in close, daily, informal contact – organisations cannot transmit their values through a computer terminal.
3. Control: managers exert control through outcomes (rewards for what is produced), behaviour (rewards for specified behaviour), social (members of the

group ensure appropriate behaviour) and personal control (self-control). Outcome and personal controls should raise few new issues in a distributed work environment, but behavioural and social controls will be more problematic.

Technology characteristics

This refers to the distributed working environment itself, such as physical facilities, information systems and security.

While distributed work arrangements are still comparartively rare, the Belanger and Collins (1998) review provides a framework within which experience can be compared and related. It indicates areas of the topic that researchers can explore, and how these studies may be linked to each other. It also indicates to those considering distributed work arrangements some of the organisational issues that will affect the outcomes.

■ Collective remote working

The spread of global organisations means that many staff need to work together, even though they are physically separate. Several technologies will help this process, such as group decision support systems, video-conferencing and computer-based scenario planning. They can, collectively, make it easier for members at widely separated locations to share ideas, draw on a wider knowledge base to meet customer or project requirements and ensure that all are working from the same information or database.

Technological solutions do not in themselves guarantee improved working among distributed staff. While they make it possible, managers need to make other changes to support the technologies. One issue is whether people work in a culture that values and encourages sharing information. If members see themselves as competing individuals rather than as collaborative players, the technology itself will not change that. People need an incentive to share information with colleagues in different locations.

The ambulance service: A threat to teamwork?

The downside is that we can go a whole shift without talking directly to an ambulance crew. Because we take a job, press the button and it goes onto a screen in the ambulance; they press status codes, which tell our computer where they are. We have experienced quite a distancing between the crews and the control staff. They're upstairs. We are all a lot busier, crews aren't around the stations as much as they used to be. Once they're out, they're out, rarely come back. The utilisation is tighter.

Source: A control manager in the service

CHAPTER CASE: PART 3

Creating a context to support remote working

The main message from the consultancy example in chapter 1 (p. 9) was that management needed to create a supportive context for the technology by:

- redesigning administrative systems to ensure staff had to use the groupware system to do their core work, including records of fee-earning work. This ensured they learned the basic operations;
- redesigning the appraisal and incentive systems to support the sharing culture that the groupware system made possible.

In work which complements that by Belanger and Collins (1998), Davenport and Pearlson (1998) studied ten firms with well-established distributed work arrangements. They concluded that in order to use the approach successfully, managers first need to recognise the functions which an office serves, summarised in the box.

Research Summary   Functions of the office

- Corporate culture – a place where people socialise, and absorb the culture
- Loyalty – creating identity with colleagues and the company
- Communication – frequent unplanned information-sharing
- Access to people – to find expertise that can quickly solve a problem
- Managerial control – managers can see the person at work; often reassuring
- Access to materials – files, documents, products
- Structure – offices signify status.

Source: Davenport and Pearlson (1998).

While technology can replace some office functions, it cannot do so for all of them. Staff who benefit from these will suffer unless managers plan to meet them in some other way. They also concluded that managers need to attend to these points to make the most of virtual offices:

- Managing people – train managers and staff in how to work in the new environment, and to manage changed family relationships.
- Managing information – institute new information arrangements to replace those lost away from the office, and train people to manage information better.
- Managing teams – explicit training on how to use groupware tools, and building processes to handle conflicts among remote workers.
- Managing processes – examine processes for possible improvements if virtual offices were implemented, and survey customers regularly to monitor satisfaction.
- Manage facilities – provide high levels of technical support for remote workers.

Other studies have reached similar conclusions on the importance of context. Examples include work by Downing and Clark (1999) and by Ciborra and Patriotta (1998) on the use of groupware in Hoffmann-La Roche and Unilever. Hutchinson et al.'s (2000) study of changes in the RAC (a UK motoring support organisation) customer services centre points in the same direction.

Activity 8.3 Remote working

Have you or your organisation any experience of remote working? If not, try to find someone who has, and ask for their views on these questions:

- *Which of the several forms of remote working did it resemble?*
- *What advantages did people expect, and what did they find, from remote working?*
- *How many of the recommendations above were put into effect?*
- *What other factors helped or hindered the change?*

Summary

- Distributed working arrangements can be either individual or collective in form.
- Individual forms (teleworking) are more likely to work if the individuals and tasks are suitable.
- Some forms of organisational control will be harder to use.
- Collective forms of distributed working depend not only on technology but also on creating an appropriate context of incentives and roles.

8.7 Implications for design – the socio-technical approach

The theme that emerges from the cases and research throughout this chapter is that IS projects need to take account of human and contextual factors as well as technical ones. This is the basis of the socio-technical approach to system design. The general message of systems theory is that in designing any kind of system it is necessary to take account of the interdependencies between the various elements of the system. The socio-technical view, in particular, argues that organisations are best understood as interdependent systems. The approach developed from the work of Eric Trist and Ken Bamforth at the Tavistock Institute in London during the 1950s. Their most prominent study was of an attempt by the coal industry to mechanise the mining system. Introducing what were in essence assembly line technologies and methods at the coal face had severe consequences for the social system encouraged by the older pattern of working. The technological system destroyed the fabric of the social system, and the solution lay in reconciling the needs of both technical and social systems – as indicated in Figure 8.6.

Studies in many different countries showed the benefits of seeing a work system as a combination of a material technology (tools, machinery, techniques, physical location) and a social organisation (people with capabilities, needs, relationships, communication patterns, authority structures and so on). Each affects the other, so people need to manage them together so that they work in harmony. Analysis should deal with both the social and technical components. The aim is to integrate them rather than to optimise one without regard to the other. A design that completely satisfied the social system while ignoring technological requirements would not survive. Similarly, a design that perfected the technological system but which ignored the needs of users or customers would soon be rejected. So the aim is to

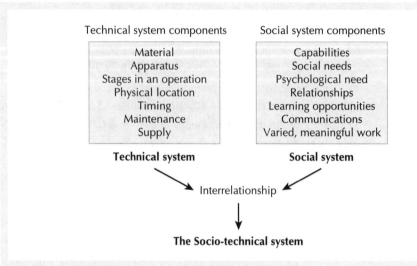

Figure 8.6 The organisation as socio-technical system
Source: Buchanan and Huczynski (2004), figure 3.4.

Research Summary   Information systems and user satisfaction

Clegg et al. (1997) studied two companies that had introduced information systems. They found that user attitudes (satisfaction, sense of ownership, commitment) were most affected by functionality, usability, skill utilisation and expectations about the impact on the company. The results led the authors to recommend that:

> *if you are managing the development and introduction of a new system, these results imply that functionality, usability, skill utilization and job demands are of critical importance; without active consideration of these, the new system may fail . . . New technologies are often used to reduce skill use and to increase job demands. The implication for practice is that managers implementing new technologies should explicitly consider the impacts on the job designs and work organization of the users. The evidence . . . is that this is undertaken only rarely and [is a major reason why new systems fail]. Managers introducing new technology . . . should spend time and effort discussing with users what they need to undertake their work, and ensuring that they understand what the new system will do and what impact it will have on them.*

Source: Clegg et al. (1997), p. 25.

develop a design approach that aims at joint optimisation of both the social and technological systems.

Clegg (2000) offered a set of principles to guide the design of new systems, including those incorporating new information technologies. He acknowledged that the use of the socio-technical approach in designing new systems had been rare, with most investments in IT being technology-led:

> *Many organizations lack an integrated approach to organizational and technical change and, in most cases, users do not have substantial influence on system development . . . Interventions often take technology as given, and the task becomes that of designing the social system around the technology.* (p. 464)

Table 8.2 **Principles of socio-technical system design**

Meta	1. Design is systemic
	2. Values and mindsets are central to design
	3. Design involves making choices
	4. Design should reflect the needs of the business, its users and their managers
	5. Design is an extended social process
	6. Design is socially shaped
	7. Design is contingent (depends on the circumstances)
Content	8. Core processes should be integrated
	9. Design entails allocating tasks between/among humans and machines
	10. System components should be congruent (should fit with related systems)
	11. Systems should be simple and make problems visible
	12. Problems should be controlled at source
	13. The means of undertaking the task should be flexibly specified
Process	14. Design practice is itself a socio-technical system
	15. Systems and their design should be owned by managers and users
	16. Evaluation is an essential aspect of design
	17. Design involves multi-disciplinary education
	18. Resources and support are required for design
	19. System design involves political processes

Source: Based on Clegg (2000).

Clegg arranges the 19 principles into three groups: meta-principles, capturing a 'world-view' of the idea; content, dealing with specific design issues; and process, dealing with how people apply the principles in practice. Table 8.2 shows these.

Those advocating the approach acknowledge that it will enable people to articulate different objectives for a system if it is to satisfy social as well as technical criteria. They recommended open discussion to resolve these conflicts, in the belief that this process is not creating the conflict but merely bringing it out into the open. Resolving it early in the process will be more productive than ignoring it.

Summary

- Organisations combine technical and social systems.
- Those advocating a socio-technical approach maintain that IS designers should deal with both, rather than give primacy to either.
- Explicit use of this approach is rare.

Conclusions

The evidence of this chapter is that information systems have widely varying effects on how people experience work. We have suggested that established and accessible theories of human motivation can guide the questions we ask about the motivational effects of information systems. Some systems have clearly been implemented in a way that reduced the motivational effects. In others the effects have been the reverse – they have enhanced motivation.

We have introduced three theoretical approaches to analysing systems from a human perspective: human–computer interaction, the technology acceptance model and theories of human needs. The work design model in particular illustrates the range of choices available to those designing new information systems. They will probably be guided by fundamental beliefs about whether they (or their senior managers) aim for a culture of control or one of commitment. We then indicated some models relevant to the increasingly common practice of distributed working arrangements, and concluded with a review of socio-technical approaches to IS design.

The chapter has also shown the importance of the interaction between an information system and the wider context. The effectiveness of distributed working arrangements (like the knowledge management systems in Chapter 2) depend on whether the prevailing culture and structure support the change. People will not use a system to share information or work cooperatively at a distance if the culture has encouraged individual competition. The outcomes of an information system depend on the interaction between the system, the people affected by it and their context.

CHAPTER QUESTIONS

1. Evaluate a system or website that you use in terms of the quality of the interface, using the criteria that this should be natural, consistent, relevant, supportive and flexible.
2. What does the technology acceptance model suggest are the main factors affecting users' willingness to use a system?
3. Staff in the Chapter Case appear to have reacted positively to the new systems. Use the work design model to identify the management actions (reported in the case) that encouraged this.
4. What forces in the wider environment may encourage managers to use IS as a means of control?
5. How important are good interpersonal skills likely to be in distributed working?

Further reading

McLoughlin, I. (1999) *Creative Technological Change*, Routledge, London. A comprehensive academic survey of several theoretical positions on the topic.

References

Belanger, F. and Collins, R.W. (1998) 'Distributed work arrangements: a research framework', *Information Society*, **14**(2), 137–52.

Boddy, D. (2005) *Management: An Introduction*, 3rd edition, Financial Times/Prentice Hall, Harlow.

Boddy, D. and Gunson, N. (1996) *Organizations in the Network Age*, Routledge, London.

Boonstra, A., Boddy, D. and Fischbacher, M. (2004) 'The limited acceptance by general practitioners of an electronic prescription system: reasons and practical implications', *New Technology, Work and Employment*, **19**(2), 128–44.

Buchanan, D.A. and Boddy, D. (1983) *Organizations in the Computer Age*, Gower, Aldershot.

Buchanan, D. and Huczynski, A.A. (2004) *Organizational Behaviour: An Introductory Text*, 5th edition, Financial Times/Prentice Hall, Harlow.

Ciborra, C.U. and Patriotta, G. (1998) 'Groupware and teamwork in R&D', *R&D Management*, **28**(1), 43–52.

Clegg, C.W. (2000) 'Sociotechnical principles for system design', *Applied Ergonomics*, **31**(5), 463–77.

Clegg, C., Carey, N., Dean, G., Hornby, P. and Bolden, R. (1997) 'User reactions to information technology: some multivariate models and their implications', *Journal of Information Technology*, **12**, 15–32.

Davenport, T.H. and Pearlson, K. (1998) 'Two cheers for the virtual office', *MIT Sloan Management Review*, **39**(4), 51–65.

Davis, F.D. (1989) 'Perceived usefulness, perceived ease of use, and user acceptance of information technology', *MIS Quarterly*, **13**(3), 319–40.

Davis, F.D. (1993) 'User acceptance of information technology: system characteristics, user perceptions and behavioral impacts', *International Journal of Man–Machine Studies*, **38**, 475–87.

Downing, C.E. and Clark, A.S. (1999) 'Groupware in practice: expected and realized benefits', *Information Systems Management*, Spring, 25–31.

Faulkner, C. (1998) *The Essence of Human–Computer Interaction*, Prentice Hall, Hemel Hempstead.

Frenkel, S., Korczynski, M., Shire, K. and Tam, M. (1998) 'Beyond bureaucracy: work organisation in call centres', *International Journal of Human Resource Management*, **9**(6), 957–79.

Hackman, J.R. and Oldham, G.R. (1980) *Work Redesign*, Addison-Wesley, Reading, Mass.

Horton, R.P., Buck, T., Waterson, P.E. and Clegg, C.W. (2001) 'Explaining intranet use with the technology acceptance model', *Journal of Information Technology*, **16**, 237–49.

Hutchinson, S., Purcell, J. and Kinnie, N. (2000) 'Evolving high commitment management and the experience of the RAC call centre', *Human Resource Management Journal*, **10**(1), 63–78.

Igbaria, M. (1993) 'User acceptance of microcomputer technology: an empirical test', *OMEGA International Journal of Management Science*, **21**, 73–90.

Lloyd, C. and Newell, H. (1998) 'Computerising the sales force: the introduction of technical change in a non-union workforce', *New Technology, Work and Employment*, **13**(2), 104–15.

Miller, G. (1956) 'The magical number seven plus or minus two: some limits on our capacity for processing information', *Psychological Review*, **63**, 81–97.

Sheppard, B.H., Hartwick, J. and Warshaw, P. (1998) 'A theory of reasoned action: a meta analysis of past research with recommendations for modification and future research', *Journal of Consumer Research*, **15**, 325–43.

Shih, H-P. (2004) 'An empirical study on predicting user acceptance of e-shopping on the Web', *Information and Management*, **41**, 351–68.

Stephanides, C. (2001) 'User interfaces for all: new perspectives into human–computer interaction', in C. Stephanides (ed.), *User Interfaces for All: Concepts, Methods and Tools*, Lawrence Erlbaum Associates, Mahwah, NJ.

Straub, D., Keil, M. and Brenner, W. (1997) 'Testing the technology acceptance model across cultures: a three country study', *Information and Management*, **33**, 1–11.

Walsham, G. (1993) *Interpreting Information Systems in Organisations*, Wiley, Chichester.

Watad, M.M. and DiSanzo, F.J. (2000) 'Case study: the synergism of telecommuting and office automation', *MIT Sloan Management Review*, **41**(2), 85–96.

PART 4

Implementation

The two chapters in Part Four concentrate on implementation – Chapter 9 on projects and Chapter 10 on programmes. Chapter 9 presents a research-based framework for diagnosing the critical dimensions of information systems projects, which enables managers to identify where to focus effort. It then compares four theoretical perspectives on change – life-cycle, emergent, participative and political – which can each contribute to the effective management of IS projects. In line with the interaction perspective of the book, it then outlines a method for identifying and influencing stakeholders, and for creating project structures to support individual action.

The idea of project structures is developed more fully in Chapter 10, which deals with the management of programmes – a collection of related projects. Clearly there are interactions not only between contemporaneous IS projects, but also with other strategic or structural changes. Companies have developed various techniques for managing these interactions within a programme, and the chapter presents and illustrates them.

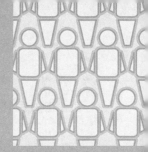

CHAPTER 9

Managing and implementing single projects

Learning objectives

By the end of your work on this topic you should be able to:

- Analyse the distinctive features of a project using a framework provided

- Distinguish four models of project management, and indicate when each is appropriate

- Conduct a stakeholder analysis

- Outline interpersonal and structural approaches to influencing stakeholders in an IS project

Freight Connect

Freight Group is a European transport and logistics company that has grown rapidly, mainly by mergers and acquisitions. All of the acquired companies had developed information systems to suit their requirements.

An IT development strategy identified the core information system requirements for the group to meet its business goals. These included freight and warehouse management systems as well as systems supporting financial, human resource and corporate management needs.

When Freight acquired Nextday – a parcel delivery business – the deal included an arrangement whereby Nextday's previous owners would maintain a proprietary freight management system for one year. This system enabled customers to enter their freight pick-up and delivery requirements to the Nextday system. Freight did not currently have a system able to do this, though managers had identified this as a priority within the IT development strategy.

Freight managers proposed developing a proprietary IS for use within the Nextday business and then across the entire Freight Group. A secondary objective was to eliminate the divisional boundaries caused by the many existing systems. The system therefore needed to be able to handle all freight requirements, from single parcels to large container loads.

The requirement to leave the Nextday system within twelve months led to new IS development priorities and the start of the 'Freight Connect' project. Managers' objectives were to develop a PC-based application that would allow customers to enter consignment information online. The system would generate documents and labels automatically. Drivers receive the pick-up information and the movement of the parcel commences. Customers can use the Internet to track parcel deliveries. Proof-of-delivery documents are scanned and can be viewed by customers. Freight Connect also allows customers to analyse and report on their shipments with Freight. The system shifts responsibility for data entry (pick-up and delivery) from Freight to the customer.

The project commenced with a brief user-needs analysis, which developed a base specification for the functions required of the system. One key objective was to differentiate Freight by developing a system that was not available to competitors. The designers used a prototype development method to build the system in an explorative way. Having sought the views of users, developers began to develop a model of the proposed system. This was then put to users for feedback regarding functionality, screen design, layout and ease of use. Responses were incorporated into a final product.

After several months, software development was largely complete and managers were putting pressure on systems staff to clear the product for rollout to customers. However, other managers were concerned that little time had been devoted to product testing, in particular user acceptance testing.

Source: Communication with Freight staff.

Introduction

Most significant information systems send ripples around the organisation. Many of these are unexpected and ensure that successful implementation requires significant project management skills. This challenge grows as information systems extend from background, internal tasks to those that affect customers, other organisations and members of the public. The issues raised throughout this book imply that those leading such projects are unlikely to have an exclusively technical background.

The chapter begins by outlining the context of information systems change, which affects the process of implementation. This is followed by a research-based account of the characteristics of IS projects, leading to a diagnostic tool that those responsible can use. We then distinguish four perspectives on the nature of IS projects, each of which contributes an insight into the task of managing such changes. Subsequent sections discuss ways of identifying and influencing stakeholders with an interest in an IS project. We conclude by introducing some themes that we develop further in Chapter 10. The aim is to provide ideas and methods that will help people implement major IS projects.

9.1 Challenges in implementing information systems

The record on implementing computer-based information systems is mixed. While many projects transform business operations and enhance company performance, others fall short of expectations. Long-term studies (Boddy and Gunson, 1996; Drummond, 1996; Currie, 1997) show that IS projects frequently fail to meet the expectations of those who initiate them, implying that much investment produces a lower return than promoters expected. Remember, however, that defining 'success' is subjective, and that initial objectives may be unreasonably optimistic. Despite that caveat, there is accumulating evidence that many managers earn a poor return on the money (shareholders' or taxpayers') which they commit to IS projects.

The Freight Connect project illustrates several possible sources of the problems faced in IS projects. It is a technologically advanced system that depends on new software. It is an intervention in an established organisation built from several existing businesses with independent systems and ways of working. And the company operates in a volatile business environment, with technical and market developments prompting competing companies to implement new processes and systems. Most IS projects occur in equally uncertain conditions, and change between conception and delivery.

These considerations are even more apparent when managers introduce systems that link them electronically with other organisations. Freight Connect spans the boundary between Freight and its customers, and will depend on customers changing the way they work. The IBM Internet procurement project described in Chapter 6 depended on suppliers being willing to make significant technical and organisational changes. Howard et al. (2003) show the strains which the automobile industry is experiencing as some players try to move from a 'sell-from-stock' to a 'build-to-order' business. Introducing an industry-wide information system to link all the major players requires an unusual degree of cooperation between independent businesses. In such projects the substantive issues will be complex, as will the process of implementing compatible change in separate organisations.

IS projects now embody strategic and organisational issues. If project managers fail to deal with them they will see 'a damaging mismatch between the capabilities of the system and the characteristics of the host organisation' (Doherty et al., 2003, p. 50). Markus and Benjamin (1997) warned against the 'magic bullet theory'. This metaphor represents the idea that information technology is the 'magic bullet' that in itself changes people's behaviour. It implies that information systems in themselves enable new work practices, displace old ones and transform organisations. The IS specialists make the 'guns' as contracted by line managers. The theory is that

Table 9.1 **Comparison of traditional and new mindsets**

	Traditional	New Wave
Organisational model	Mechanistic, goal-oriented	Multiple constituencies
View of IT	Discrete systems	Integrated systems
Causation and outcomes	Consistent causes, technologically determined outcomes	Countervailing forces, unpredictable outcomes
Knowledge	Well-defined, explicit, articulate	Ill-defined, tacit, diffuse, embedded
Status quo and organisational change	Dispensable status quo, change by design	Status quo valued for embedded knowledge, change emergent
View of business and competitive advantage	Design school, design for strategic position	Resource-based view, advantage through learned competences

Source: Sauer and Yetton (1997), p. 19.

the magic bullets will hit the target and do what managers required – everything will fall into place. Reality is evidently more awkward, and changes on the scale required by modern IS need substantial effort to implement them.

Sauer and Yetton (1997) observed a similar misconception. This arises when managers view IS as if its role is confined to supporting the traditional drivers of competitive advantage such as market differentiation or total quality management. This support role is a valuable but partial view of the IS contribution, in that it ignores the possibilities of using information systems to redefine the business a company is in. They believe that this more radical view of the potential effects of information systems calls for an equally radical approach to managing IS projects: Table 9.1 compares traditional and 'new wave' approaches.

The 'new wave' perspective on IS-based change implies a new approach to implementation since the issues are wide, ambiguous and linked. This chapter offers perspectives and tools with which to analyse how people interpret and deal with these issues.

9.2 The context of change

People implement an IS project within a unique context made up of external, internal and often historical elements. These shape how players react to proposals, and whether they seek to help or hinder the project.

The external context is the mass of political, environmental, economic and other factors outside the firm that shape, and are shaped by, management activities. These include commercial developments, changes in customer habits, legal framework, technology infrastructure and so on. IS projects typically arise when someone observes something in this external world that is a significant threat or opportunity, links that to an IS solution and persuades others to back the change.

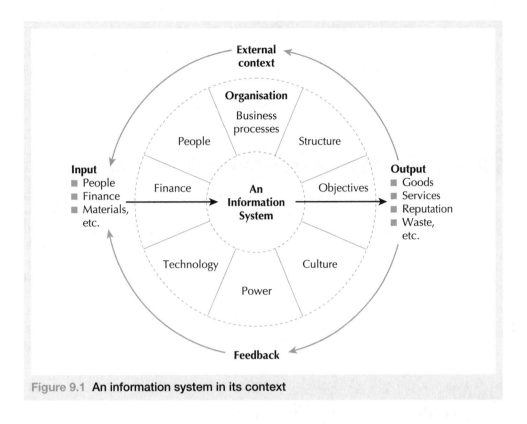

Figure 9.1 An information system in its context

The internal context is made up of the existing state of the organisation into which someone is introducing a project. The model in Figure 9.1 (which repeats Figure 1.5) is a convenient way of describing the setting into which those driving the project are trying to change. This context can help or hinder their efforts. For example, Chapter 6 showed how the prevailing culture and structure of an organisation affect attitudes towards an information system, as well as how they in turn are affected by the system if it is implemented.

However modern and technologically advanced a system, historical factors affect how people view it. A history of successful and beneficial changes will usually mean that people react favourably to a proposal. A history of badly managed projects or expensive failures will have the opposite effect. While those promoting the change hope to change aspects of the context, they are inevitably working within this inherited context.

The context is not an objective thing, but is created in the minds of those involved with the project. Not everyone attends to the same elements of the context, and those who do are likely to interpret them in different ways. Some interpret an event as threatening the business whereas others minimise its significance – and this affects their response. People influence how others respond by managing the flow and nature of information about external events. They can exaggerate customer complaints or competitor actions to shape opinion towards a proposal they favour. Or they can play down potential problems with a project and suggest that others are deliberately magnifying them to block progress.

▨ Summary

- ▨ Managers introduce IS projects into an established organisational context.
- ▨ How people interpret the inherited and proposed context affects their view of change.
- ▨ People try to shape how others interpret that context and their view of the change.

9.3 Diagnosing a project's critical dimensions

How do IS projects relate to established methods of managing projects? They will be similar in being a 'projection of ideas and activities into new endeavours', a step into the unknown. Project managers support the endeavour by trying to foresee the tasks required to complete the project and then planning, organising and controlling the job to completion. There will also be similarities to conventional projects in balancing the competing criteria of performance, time and cost – with priorities shifting as the project is defined and planned (see Figure 9.2).

We can see these tensions at Freight. Initially there was great pressure on time – but later this appears to have changed to a concern over costs. This has slowed the project down and contributed to anxiety about the performance of the system because of limited testing – as described below.

Freight Connect: Conflicting priorities

As the delivery date came closer the project was experiencing difficulties. An important potential customer was pressing for the system to be released. Yet Freight Connect had not yet been cleared for rollout, and conflicting priorities were appearing.

Should an underdeveloped system be rolled out? The physical rollout would require approximately two months to complete (even when additional resources were employed). The plan was that the rollout team would install the software at each customer's premises and individually train the users. This was being questioned as to the efficient use of resources given the shortage of time.

Yet the system was the customer's interface to Freight. Consequently, rollout would be more sensitive than an internal system development and the risks higher. There was a substantial risk that an underdeveloped product could be placed with customers. The product had not been thoroughly tested to eliminate any bugs. There was insufficient user support and training materials were underdeveloped. Managers were concerned that any problems encountered would directly affect the customers and could potentially have an impact on their image of Freight.

Source: Private communication from a manager in the company.

CASE QUESTIONS 9.1

Which of the challenges mentioned can you see in the Freight project?
Where would you locate the project in Figure 9.3?
When you have read the next section, use Table 9.2 to analyse the project.

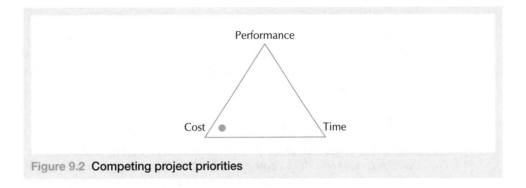

Figure 9.2 **Competing project priorities**

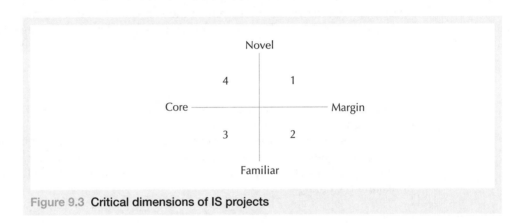

Figure 9.3 **Critical dimensions of IS projects**

Projects vary in the problems they present to those responsible for implementation. Boddy (2002) reported a study in which a team worked closely with project managers implementing a wide range of changes. The study showed that managers believed two dimensions of their projects had a strong influence on the scale of the task. The first dimension was how central the change was to the primary task of the organisation – core or marginal. The second was the novelty of the change – novel or familiar. This gave four quadrants representing significantly different types of project (see Figure 9.3). Those which are core and novel will be more risky, and more difficult to implement, than those which are marginal and familiar.

A project in quadrant 2 is one that is marginal to the main task and is also an incremental change to existing practices. A project to enhance the computer system for paying pensions to retired employees would be an example. Such projects carry little risk and are fairly easy to implement. In contrast, quadrant 4 projects affect the core activity and are a radical departure from what exists. A project to set up an Internet banking operation in an existing bank would be an example. These are the most risky types of change as they present major implementation problems – both organisational and technical. These categories are relatively subjective, and so fluid. People may have different views about which type of project they are dealing with, and may change their views as the project proceeds.

The study identified five other project dimensions that managers perceived to affect the task, and which we outline below.

Controversy

Some changes are vigorously opposed from the start by one or more of the parties, who seek to undermine them by overt or covert means. Others are seen as desirable by all concerned who work together to make them happen. There will also be conflicting priorities (as at Freight).

Changing goals

The goals of change projects often continue to evolve as the project itself is planned and implemented: 'my project is only half-way through implementation, but already we're introducing significant changes to cope with new areas of business which the sales and marketing people have obtained'. Sometimes these changes reflect poor initial planning. More often they reflect the fact that the business world has changed since the project began. Management then needs to change the change itself to keep it relevant.

Senior stance

The attitude of senior management towards the change is critical. They cannot give detailed guidelines to change managers, and may not even set a blueprint for change. They can affect the outcome by the scale and consistency of their support. Where difficulties or resource problems arise, someone managing a change needs adequate and consistent support from senior managers if they are to have a chance of making the change.

Outside links

Many projects depend on either physical or organisational changes in areas beyond the immediate authority of the project manager. They need the cooperation of people in other departments or organisations who are not necessarily as committed to the change as the company leading it.

Clusters of change

Volatile environments mean that change is more frequent and so comes in clusters. Most projects take place at the same time as other major changes. Sometimes these support the direction of the IS project – but at others they cut across it and distract attention.

Figure 9.4 summarises these dimensions.

Activity 9.1   Diagnosing a project

Use Table 9.2 to analyse a project you know. Circle the number in each row that best represents the situation. The greater the score, the more problematic that issue is likely to be.

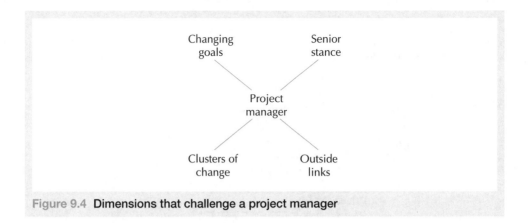

Figure 9.4 Dimensions that challenge a project manager

Table 9.2 **A method for identifying project dimensions**

Significant change?	Margin	1	2	3	4	5	Core
Solution	Familiar	1	2	3	4	5	Novel
Changing goals	Rare/Minor	1	2	3	4	5	Often/Major
Senior stance	Supportive	1	2	3	4	5	Unsupportive
Outside links?	Few	1	2	3	4	5	Many
Other changes	Few	1	2	3	4	5	Many
Will there be a fight?	Uncontroversial	1	2	3	4	5	Controversial

Summary

- Projects vary on a small number of significant dimensions.
- Diagnosing these alerts the project manager to potentially difficult areas.
- These dimensions are subjective, so others may make different interpretations.

9.4 Models of change – life cycle, emergent, participation and politics

People can view significant IS projects from four alternative, but complementary, perspectives. Each has different implications for those implementing the change.

Life cycle

Much of the advice given to those responsible for managing projects uses the idea of the project life cycle. Projects go through successive stages, and results depend on conducting the project through these stages in an orderly and controlled way. The labels vary, but major themes are:

- define objectives clearly;
- allocate responsibilities;

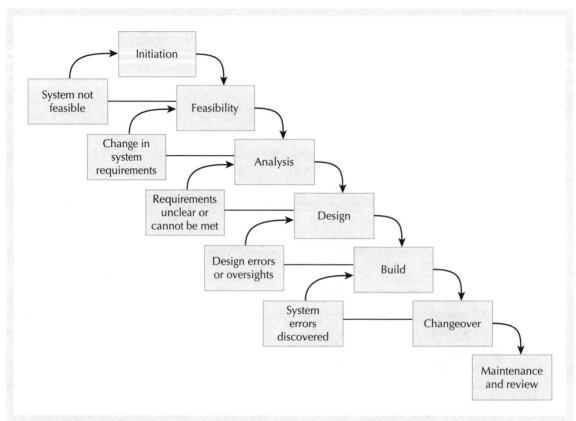

Figure 9.5 **The traditional waterfall model of information systems development**
Source: Based on Chaffey (2003).

■ fix deadlines; and

■ set budgets.

People often refer to these approaches as 'rational–linear' models of change. They reflect the assumption that planned change in organisations unfolds in a logical sequence, that people work to the plan and that they notice and correct deviations from the plan. In relation to IS projects, advocates of tools such as the 'system development life cycle' make similar assumptions. Designers created this model to bring some order to the task of developing computer-based information systems and advocate following steps such as those shown in Figure 9.5.

While this approach has many advantages and is widely used, taking it too literally embodies the fallacy that a project goes through these stages once, with any faults or misunderstandings about user needs being fixed at the testing stage. This isolates designers from the reality of the users' world, whereas 'experience and ideas from each downstream part of the construction process must leap upstream, sometimes more than one stage, and affect the upstream activity' (Brooks, 1995, p. 266). This implies using the model not in a linear way, but iteratively – as shown in the figure.

Linear methods can work well with specific, structured requirements such as those in accounting and stock control where the activities themselves flow in a

MIS in Practice   PRINCE 2 methodology

This method was developed for the UK government and is intended to be used for planning major projects, especially those based on information systems. The method applies three key elements to each project: processes, techniques and components.

- **Processes.** The approach advocates seven 'fundamental processes': start-up, initiation, directing, managing stage boundaries, controlling a stage, managing product delivery and closing a project. All of these processes link to techniques.

- **Techniques.** Those listed within the method are: product-based planning, change controls, quality reviews, project filing arrangements and configuration management.

- **Components.** The method includes eight components: organisation, planning, controls, stages, risk management, quality, configuration management and change control.

Each of these aspects is specified in considerable detail, giving clear guidance on how major projects should be structured and managed. For example, the organisation component sets out the responsibilities of structures such as the project board, project support and project support office. A PRINCE project is divided into a number of stages, each forming a distinct unit for management purposes. PRINCE defines the organisation of the project and its stages, the processes which drive the task, the structure and content of project plans, some basic project management techniques and a set of controls.

logical, orderly sequence. For some projects, and for some parts of other projects, people can plan like this, and in such cases life cycle models are useful. They are less useful where requirements are ambiguous and where the work is being done in a constantly changing environment. In these circumstances, managers who rely too much on a linear approach will run into difficulty. They may draw on a different perspective, one which gives more emphasis to the emergent rather than the planned nature of change.

Freight Connect: Project management

The rational project management approach may also be inappropriate in terms of the overall mindset which it embodies. Bensaou and Earl (1998, pp. 122–3) observed that

> the cumulative and pervasive value-for-money mind-set can be destructive. It can bias investment decisions toward cost-saving automation projects; it can deter ideas for revenue generating IT applications; and it can lead to the dangerously late adoption of IT infrastructure improvements.

The Freight project illustrates this. Someone close to the project commented:

> The capital expenditure process has been the major hold-up in the development process. Instead of focusing on the benefits that could be achieved through an early and well-planned and financed implementation, there has been an excessive concern over the cost of the investment. We are now in a predicament due to the slow development process undertaken [in order to reduce costs] and the slow approval of capital expenditure requests. Moreover, the IT specialists involved at Freight are just that – they are not highly involved in operational business activities, therefore they are not in touch with the detailed requirements of the customer.

CHAPTER CASE: PART 3

■ Emergent or incremental approaches

As outlined in Chapter 3, Henry Mintzberg (1994) takes the view that developing an organisational strategy, far from being a logical and rational process, is better described as one which is *emergent* or adaptive. Some departure from a plan is inevitable due to unforeseeable changes or new opportunities. He distinguishes between *intended* and *emergent* strategies. He acknowledges the value of a plan that sets out intended courses of action, and recognises that managers will achieve some of their intentions. However, they will fail to implement some of their intentions (unrealised strategies), while implementing some changes that they did not expressly intend (emergent strategies). These emergent strategies result from 'actions taken one by one, which converged in time in some sort of consistency or pattern' (Mintzberg, 1994, p. 25). The 'realised' strategy combines (some) intended strategies and other, unintended, 'emergent' strategies. A flexible approach to strategy is one which recognises that 'the real word inevitably involves some thinking ahead of time as well as some adaptation en route' (p. 24).

The view of strategy as an emergent process applies equally well to IS projects. Many observe that they are not the result of a scientific, comprehensive or rational process, but an iterative, incremental process, characterised by restricted analysis and bargaining between the players involved. They take place in exactly the same volatile, uncertain environment as does the organisation as a whole. People with different interests and priorities try to shape both the ends and the means of projects. The Kwik-Fit case in Chapter 6 shows how the initial plan for a simple administrative system evolved into an IS that was very different, and very much more effective, than the original plan.

At the system development level, an incremental approach implies dividing development work into sub-tasks that IS staff can complete quickly and test with users. 'If you don't know what you are doing, keep it small' summarises this approach. Developers who use this approach often use prototyping, whereby they offer the user a prototype, or working model, of the end-product. This will include how it interfaces with users – such as through the screen layout or paper reports. A related approach is known as Joint Application Development (JAD) – a method in which users and designers discuss requirements in workshops and use this information iteratively in designing and trialling successive systems. Figure 9.6 shows the prototyping technique of systems development.

Developing a working system as soon as possible allows users to gain experience thereby enabling them to make informed comments about the system and how it fits into their work. Developers can take account of these comments as they adapt the system. Working this way demands a very close and natural degree of cooperation between users and designers, resulting in an incrementally designed system. It reflects the idea that IS projects need to be able to evolve to meet changing needs and circumstances, rather than follow a pre-determined plan.

■ Participative models

Those viewing projects from this perspective emphasise the benefits of establishing a sense of ownership of the change among those whose support will be needed, or who will have to live with the change when it is implemented. Typically this includes involving those affected in the design of solutions; consulting widely about possible

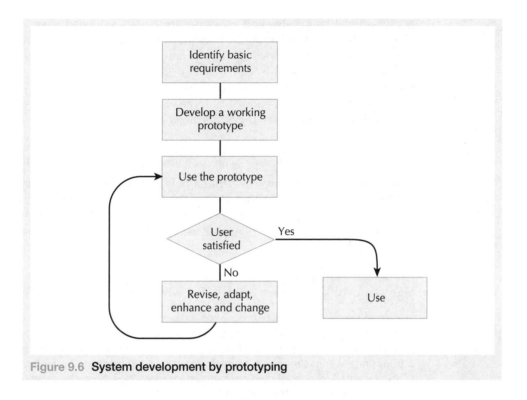

Figure 9.6 **System development by prototyping**

options; ensuring that information is widely communicated; providing training and support; and ensuring that conflicts or disagreements are openly and skilfully dealt with. Participative ideas have become an established aspect of the management literature and few openly argue that it is not an effective way of implementing organisational change. People expect such an approach to overcome resistance and to win commitment to new ideas. The underlying and wholly reasonable assumption is that if people can say 'I helped to build this,' they will be more willing to live and work with it, whatever it is.

In the IS field, Enid Mumford developed the ETHICS system design methodology (Mumford and Weir, 1979). This includes involving users in system development, recognising the social issues in implementation and using socio-technical principles to redesign work. More recently, Clegg (1996) developed five tools that those involved in system development could use to give explicit consideration to human issues. The tools support:

- organisational scenarios: to identify and evaluate the choices facing an organisation;
- task analysis: to record information about the tasks undertaken in a work system;
- task allocation: to help allocate tasks between people and technology;
- job design: to help design jobs that meet organisational and individual needs;
- usability: to evaluate the usability of a planned or actual computer system.

However, people rarely use participative methods in a formal way, or they do so at a relatively late stage in the system development cycle. 'The focus of interest and expertise [of system developers] is predominantly technical; psychological and organisational knowledge and expertise are largely excluded from these processes' (Clegg, 1996, p. 485). For all the potential advantages, there will sometimes be valid arguments for not encouraging users to participate in development – such as lack of user knowledge, widely dispersed users or lack of time. There may also be political reasons either when there is already full agreement on how to proceed, where management is powerful enough to force changes through, or where there is fundamental disagreement which the opportunity to participate would not in itself resolve.

■ Political models

Those who see change projects from a political perspective (such as Markus, 1983; Pfeffer, 1992; Knights and Murray, 1994) start from the assumption that IS projects inevitably affect people with different interests. They will pull in different directions, and pursue personal and local as well as organisational goals – as the example in the box shows.

MIS in Practice   Eastern Electronics

In 1998 the company had 150 staff who design, manufacture and sell various kinds of electronic equipment. It is part of the Asia Industrial Group (AIG), a major holding company in the subcontinent. AIG had had increasing problems in gathering financial data from units within the group as each company had adopted its own methods. Head office wanted to control the financial system more closely so that it would reduce their workload and give more insight into group performance. They decided to introduce a computer-aided production management (CAPM) system.

Head office decided to establish CAPM systems without consulting the group companies, which resulted in little response from them. The implementation ran into these problems:

1. CAPM is an integrated system that cannot simply replace the existing manual system. Other organisational changes are needed. These include changes in the way Eastern staff handle and process information and how departments cooperate.

2. Eastern felt no ownership of the system because the investment and selection decision had been imposed by AIG.

3. Eastern managers often argued that their company was not big enough for such a sophisticated system.

4. Eastern had an organic management structure, with little definition of responsibilities, unclear tasks and a belief that change occurs at its own pace.

However, a manager in the company noted that departments within Eastern were divided in their view of CAPM. The purchasing department disagreed strongly with the system. The purchasing manager had created the current manual system and believed that CAPM was created for group needs, rather than to benefit the companies. The engineering department did not at first see the value of the system. But when they saw some of the functions it could provide, they rapidly became supporters of the change. The production department was strongly in favour. Both the director and manager had previously worked in a computerised environment and could see the advantages. After two years of work the system was still not implemented, though considerable work had been done.

Source: Personal communication from a manager in the company.

In the same vein, Pfeffer (1992) argues that power is essential to get things done. Decisions in themselves change nothing – it is only when they are implemented that anyone notices a difference. He proposes that change, including IS projects, requires more than an ability to solve technical problems. An IS system frequently threatens the status quo and people who benefit from the present arrangements are likely to resist it. Innovation depends on those behind a change developing political will and expertise – to ensure it is on the agenda, and that senior managers support and resource the change. Promoters need to build and use their power.

From a political perspective, two approaches are necessary to implement large-scale IS changes. Those promoting the change have to produce a 'public, front-stage performance' of logical and rationally planned change linked to widespread and convincing participative mechanisms. Senior management and expert staff have to be convinced that the change is technically rational, logical and also congruent with the strategic direction of the organisation. Established project management techniques are widely recognised tools for managing IS projects. They also sustain the image of the project manager by reassuring senior management that the right things are being done in their name.

Project managers also have to pursue 'back-stage activity'. They have to exercise power skills: influencing, negotiating, selling, searching out and neutralising resistance. A classic article by Peter Keen (1981) highlighted how stakeholders who oppose a project can try to put it off course. Since overt resistance to change is risky, those

---

MIS in Practice   Peter Keen on the tactics of counter-implementation

- **Divert resources.** Split the budget across other projects; have key staff given other priorities and allocate them to other assignments; arrange for equipment to be moved or shared.

- **Exploit inertia.** Suggest that everyone wait until a key player has taken action, or read the report, or made an appropriate response; suggest that the results from some other project should be monitored and assessed first.

- **Keep goals vague and complex.** It is harder to initiate appropriate action in pursuit of aims that are multi-dimensional and specified in generalised, grandiose or abstract terms.

- **Encourage and exploit lack of organisational awareness.** Insist that 'we can deal with the people issues later', knowing that these will delay or kill the project.

- **'Great idea – let's do it properly'.** And let's bring in representatives from this function and that section, until we have so many different views and conflicting interests that it will take for ever to sort them out.

- **Dissipate energies.** Have people conduct surveys, collect data, prepare analyses, write reports, make overseas trips, hold special meetings . . .

- **Reduce the champion's influence and credibility.** Spread damaging rumours, particularly among the champion's friends and supporters.

- **Keep a low profile.** It is not effective openly to declare resistance to change because that gives those driving change a clear target to aim for.

These inertial forces may make the implementation of the structural and organisational issues identified earlier that much more difficult to implement.

Source: Based on Keen (1981).

wanting to block a change may use covert tactics – even while appearing to support the change. The box summarises these 'tactics of counter-implementation'.

Keen recommends a 'counter-counter-implementation' strategy that establishes who can damage the project, co-opts likely opposition early on, provides clear incentives and benefits from the new system, and tries to create a 'bandwagon' effect. This is a 'back-stage' political strategy and depends heavily on the presence of a 'fixer' with prestige, visibility and legitimacy.

These four views (life cycle, emergent, participative and political) are not necessarily competing with each other. They are complementary in the sense that a large IS project is likely to require elements of each. Each perspective can be linked to a series of management practices, which can help or hinder the implementation of change.

Summary

- We have identified four complementary perspectives on IS projects, each of which can be useful within a project.
- Each has different implications for managing the project, and requires the project manager to exercise a different set of skills.
- These skills include the ability to decide when each perspective is appropriate.

9.5 Identifying a project's stakeholders

Stakeholders are the people and groups with an interest in the project, and who can affect the outcome. They may be active promoters or supporters of the change, keen to have it succeed. They may be affected by it, though some will not be aware of it. Stakeholders have an interest in the substance and results of change, and in how the change is managed. They can make a difference to the situation, and project managers need to gain and keep their support. Stakeholders can be within the organisation – functional or departmental groups, users, the IS department and so on. External stakeholders will also have an influence – customers, suppliers, hardware and software vendors or consultants – as discussed by Howard et al. (2003).

The difficulties arise because stakeholders are likely to have different interests and will interpret an IS project from its likely effects on those interests. Their power to influence the direction of the project will also vary. Strong stakeholders need more attention than weak ones, so thinking of this allows them to decide where it is most useful to concentrate effort. Understanding stakeholders also helps the project manager to discover possible allies whose help may be useful during the project. Important tasks for the project manager therefore include:

- identify stakeholders, pressure groups, interested parties;
- assess their commitment;
- assess their power to help and hinder the change;
- assess their interests, what they will think and do about the change;
- manage relations with them – to gain their support, or contain opposition.

Activity 9.2 sets out a method for analysing stakeholders in a project.

Activity 9.2 Analysing stakeholders

Identify stakeholders

Write the name of the project in a circle at the centre of a sheet of paper. Draw other circles around the sheet, each identifying an individual or group with a stake in the project. Place the most significant nearer the centre; others around the edge.

Assess their commitment

Use a scale such as that shown in Figure 9.7, to assess the 'present' (X) and 'hoped for' (Y) level of commitment of each stakeholder to the project 'present'.

Key stakeholder	Vigorous opposition	Some opposition	Indifferent towards it	Will let it happen	Will help it happen	Will make it happen
Freight Nextday				X		Y
Freight IT				X	Y	
Freight Group board			X		Y	
Vendor				X		Y
Customers		X	X		Y	

Figure 9.7 Stakeholder commitment at Freight

Assess their power

Rate each stakeholder on whether their power to affect the project is high or low.

Assess their interests

Use a grid like that shown in Figure 9.8 to note your answers to these questions for the main (powerful) stakeholders:

Stakeholder	Their goals	Current relationship	What is expected of them?	Positive or negative to them?	Likely reaction?	Ideas for action

Figure 9.8 Grid for summarising stakeholder interests and reactions

- *What are their priorities, goals, interests?*
- *What is the general tone of our present relationship with them?*
- *What specific behaviour is expected of them, in relation to this project?*
- *Are they likely to see this as positive or negative for them?*
- *What is their likely action to defend their interests?*
- *What actions can we consider to influence them?*

Source: Based on Boddy (2002).

Freight Connect: Assessing stakeholder commitment

Freight Nextday were clearly the project owners. However, poor project management had resulted in a lack of control and direction being maintained – hence the slip into a very relaxed 'will let it happen' mode by the key stakeholders instead of a proactive 'will make it happen' approach. Other business priorities had encroached on the other divisions and, because they were not pressured by the key stakeholder, the project slipped in priority and focus.

Very little communication was provided to customers about the new product, nor was the additional future benefit, that the product can be used for all dealings with the Freight Group, explained. Customers were therefore unclear about the benefits to them, and were reluctant to release staff for training (even though this, and the product, would be provided free of charge). The software vendors too had not been convinced of the value of the project, and took an indifferent approach to it.

Source: Commentary by a Freight manager.

Considering the project from the stakeholders' point of view is likely to identify some practical steps the project manager can take to influence the stakeholders to increase their support. This can include identifying what benefits can be offered to the stakeholders and how best those benefits can be sold to them.

Summary

- Conducting a stakeholder analysis is a simple but effective way of identifying targets upon which it will be best to focus effort.
- It enables project managers, and their teams, to look at the project from the stakeholders' point of view.
- This awareness is likely to be an essential first step in influencing stakeholders towards a supportive position.

9.6 Influencing stakeholders

Having identified the most important stakeholders in a project, those driving it will seek to influence them to act in ways that support the project. They may want them to work in new ways, change where they work or change what information they receive. Project managers need to consider which perspectives on project management best match the circumstances, and then use an appropriate range of influencing tactics. The role of the change agent in major projects is inherently manipulative and political. While the 'front-stage' activities of technical and strategic logic and user-participation strategies provide credibility, the 'back-stage' activity is key to success or failure. If back-stage techniques are to be successfully employed it is important that the change agent has access to the back-stage politics of the organisation. A change agent who has little insight into internal power politics will be unable to operate this type of strategy successfully.

Table 9.3 **Content and process skills for managing IS projects**

Approach to project	Situation in which most likely to be appropriate	Influencing tactics
Life cycle	Uncontroversial projects with limited scope in stable conditions	Setting objectives; allocating tasks; setting milestones; monitoring progress and exercising control
Emergent	Projects where conditions are changing rapidly and there is high uncertainty about the future of the business	Observing changing conditions and being able to adapt; identifying changing user needs and interests; adapting projects to meet changing circumstances
Participative	Where users are knowledgeable about the project, do not feel threatened by it and have ideas to contribute	Identifying stakeholders, their interests, commitment and power; exchanging ideas, encouraging contributions; presentation and communication; consulting and negotiating; resolving differences and reaching agreement
Political	Where the project threatens established interests of players who have the power to defend their position	Identifying stakeholders, their interests, commitment and power; building coalitions; manipulating information; identifying and blocking opposition; negotiating

Combining suitable models

Table 9.3 summarises the conditions in which the four approaches to managing an IS project are likely to be suitable, and the tactics a project manager may use to influence key stakeholders. It is important that those driving the project are able to assess the situation reasonably accurately and choose the right combination of tactics.

Tactics for influencing others – interpersonal methods

Yukl and Falbe (1990) identified the influencing tactics which managers used in dealing with subordinates, bosses and co-workers, shown in Table 9.4.

The nine tactics cover a variety of behaviours that managers use as they try to influence others – whether subordinates, bosses or colleagues. Yukl and Tracey (1992) extended the work by examining which tactics managers used most frequently with different target groups. They concluded that managers were most likely to use:

- rational persuasion when trying to influence their boss;
- inspirational appeal and pressure when trying to influence subordinates; and
- exchange, personal appeal and legitimating tactics when influencing colleagues.

We can relate these tactics to the earlier discussion of project characteristics. Rational persuasion would clearly be consistent with the life cycle approach, while those of exchange, coalition, legitimacy and pressure would support a political approach. Ingratiation, personal appeal, exchange and consultation would usually be suitable tactics to use in situations where a participative approach was appropriate. In the uncertain conditions of emergent projects, a combination of all tactics may be appropriate, depending on the issues and time available.

Table 9.4 **Influence tactics and definitions**

Tactic	Definition
Rational persuasion	The person uses logical arguments and factual evidence to persuade you that a proposal or request is viable and likely to result in the attainment of task objectives.
Inspirational appeal	The person makes a request or proposal that arouses enthusiasm by appealing to your values, ideals and aspirations or by increasing your confidence that you can do it.
Consultation	The person seeks your participation in planning a strategy, activity or change for which your support and assistance are desired, or the person is willing to modify a proposal to deal with your concerns and suggestions.
Ingratiation	The person seeks to get you in a good mood or to think favourably of him or her before asking you to do something.
Exchange	The person offers an exchange of favours, indicates a willingness to reciprocate at a later time or promises you a share of the benefits if you help accomplish the task.
Personal appeal	The person appeals to your feelings of loyalty and friendship towards him or her before asking you to do something.
Coalition	The person seeks the aid of others to persuade you to do something, or uses the support of others as a reason for you to agree also.
Legitimating	The person seeks to establish the legitimacy of a request by claiming the authority or right to make it or by verifying that it is consistent with organisational policies, rules, practices or traditions.
Pressure	The person uses demands, threats or persistent reminders to influence you to do what he or she wants.

Source: Yukl and Tracey (1992), Table 1.

Tactics for influencing others – formal structures

IS projects can be implemented either by people acting on their own initiative or by people acting through institutions. There are limitations to what people acting on their own to solve a problem or improve a process can achieve. These can to some extent be overcome by supporting individual action with appropriate structures and mechanisms. There are advantages and disadvantages in both. Without some human agency, without someone putting personal effort into the problem, nothing will change. People acting on their own to solve a problem or improve a process can produce the quick results so often needed. It is a sign of commitment and enthusiasm and can be highly rewarding – helping to ensure that creative and energetic people stay with the business. The possible disadvantages are that wider considerations may be ignored and that the system may be over-dependent on individuals, making it less robust.

Individual effort can be supported by institutions. The value of creating appropriate structures through which to manage major organisational change has received strong statistical support (Boddy and Macbeth, 2000). Those promoting change use such institutions to raise their concerns and ensure that issues are debated. The lack of a legitimising forum for discussion impedes change. Institutions of various forms (teams, boards, rules, procedures) have the advantage that they allow a wider range of views to be brought together, balance a range of considerations and ensure continuity. Whatever is agreed outlasts any of the individuals involved in creating it and can be more easily transmitted to many places and people. Learning is captured and widely available.

McDonagh (2003) identifies a broader advantage in such institutions. Observing that projects are frequently managed with a technical rather organisational focus, he concludes that a major reason for this is the relative isolation of the executive, IS and organisational development communities.

> *Executive management view the introduction of IT as an economic imperative while IT specialists view it as a technical imperative. The coalescent nature of these two imperatives is such that human and organisational considerations are regularly marginalised and ignored [during IS projects].* (pp. 14–15)

Senior management wishing to take into account the contribution of all three perspectives can only do so if they create institutions in which each is adequately represented.

The possible disadvantages are that institutions take time to develop, may have the wrong people in membership and may not be sufficiently flexible to cope with varying local circumstances. They may slow the process, blunt initiative and demotivate creative and energetic staff. One widely used structure is the project team, discussed in the next section. Some further aspects of structure, particularly relevant in a multi-project environment, are discussed in Chapter 10.

Project teams

The membership and leadership of project teams have a crucial effect on the range of issues that are placed on the agenda, and hence on the quality of the outcomes achieved. Teams bring many advantages if they are well managed, including:

- **Providing a structure** to deal with complex problems. They provide a mechanism or a forum in which issues or problems can be raised, put on the table and dealt with – rather than being left unattended.

- **Increasing the perspectives** available. While an individual may find a solution on their own, no one can be familiar with all sides of an issue. So, by bringing in more people, ideas can be tried on other members and encouraged or discarded in the light of their reactions and other sources of knowledge.

- **Encouraging acceptance and understanding** of the problem and the solution proposed. If those closely affected by a decision have been able to express their views they are more likely to accept the result than if it were imposed. They will know more of the constraints and limitations, and probably be more committed to implementing the result. Taking part in a group effort usually builds a sense of ownership in overcoming difficulties and achieving a result.

- **Promoting learning**. As people work together to solve problems, they not only deal with the present task, but may also reflect on what they can learn from the experience, and perhaps see how they could do the job differently next time. People often use tacit, taken-for-granted knowledge to reach solutions; working in a team is more likely to lead to those assumptions being challenged and tested against reality, rather than continuing to be applied in an established way.

Project teams also have disadvantages, and are a source of failure if they are not managed well. Members have varied technical skills, and those less familiar with the technical aspects, perhaps because they come from a user department, will usually be reluctant to air their questions in the public forum. Most members have other jobs to do, because in most cases they will only be part-time members of the project team. Members will also have political and possibly personal agendas, being there as representatives of a department or function rather than as individuals. These problems do not negate the argument for teams where these will add value, they merely put the point that teams need to be managed (see Boddy, 2002, for a fuller discussion of teams).

CASE QUESTIONS 9.2

What does the stakeholder analysis above imply for the project manager?

Does it suggest anything about the composition and management of the project team?

In terms of Table 9.1, has Freight management shown a traditional or a 'new wave' mindset?

Summary

- A fundamental skill for managing an IS project is to be aware of the four models of change, and the conditions in which each can be used.

- A range of interpersonal approaches to influencing others in a project has been identified.

- Interpersonal tactics can be supported by formal structures, such as documentation, teams and steering groups.

Conclusions

In this chapter we have introduced ideas about implementing information systems. As is clear from the argument throughout the book, this is more than a matter of technology planning. It requires the ability to manage a range of often unpredictable interactions between the factors set out in Figure 9.1 – the context in which the IS project takes place. Managers need to be aware of the strategic implications of what they are undertaking, and how these will interact with issues of structure, culture and human motivation – as reflected in 'new wave' mindsets suggested by Sauer and Yetton. They also need to be aware that the links are interactive. People are not passive recipients of change elsewhere – they can shape it through their interaction with the contextual factors we have outlined.

We have therefore introduced some tools and techniques to help project managers analyse the situation in which they are working. They help them to understand the driving and restraining forces working on an information systems project, and the range of stakeholders involved. Another major theme has been the theoretical perspective on change. Information systems projects often seem well suited to rational, life cycle approaches to change. In some respects they are – but the emergent, participative and political perspectives are likely to be equally relevant.

Project managers can use the techniques we have suggested as individuals, but other research we have done suggests they often require the support of more formal structures. Some ways of providing such structures are outlined in Chapter 10.

CHAPTER QUESTIONS

1. Review Table 9.1 ('traditional' and 'new wave' mindsets towards IS projects). Which of the elements listed under each heading are supported by the ideas and evidence presented in this book?
2. Use Table 9.2 to analyse where the Freight project was most likely to experience difficulty.
3. Summarise the four perspectives on project management (about two lines each). How would a project manager be able to assess which approach was likely to be most help in dealing with issues during a project?
4. How relevant are Keen's views likely to be in major IS projects? Justify your views by reference to examples or experience.
5. What do you believe is likely to be the greatest problem in making a project team work effectively?

Further reading

Brooks, F.P. (1995) *The Mythical Man-Month*, Addison-Wesley, Reading, Mass. A very readable collection of essays by a distinguished member of the IS community. Draws on vast experience to provide thought-provoking insights for anyone involved with IS projects.

Buchanan, D. and Badham, R. (1999) *Power, Politics and Organisational Change*, Sage, London. A detailed and empirically based analysis of the politics of change which implies that project managers who lack political skill will fail.

Collins, T. (1997), *Crash: Learning from the World's Worst Computer Disasters*, Simon and Schuster, London. Draws on the experience of many high-profile cases to identify some common factors and the warning signs that project managers should look out for.

Drummond, H. (1996) *Escalation in Decision-making: The Tragedy of Taurus*, Oxford University Press, Oxford. An absorbing account of a high-profile project failure at the London Stock Exchange.

References

Bensaou, M. and Earl, M. (1998) 'The right mind set for managing information technology', *Harvard Business Review*, **76**(5), 119–28.

Boddy, D. (2002) *Managing Projects: Building and Leading the Team*, Financial Times/Prentice Hall, Harlow.

Boddy, D. and Gunson, N. (1996) *Organisations in the Network Age*, Routledge, London.

Boddy, D. and Macbeth, D.K. (2000) 'Prescriptions for managing change: a survey of their effects in projects to implement collaborative working between organisations', *International Journal of Project Management*, **18**(5), 297–306.

Brooks, F.P. (1995) *The Mythical Man-Month*, Addison-Wesley, Reading, Mass.

Clegg, C.W. (1996) 'Tools to incorporate some psychological and organizational issues during the development of computer-based systems', *Ergonomics*, **39**(3), 482–511.

Currie, W. (1997) 'Computerising the Stock Exchange: a comparison of two information systems', *New Technology, Work and Employment*, **12**(2), 75–83.

Doherty, N.F., King, M. and Al-Mushayt, O. (2003) 'The impact of inadequacies in the treatment of organisational issues on information systems development projects', *Information and Management*, **41**, 49–62.

Drummond, H. (1996) *Escalation in Decision-making: The Tragedy of Taurus*, Oxford University Press, Oxford.

Howard, M., Vidgen, R. and Powell, P. (2003) 'Overcoming stakeholder barriers in the automotive industry: building to order with extra-organisational systems', *Journal of Information Technology*, **18**, 27–43.

Keen, P. (1981) 'Information systems and organization change', in E. Rhodes and D. Weild (eds), *Implementing New Technologies*, Blackwell/Open University Press, Oxford.

Knights, D. and Murray, F. (1994) *Managers Divided: Organisation Politics and Information Technology Management*, Wiley, Chichester.

McDonagh, J. (2003) 'Not for the faint hearted: social and organizational challenges in IT-enabled change', *Organization Development Journal*, **19**(1), 11–19.

Markus, M.L. (1983) 'Power, politics and MIS implementation', *Communications of the ACM*, **26**(6), 430–44.

Markus, M.L. and Benjamin, R.I. (1997) 'The magic bullet theory in IT-enabled transformation', *MIT Sloan Management Review*, **38**(2), 55–68.

Mintzberg, H. (1994) *The Rise and Fall of Strategic Planning*, Prentice Hall International, Hemel Hempstead.

Mumford, E. and Weir, M. (1979) *Computer Systems in Work Design: The Ethics Method*, Associated Business Press, London.

Pfeffer, J. (1992) *Managing with Power*, Harvard Business School Press, Boston.

Sauer, C. and Yetton, P.W. (1997) *Steps to the Future: Fresh Thinking on the Management of IT-based Organizational Transformation*, Jossey-Bass, San Francisco.

Yukl, G. and Falbe, C.M. (1990) 'Influence tactics in upward, downward and lateral influence attempts', *Journal of Applied Psychology*, **75**(2), 132–40.

Yukl, G. and Tracey, J.B. (1992) 'Consequences of influence tactics used with subordinates, peers and the boss', *Journal of Applied Psychology*, **77**(4), 525–35.

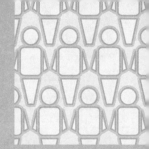

CHAPTER 10

Managing a programme of projects

Learning objectives

By the end of your work on this topic you should be able to:

- Describe how the management of programmes differs from that of projects

- Explain how programmes enable sets of related projects to retain overall strategic alignment through a common, shared approach

- Describe the tools of the programme manager, and the practical constraints in their use

- Define an appropriate organisation structure for the management of a programme

- Explain the importance of management information to the long-term success of a programme

- Describe why Quick Wins are important to the long-term success of a programme

- List the key aspects of a successful programme environment

NatWest Bank and The Royal Bank of Scotland

On 6 March 2000, The Royal Bank of Scotland Group (RBS) formally acquired the National Westminster Bank (NatWest) after a six-month period of intense market bidding between the two banks and a second potential acquirer – the Bank of Scotland (BoS) (now the Halifax Bank of Scotland plc). To win the bidding process, RBS had to demonstrate its ability to extract major cost savings from the combined operations and to drive greater income from the combination of brands, customers, products and skills. The RBS bid promised to deliver a 'new force in banking' with the scale and strength to exploit new opportunities in the UK, Europe and the USA.

Many industry analysts doubted the ability of RBS to deliver on its bid promises:

- 'Most banks have simply not anticipated the difficulties in integration and streamlining IT systems.' (Deloitte Touche Tohmatsu, December 1999)

- 'We believe execution risk is significant given the hostile nature of the deal and the high level of cost savings.' (Morgan Stanley Dean Witter, February 2000)

RBS was therefore under extreme pressure to complete the integration process on time and to meet the cost savings and income benefits quoted during the bid.

The integration programme was quickly established following the takeover, dividing the task into 154 integration initiatives to be completed in three years. These were expected to yield £1.1 billion in annual cost savings and reduce staff by 18,000. Programme Management teams were established in each of the delivering business and technology areas, and control and reporting procedures were put into place. The key elements of the integration strategy were agreed and communicated across the Group and to external stakeholders:

- To use RBS information systems as the single platform for operations across the merged bank;

- To migrate customer-facing systems such as credit cards, ATMs and Internet screens to RBS systems early;

- To transfer the NatWest customer and accounting data to the RBS systems in a single weekend.

Within 90 days of the acquisition, real progress was being made. The NatWest Group head office had been closed and vacated, and 400 staff were deployed on integration project work. Control procedures had been established. A monthly reporting process had commenced to report on achievement of actual costs and benefits against budget, summarising the progress made so far and the main achievements and difficulties being encountered.

The integration programme was under way.

Introduction

Information systems projects do not happen in isolation. They are often one of many projects taking place to support a larger initiative. This collective set of projects makes up a programme. Many of the projects will depend on each other, and at times will compete for scarce resources or senior management support. While the organisation needs to manage the individual projects well, that is not enough. The links between them mean they cannot work in isolation. They affect each other, and senior managers must ensure that they work together towards the aims of the overall programme.

Moreover, a project to develop and implement an information system will have an effect throughout the organisation. There are likely to be structural changes,

changes to business processes, new work patterns and perhaps new electronic links to other organisations. This is illustrated in the Chapter Case on the integration of the NatWest Bank with The Royal Bank of Scotland where the integration of the main IT systems required the alignment of the operational procedures, staff roles and the outsourcing of a major activity to a third party supplier.

To make the integration of NatWest with The Royal Bank of Scotland happen required many coherently linked projects. This chapter extends our analysis from the individual projects considered in Chapter 9 to the wider programme management structure. It reviews the tools, techniques and considerations managers can use in a connected set of projects.

The chapter begins by outlining the pieces in the programme management toolkit, and then describes a typical programme management structure. The following section shows how effective programmes manage information to help control rapidly changing situations. Concluding sections show the benefits of Quick Wins and an energised environment. The aim is to identify the management tasks involved in leading a group of projects – a programme.

10.1 The programme management toolkit

The essence of programme management is to take a high-level view of the planned changes. It sees them in the wider context – what has stimulated the change, and where the change will be implemented. It aims to monitor and control the big picture.

The project manager is concerned with the detail of individual activities and tasks – who will do what by when. The programme manager aims to understand the high-level timetable and deliverables of that project, and how they fit with other projects. He or she also relates these to the wider strategy – such as the launch of a new product or entry to a new line of business. The programme manager focuses on the interdependencies between and around the individual projects. This role can also include responsibility for 'de-escalation' (Keil and Robey, 1999) to prevent failing projects taking ever more resources.

Project plans define and display every task and activity, but a programme manager would soon become swamped with such detail. Thus the standard project management tools, such as Gantt charts, are of little use when managing several projects at once. Each has its interdependencies, resource requirements, deadlines, milestones, issues and delivery phases. The office wall is simply not big enough. Programme management needs a new toolkit. It needs to be able to deal with a large amount of rapidly changing information and to track progress in the projects. The toolkit takes data from project managers and distils it to show the overall situation. Tools include the overview chart, reporting systems and an issues management system.

The programme overview chart

The programme manager needs to maintain a quick-to-understand snapshot of the programme. This should show progress to date, the main events being planned, interdependencies, issues and expected completion dates. This also helps the programme manager to communicate with senior management and project managers.

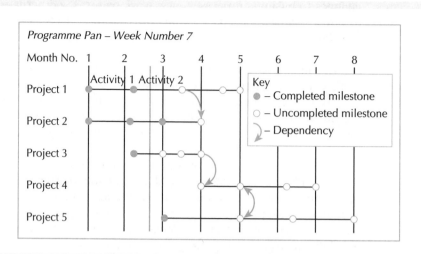

Programme Pan – Week Number 7

Figure 10.1 **The programme overview chart**

One way to do this is to create a single chart with a simplified view of each project on an indicative timeline. Figure 10.1 illustrates this.

Details vary but the main features are usually:

- an indicative timeline, along which the individual projects are plotted;
- a simplified representation of the major milestones in each project, or change area;
- descriptions of actual progress against expected progress for each project;
- indications of interdependencies between projects.

Weekly project reports and the composite plan report

Senior managers will also expect the programme manager to provide a written report on progress. This will be at a high level, but will draw information from the

---

MIS in Practice   **Web-based reporting at a semi-conductor company**

A multinational firm in the electronics industry reorganised its worldwide facilities during 1999 and 2000. This involved rearranging capacity between the sites and implementing various information systems to support manufacturing. The IS department designed a web-based reporting system, in which each sub-project manager completed a standard report showing progress against actions. The site also contained standard programme documents that would previously have been paper files.

The information entered by each project manager was visible to everyone with access to the site (most staff). In addition, the programme manager called a weekly meeting of all project managers. Each brought up their report on a large screen in the conference room and talked the programme manager through the report, together with any issues on which they needed support.

The system worked so well that it has now been adopted as standard programme management practice throughout the company.

Source: Personal communication from a project manager.

projects. A common method is to establish a weekly reporting mechanism whereby project managers feed details on their progress into the overall report. This used to be a paper exercise, but is now likely to use shared files on a computer network or an intranet site.

Figure 10.2 shows an example weekly project progress report that would feed into the composite progress report, shown in Figure 10.3.

The composite progress report can then provide the programme owners (the budget holders and executive decision-makers) with a quick and accurate update on the overall programme situation.

The issues and risks management system

In reviewing progress with project managers, the programme manager will inevitably meet problems that he or she cannot resolve with current resources. This will often involve scarce staff being required by two or more projects at the same time. They usually require a senior-level decision on the relative priority of two conflicting tasks, or to agree to move a deadline. People refer to problems that have arisen as 'issues'. Risks are 'issues' that may occur in the future if someone does not take the necessary actions in time.

A key task for the programme manager is to record, report and resolve issues and risks in a reasonable time. Figure 10.4 shows a form for documenting this. It includes:

- a unique reference number for each issue or risk;
- a brief description of the issue or risk;
- the name of the person raising the issue or risk – the owner;
- suggested resolution, or actions undertaken;
- the name of the person assigned to resolve the issue or address the risk;
- comments on progress made.

The issues and risks management system, which can vary in complexity from a simple paper-based system to a fully networked web-based computer system, encourages the entire programme management team to be open and rapid in handling issues. It can also be a vital support for project teams and their project managers. They can be confident that issues put into the system will be visible to the steering group or similar body.

The programme office

The programme manager's job involves a great deal of information handling and processing. Information on the status of the projects is continually flowing to the programme manager, who must be able to distil this into a meaningful picture. They require adequate space and facilities to handle this cascade of information effectively. A separate programme office is a good way to achieve this. This will be a visible area central to the project teams where the programme manager can receive information, update status displays and prepare reports for senior management on the current situation.

Programme Office
Weekly Progress Report

Project: System Development Phase 2 – Functionality Enhancements
Project Manager: Allana Carruthers
Week Ending: – 7 April 2004
Project Status (Red / Amber / Green): AMBER

Reasons for Amber/Red: Difficulties with retaining key staff are impacting on deadlines.
Recruitment programme commenced with HR and new team members expected to be available by mid-May. Meantime, overtime being offered to minimise slippage.

Activities This Week:
- On-going discussions with respective parties (auditors, SE, bankers, management) to firm up on the exact forms of reporting
- Meeting to analyse accounting policy differences and consider approach to address them
- External/internal recruitment under way
- Commenced detailed analysis of acquisition implications
- Initial legal issues meeting held

Activities Planned for Next Week:
- Progress completion coding and test scripting
- Conclude external reporting formats
- Legal meeting and identification of issues and approaches
- Analysis of detailed accounting implications

Forthcoming Milestones	Completion Date:		
	Baseline	**Estimated**	**Actual**
Preliminary coding modules completed	4 April	7 April	7 April
Summary report formats completed	15 April latest		
Legal issues, including decision on deal making processes defined	15 April		7 April
Decide on processes for maintenance of account figures	20 April	25 April	
Completion reports defined	30 April		
Completion reports coded	5 May		
Test scripts agreed	15 May		

Issues / Actions Required
1. Fast-track internal recruitment processes to allow earliest possible start dates.
   Project Director to discuss with HR Director.
2. The uncertainty of external reporting requirements impacts a number of areas.
   Conclude discussions as fast as possible.

Figure 10.2 Example of a weekly project progress report

Programme Office
Composite Progress Report

Week Ending: – 7 April 2004
Programme Status (Red / Amber / Green): Green

Summary:
Product tables for database delayed six weeks due to marketing replanning.
Communications plan rescheduled. Systems Development Phase 2 at Amber due
to resourcing problems, but no major impact expected.

Major Activities Carried Out This Week

- Consolidated March results produced and completed monthly report.
- Risks Workshop held, and Risk Log distributed for comment.
- Most Union submissions are now complete.
- Finance re-forecasts completed.
- High-level plan for property agreed.

Major Activities Planned for Next Week

- Issue Board papers for May.
- Complete population of database with YTD May information, actual and budget.
- Input to systems work on tactical solutions – consolidation.
- Union consultations.
- Follow-up Risk Log to confirm gaps and establish action plans to close gaps.

Missed / Slipped Milestones Reported This Week

	Completion Date:		
	Baseline	Estimated	Actual
Database Build			
Create entities on system for customer data and populate YTD April actuals.	1 April		6 April
Create integrated product tables	20 March	30 April	
System Development Phase 2			
Preliminary coding modules completed	4 April	7 April	7 April
Decide on processes for maintenance of account figures.	20 April	25 April	

Issues / Actions Required
1. Fast-track internal recruitment processes to allow earliest possible start dates for
systems development team members.
Project Director to discuss with HR Director.
2. The uncertainty of external reporting requirements impacts a number of areas.
Conclude discussions as fast as possible.

Figure 10.3 **Example of a composite progress report**

Issue/ Risk No.	Date Raised	Raised By	Dept	Description	Priority	Action Required	Action Owner	Target Date	Progress/Comments
12	30-Apr-04	Fiona Cooper	Legal	Current reporting requirements are impacting on resource availability. Negotiations needed with Audit and Board on the form and extent of reporting to be incorporated.	Medium	Arrange Audit meeting to review requirements and prepare paper for Board presentation.	Fiona Cooper and Alan Duncan	30-May-04	Meeting with Audit arranged and discussion paper circulated in advance. Need to book Board presentation slot.
21	23-May-04	Raj Kapul	Systems Development	Accounting policies not yet confirmed. Confirmation required urgently to allow final coding.	High	Finance Department to provide policy documentation to project team.	Sally Forrest (Finance)	30-May-04	Note issued
22	23-May-04	Alistair Sanderson	Marketing	It is proving difficult to make decisions on how to manage copyright issues.	Medium	Agree with Legal how to fast-track decisions with Marketing	Alistair Sanderson	15-Jun-04	Some high-level decisions expected by 15/6, but issues likely to remain for short term.
23	25-May-04	Sheila Provan	Programme Office	Staff morale could be impacted by latest Board decision on programme life-expectation.	Low	Maintain watching brief on attrition rates and raise any specific problems through line management.	Dan McGulliver (HR)	4/7 (Review)	See update provided by DMcG 28/5

Figure 10.4 Example of an issues and risks log

▨ Summary

▨ Programmes contain a set of projects with a common aim.

▨ Programme managers need to understand how individual projects contribute to the overall programme.

▨ Programme management requires a separate set of tools to assist with control.

▨ Programme overview charts help to illustrate progress at a high level.

▨ Regular reporting forms, feeding into a composite form, help to coordinate information feeds from the individual projects to provide a consolidated view of progress.

▨ Issues and risks systems provide a controlled mechanism for raising and resolving problems.

▨ The programme office provides a single source for information and a focus for managing day-to-day issues.

Activity 10.1 Project and programme managers

Make two lists of the skills that you would look for in a project manager and a programme manager. Highlight the common skills and consider the ways in which the roles differ and are similar.

▨ *In what ways might conflicts arise between the roles?*

10.2 The programme management structure

To control a series of projects successfully the programme manager requires a supportive organisation structure. Figure 10.5 shows the typical components of this structure.

▨ Groups and roles

The programme steering group

This usually consists of 6–10 senior managers representing the main business and user interests affected by the programme. It meets regularly to receive reports on progress from the programme manager, and give guidance on outstanding issues.

The executive chairperson

This is usually a senior figure; their status signals that the project is being taken seriously. It is essential that the programme manager maintains their confidence and support – the chair will be receiving any bad news through their own networks.

Board of directors

The executive chairperson will report directly to the board. The board provides the direct link to the strategy and operations of the organisation. The quality of this link determines how well the programme contributes to broader strategy.

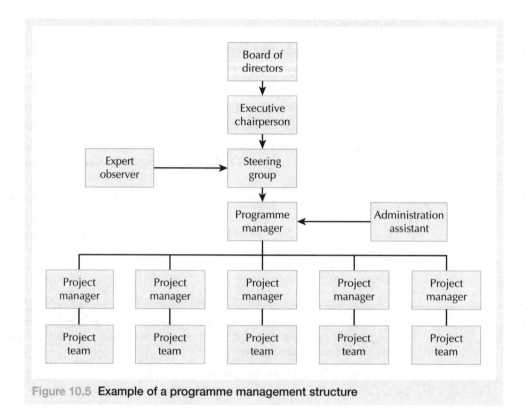

Figure 10.5 **Example of a programme management structure**

Expert observer

An informed outsider can give valuable impartial observations on difficult dilemmas facing a programme or project within it. They can help the group avoid believing its own publicity, and take a critical view of reported achievements. This is especially important when a programme is beginning to escalate and is seeking more resources than can be justified by progress. They can more easily advise termination than an insider. The best expert observers contribute only when asked for an opinion, or when the group has reached an impasse. They can then state the relative merit of each option to help the steering group take a more informed decision.

The programme administrator

Someone needs to keep the books – meticulously maintaining the minutes of meetings and background notes with clear and accurate filing. An experienced administrator to manage information in support of the programme manager is essential. They will prompt others for progress reports before meetings and handle all the usual support work.

▧ Management information

Programmes need the support of good information. The benefits of an effective management information system (MIS) include:

NatWest Bank and The Royal Bank of Scotland: Integration programme – some structural considerations

The early stages of the programme to integrate NatWest with RBS involved some challenging decisions about the organisation structure for the programme teams.

Centralised versus decentralised control

Once the initial programme strategy had been devised, the individual parts of the integration programme were allocated to local business areas to deliver. At this stage it would have been easy to devolve control and monitoring of the programme to the individual areas. Local areas understand their particular problems better and so can tailor their review processes to suit their local environment.

However, the importance of maintaining a central function to control and review progress across the whole organisation was demonstrated many times throughout the programme. Central control functions increase efficiency by developing a standard set of control procedures to be used by all areas. These simplify the process of compiling progress updates for the whole programme, and develop a common level of rigour to be applied by all areas. This ensures that progress updates and issues are communicated effectively to the senior executive and that appropriate levels of prioritisation are applied across the whole programme.

Business versus technology control

While much of the work of the integration programme was IT-related (i.e. the transfer of NatWest data to the RBS systems platform), it was critical for the business areas to have a strong say in what could be done when. It is the business areas that deliver the income, and their knowledge of customer requirements and operating principles must be taken into account when planning IS changes.

Programme steering groups therefore contained a mix of representatives from the impacted business areas and the appropriate Technology teams. Project plans were required to contain an appropriate selection of both Business and Technology activities and milestones. Key steps in the systems transfer process were assessed for impact on business areas prior to acceptance.

The aim was to achieve the integration without adversely impacting customers or even making them think that changes were happening. In a competitive market, it was realised that high levels of customer attrition could easily be triggered by clumsy integration activities. That customer satisfaction levels were retained at a high level throughout the integration programme was largely due to the fact that the large-scale IS changes were kept in the background of the business operations.

- more efficient use of staff and equipment;
- earlier recognition of problems;
- clearer communication of progress;
- improved learning from past activities;
- more justification for continued or increased resources;
- greater support from executives (from their increased confidence);
- more motivated staff.

The most useful management information will include nothing more complicated than:

- time expended by project staff;
- actual costs incurred against budgets;
- progress made against plans; and
- issues being encountered.

Trying to gather more sophisticated information than this will probably waste time and money. It can become a major distraction from project activities. Accuracy, presentation and timeliness are more important than detail in programme management.

Accuracy

The information will guide decisions and present a picture of the programme to outsiders. Incorrect information leads to mistakes and contradictions, with confusion or climb-downs in front of senior management.

Presentation

Senior people need to see the main points quickly so they can concentrate on the areas that most need their attention. Detail obscures the message. Good use of symbols, graphs and colours will help.

Timeliness

Information provided too frequently wastes time and alienates people; too infrequently and problems will go unnoticed for too long. Striking the right balance is a matter of judgement – frequently in a crisis or time of rapid change, infrequently in stable conditions.

> **MIS in Practice   Cross reference – reporting by exception**
>
> A useful analogy for presenting good programme management information is the dashboard of a car. This clearly and simply shows the driver the most important information about the car – speed, engine temperature, oil pressure, fuel. Major problems such as overheating are indicated immediately with red lights or warning sounds. The driver need only occasionally glance at the dashboard to obtain all of this information. So it should be for the 'drivers' of an IS programme.

Summary

- The programme management function should provide:
    - direct links to the rest of the organisation and its strategy;
    - sufficient seniority to the decisions being taken;
    - impartial and experienced advice;
    - regular reviews of progress with involved parties;
    - strong administrative support.
- It is critical to clearly define the structure of the programme management function to involve the appropriate business and IT areas to be represented.
- Management information takes time and quality staff to produce but, done well, will be hugely valuable to the success of the programme.
- The key to popular management information is to keep the presentation simple and attractive, rapidly drawing attention to those areas that most require it.
- It is important to match the frequency of information to the rate of change.

10.3 Quick Wins – the fuel for long-term development

Since programmes usually last for several years, they face the risk of project fatigue. This damages a programme in several different ways:

- staff and managers become demotivated;
- executive sponsors lose interest;
- end-users become resistant to the outcomes;
- the programme loses credibility, and becomes a target for criticism.

Project fatigue occurs when the enthusiasm of working on a programme wears off. The pressures of day-to-day problems and new issues take precedence over the long-term benefits. People have done the work but see no benefits. Their belief in the value of the project falls.

The risks of this happening reduce if the programme manager can produce short-term deliverables that have clear benefits. People respond to such 'Quick Wins', and the wise programme manager will build several into the overall programme plans. They can take many forms – for example a new process that will generate new income, cut costs or improve conditions for a visible unit. This has a number of benefits:

- staff gain a sense of achievement;
- management can claim a success for the programme;
- board members see a return on their investment;
- end-users gain an improvement to their working processes;
- customers get an improved service.

If they can build enough Quick Wins of real value into the programme, management can claim that the programme is self-funding. This sends a powerful message to the stakeholders about the overall value of the programme, and severely weakens objectors. One danger of Quick Wins is potential to distract staff from the longer-term issues of the programme. Programme management is balancing short-term and long-term objectives.

Summary

- Quick Wins – short-term, tangible deliverables – can be an excellent way to maintain support for a long-term programme.
- Care must be taken to ensure that Quick Wins do not distract project staff from the long-term aims of the programme.

Activity 10.2 Quick Wins

Imagine that you have just bought a dilapidated farmhouse as your new family home. Aware that your family will have to put up with many months of disruption while an extensive rebuilding programme takes place, you are keen to identify some Quick Wins to retain their support. List some of your ideas.

NatWest Bank and The Royal Bank of Scotland: Quick Wins in the integration process

The first six months of the integration programme focused on the most obvious duplications and overlaps between RBS and NatWest. The integration of the two banks had brought about some significant duplication of centralised processing centres dealing with the maintenance of customer accounts. These centres dealt with the setting-up and day-to-day management of accounts, payments processing, controlling of loans and mortgages, cheque and cash handling for both personal and business customers.

Combining work and driving process efficiencies enabled the closure of nine of these processing centres in the first six months of integration alone. This work contributed to a total figure of over one million square feet of property being vacated, almost all in back-office or administrative functions.

A further key area for generating integration benefits in the initial period was in the rationalisation of contracts with suppliers. The two banks had separate contract agreements with thousands of suppliers for everything from paperclips to computers, from cleaning services to hotel rooms. Integration provided the opportunity to renegotiate supplier contracts with a reduced number of suppliers for an enlarged, single organisation. In the first six months alone, almost 100 key supplier contracts were rationalised between the two banks leading to annual savings in excess of £35m.

The largest integration task of all was that of moving all NatWest data onto the RBS computer systems and shutting down the NatWest systems. This was an enormous programme in itself, involving the migration of 18 million customer accounts worth £158 billion and with huge daily transaction volumes. The preparation work would take over two years to complete, so the transfer itself could not take place until well into the year 2002. However, much important preparatory work was completed in the initial stages of the programme, including:

- acquisition of a major new building to house computer systems, and installation of additional computer capacity for the scaled-up IT operations;

- alignment of NatWest ATM screen flows with those of RBS;

- merging of year-end financial reporting onto a common platform.

The Quick Wins achieved in the first six months provided £230m of Run Rate Cost Savings and a reduction in headcount of 3,500 in the Manufacturing Division. These benefits were higher than had been anticipated at the start of the programme, and demonstrated tangibly to staff and market analysts that the integration programme was producing results.

10.4 Rollout planning and implementation control

All the work of designing, developing and testing an information system is lost if its introduction into the real environment is not carefully managed. The rollout is where reality strikes, and it is here that any hidden failures in the earlier stages appear. Rollout is where actual end-users operate the new system in a real working environment with real customers and real data for the first time. Users who were reluctant about the changes now have their opportunity. They can demonstrate how badly the new system works ('I told them at Head Office that this wouldn't work and now look – I've been proved right!'). It is one of the most stressful areas of programme management.

Management needs to roll out completed projects in an orderly, planned way. In practice this is difficult to do as it involves integrating many linked factors. In technical terms alone the following list of tasks is daunting:

- hardware purchase and installation;
- software installation;
- property surveys and modifications, including cabling, furniture, security;
- staff training, and cover for staff absent on training;
- asset control procedures;
- health and safety measures;
- financial control;
- installation contractor selection and management;
- communications with staff, contractors, customers;
- activity planning and progress tracking;
- contingency planning, including fallback on previous systems in cases of failure.

In addition there are the many organisational, cultural and structural ripples that we have examined throughout this book. The programme is rolling out a change in organisation, not a change in technology. Without careful management, it will produce frustrated staff, confused customers and a general lack of confidence in the new system.

The central dilemma is between the Big Bang approach (installing at all your operational sites at once) or a phased introduction. A key issue is the extent to which the operational areas can cope. Do they prefer large amounts of change in a short period or small changes over a long period? Table 10.1 compares the advantages and disadvantages.

The decision depends on circumstances. Where reliability is critical, a slower pace offers less chance of large-scale failure. Where speed to market is critical, the Big Bang may be essential.

Active communication is vital during rollout. Staff need to know what is happening to their area, when it will happen and how it will affect them personally. Local management must also understand and approve the process or they will be unable to promote the project to their staff. Surveys of completed areas will provide the rollout team with vital information on how to improve by learning from the experiences of end-users and their managers.

Table 10.1 **The advantages and disadvantages of the Big Bang approach to rollout**

Advantages	Disadvantages
The benefits are gained by the whole organisation immediately	High-risk approach since if the new system fails there is no fallback
The period of operational disruption is minimised	Are sufficient contractors available to do the work simultaneously across the whole business?
No need to support the old and new systems at the same time	Not possible to develop 'best practice' techniques by learning from earlier installations
Bulk purchase of equipment ensures discounts and same specification	

| MIS in Practice | New Branch rollout at The Royal Bank of Scotland |

The development of a new IT platform for branch banking was a major programme for The Royal Bank of Scotland. A series of projects delivering an integrated suite of front-office applications, the New Branch system was a £100m investment vital to the future of the retail banking business.

The rollout of the New Branch programme was in itself a major undertaking. It involved installing over 5,000 workstations in 650 branches across the UK, and providing 18,000 days of staff training.

To control more than 21,000 activity milestones, the team developed a database of key activities and dates to enable them to plan and track rollout events in each location. The database provided a structure for the tasks to be completed at each location. It highlighted those that were due and overdue, assigned ownership of each task to a member of the rollout team and produced management information on progress.

Rollout was phased, with the last branch being installed two and a half years after the first. The team deliberately applied lessons from the earlier installations to the later ones, so that these went more smoothly. They also undertook an intensive programme of communication with branch staff and management. They made hundreds of presentations to staff, and visited every branch to answer questions. Following each installation, surveys of staff satisfaction were carried out. The results influenced part of the pay of the rollout staff involved.

Through tight control, and taking time to understand and address the needs of the local workforce, the New Branch rollout team implemented the system exactly to schedule. They also maintained good relationships with branch staff and customers throughout the rollout. This contributed significantly to the overall success of the system.

Summary

- High-quality rollout management is critical to gaining the support of end-users.
- The pace and extent of rollout should be matched to the ability and willingness of the end-users to cope with change.
- Communication with all affected staff should prepare them for the changes that will take place.

10.5 Building the energised environment

Throughout the life of a programme, it is important to develop and maintain an environment that encourages its members to continually improve their capabilities and those of their colleagues. Staff should feel that they are being given the opportunity to increase their value to the organisation, while being valued for the contributions they are already making.

Within such an environment, staff will feel confident of their positions and their ability to try new approaches without fear of retribution for mistakes, or for failing to 'toe the party line'. They will fully understand their role, what is expected of them and what they need to do to excel in that role. The reward for their efforts will be transparently commensurate with the contributions they have made to the aims of the programme and to those of the organisation as a whole.

When the programme manager has developed an energised environment of this type, in which staff want to surprise and delight their colleagues and are willing to work hard to do so, then he or she will have gone a long way to ensuring the successful outcome of the overall initiative. Some of the vital components of the energised environment are discussed below.

Clearly understood strategy and vision

For programme staff to be able to work cohesively towards the overall aims of the initiative, they must understand what those aims are and how they can contribute towards them. Defining and communicating the programme strategy and how it will support the organisation is essential.

NatWest Bank and The Royal Bank of Scotland: Creating a shared vision for the integration programme

CHAPTER CASE: PART 4

To create a shared vision for the integration programme across all staff in the new RBS Group, including many NatWest staff members who felt vulnerable following the hostile takeover, a series of steps were undertaken.

- 'Creating a New Force in Banking' was a key message used by RBS during the bid process to describe the positive outcome of the integration. This was also used during the early stages of the integration programme in staff and public communications. Use of a simple catchphrase gave a focus and sense of purpose to the programme for all staff to follow.

- As stated earlier, overall targets for cost savings and new income generation for the programme were published. This gave a clear message about what had to be achieved – and monthly reviews showed what progress had been made towards completing the integration.

- Additionally, overall integration targets were broken down into individual monthly targets for each business area. This gave staff at local levels clarity and accountability for what they had to achieve to contribute to the integration, and regular updates on how they were doing against targets.

- Early communications to staff included statements on the key elements of the integration strategy. Sharing this level of information with staff gave a common understanding of what was being done and how individual projects fitted with the overall approach.

- Throughout the programme, a regular set of communications were made to staff by directors describing the achievements to date and the plans for the future. These included question and answer sessions that staff could contribute to. Keeping staff well informed reduces the opportunity for negative messages to spread.

Clear personal objectives, regularly reviewed

Closely aligned to the strategy for the programme with an energised environment will be a set of clearly defined personal objectives for each member of staff. These will carefully describe the behaviours and results that are expected from that individual, and how these will be measured and rewarded.

Achievement of these individual objectives will demonstrably contribute to the achievement of the overall strategy for the programme. Ideally, a Balanced Scorecard of objectives for the programme will be prepared from which the individual objectives are derived (Kaplan and Norton, 1996). Personal objectives can be set at the start of a review period and reviewed regularly throughout that period by the individual's line manager. High-quality feedback recognising the value of the individual's contribution, and pointing out areas for development, will be backed up with practical examples from recent project work. Ideally, feedback will also be received from the individual's peer group and reportees, providing a 360-degree perspective on performance.

Of course, attempting to define precisely the performance requirements of an individual a year ahead can be difficult in the turbulent atmosphere of a change programme. Indeed, this approach runs the risk of being over-prescriptive and rigid when what is really required of staff is flexibility and a can-do attitude to whatever events transpire. Currie and Willcocks (1996) identified this problem as affecting morale in a major programme.

While no simple answer exists to this problem, it is clear that a balance has to be struck between clearly informing individuals of what is required of them and how they will be rewarded, and allowing objectives and measures to flex around changes in the environment.

Activity 10.3 Personal objectives

List the personal objectives that should be set for a project manager working as part of a large-scale change programme.

- *How would you ensure that these are motivational and will remain relevant in a dynamic environment?*

Reward and recognition

Having taken the time to clearly define and review the work of the individual programme members, it is necessary to ensure that they receive a reward for their performance that fits with their contribution to the programme aims. This reward will most commonly take the form of money and recognition among peers, and it is critical that this is provided in a fair and transparent way to everyone. Performance-related pay is a powerful motivational tool and can form a significant amount of the programme members' remuneration package.

A learning culture

No programme of any meaningful content or duration will exist without mistakes being made. These should be viewed positively as learning opportunities from which competitive advantage will be derived. To realise this competitive advantage, it is necessary to recognise and understand these mistakes as they occur and apply the lessons that accrue from them immediately into subsequent programme activities.

Regular interaction among the project staff, frequent review sessions and, in particular, post-implementation reviews are all sources of fascinating and invaluable knowledge on how to improve performance. However, studies of companies in the USA revealed a low incidence of post-implementation reviews. The main reasons were:

- too busy: no time to follow up on past projects and too focused on future projects to dwell on the past;
- too difficult: there are so many variables that can affect the outcome of a project it is difficult to say that any one was the main cause of a problem;
- no constituency: once the projects are approved, there are no formal procedures which enforce a review;
- pride: a general feeling that there is enough robustness in planning to foresee and overcome any future problems without thinking about what has gone before.

Having reviewed and refined project performance and behaviours, an organisation with a learning culture will record and store a set of ideal methodologies in a knowledge database. This can take a very simple form, such as a set of hints and tips for future work, or can be a large and sophisticated set of instructions for detailed project activity planning. Whatever method is chosen, the determination to learn from ongoing activities can only enhance the performance of the organisation.

Summary

- The chances of the successful delivery of a programme will be greatly enhanced if the people working there are given a positive, or energised, working environment.
- Elements of an energised environment will include a shared vision, rewards and recognition linked to performance, and positive support for personal development and a learning culture.

Conclusions

This chapter has described some of the techniques that help those responsible for managing programmes – a series of related projects. As Currie and Willcocks (1996) pointed out large-scale programmes face acute challenges. These include:

- a lack of cohesion between the business and technology departments;
- a lack of understanding among senior management on the technical issues involved with achieving the desired systems changes;
- difficulty in communicating the aims of the programme as a strategic imperative for the organisation;
- emphasis towards lower-level decision-making, rather than the top-down approach normally suggested for large-scale change programmes;
- lack of structured methodology for the overall re-engineering approach;
- difficulties in managing contract IT staff.

All programmes face these difficulties, which are symptomatic of the complex and dynamic nature of such initiatives.

They are not just large-scale initiatives – it is the links between the changing elements that makes them unpredictable. Managing these interactions between elements of the change and their context requires a 'helicopter view' of the type that

NatWest Bank and The Royal Bank of Scotland: Successful completion of the integration

The integration programme completed early in 2003 – within three years of the acquisition date as originally planned and promised. The biggest single event in the programme – the transfer of NatWest customer and account data to the RBS computer platform – happened over a single weekend in October 2002. In summary, the programme achieved the following:

- 154 integration initiatives across five divisions with a total of 100,000 staff;
- achieved £1.4bn of annual cost savings;
- achieved revenue benefits of £890m;
- 4,200 staff working on the programme at its peak;
- total costs of £1.2bn;
- 18 million NatWest accounts worth £158bn migrated to RBS systems – and balanced to the penny!

By all measures, the integration of NatWest with RBS can be considered a remarkable success. During the initial bid process in late 1999, it was considered by many as foolish to try to integrate such a large organisation as NatWest with a relatively small one. Many examples were cited of failed integrations, and the achievability of moving such a large amount of critical data from one mainframe platform to another while maintaining full operations was considered by many experts not to be possible.

Nonetheless, the biggest IT integration project of its kind ever undertaken in the financial sector was completed successfully on schedule. The benefits quoted in 1999 – over £1.1bn of repeatable cost savings – were overachieved. In addition, RBS can point to several other benefits achieved from the integration programme, including:

- A 'battle hardened' change management capability. The integration work developed a tried and tested approach to managing change on a large scale, across business units and across

functions, which can be used to support future changes.

- A single platform that can operate multiple front-ends – build once, use many times. The main RBS systems platform – eight mainframe computers operating as one and capable of handling over 16 billion instructions per second – can now be applied to supporting many different brands and businesses throughout the RBS Group on a highly efficient basis.

- A single network supporting 95,000 connected PCs. The widespread RBS computing network enables business to be conducted in a connected fashion throughout many different centres and offices in the UK. This enhanced network enables many more efficiencies in working practice, and future developments will include reduction of paper handling through imaging and workflow systems.

- Excellent systems availability. The scaled-up systems platform has proved to be robust and to have excellent performance to support the Group-wide operations.

- Enhanced disaster recovery. New data centres developed to support the integrated organisation include a more robust disaster recovery procedure than was possible before.

- Better knowledge of operating processes. Integration activities forced a rigorous review of operating processes, driving the bank as a whole to a new level of efficiency and effectiveness.

With RBS now operating on a large-scale, stable technology platform that can handle multiple businesses, and with proven experience in managing major integration programmes, the Group finds itself as an admired and feared competitor in UK banking. RBS is now in a strong position to manage further acquisitions in the UK financial services industry, and international expansion in the USA and Europe.

programme management introduces. These provide invaluable structures to support the work of the individuals working on the separate components of information systems projects.

CHAPTER QUESTIONS

1. Large-scale IS programmes are often long term in nature, but objectives will become blurred as circumstances change over time. What can a programme manager do to maintain momentum and focus throughout the life of the programme?

2. The 'expert observer' member of the programme steering group is normally from outside the organisation, and has little at stake in the success or failure of the programme. Why, then, is he or she often such an influential member of the group?

3. You are the programme manager for a large set of projects taking place across your organisation. What will you do to encourage a shared set of values? Why might individual project managers actively resist your well-intentioned actions?

4. IS programmes need executive support, but studies show that executives are often 'e-illiterate'. What problems can this raise for the programme, and how can they be addressed, given the power of these individuals?

5. Compare these two statements:

   (a) 'We must communicate openly and honestly at all stages.'

   (b) 'Communicating too early can cause unnecessary alarm – we need to keep a tight lid on things until we're in a position to advise people in full knowledge of the facts.'

   What are the benefits and risks associated with each approach to communication in an IS programme.

Further reading

Brooks, F.P. (1995) *The Mythical Man-Month*, Addison-Wesley, Reading, Mass. A very readable collection of essays by a distinguished member of the IS community. Draws on vast experience to provide thought-provoking insights for anyone involved with IS projects.

Buchanan, D. and Badham, R. (1999) *Power, Politics and Organisational Change*, Sage, London. A detailed and empirically based analysis of the politics of change which implies that project managers who lack political skill will fail.

References

Currie, W.L. and Willcocks, L. (1996) 'The new branch Columbus project at Royal Bank of Scotland: the implementation of large-scale business process re-engineering', *Journal of Strategic Information Systems*, **5**, 213–36.

Kaplan, R.S. and Norton, D.P. (1996) *The Balanced Scorecard: Translating Strategy into Action*, Harvard Business School Press, Boston, Mass.

Keil, M. and Robey, D (1999) 'Turning around troubled software projects: an exploratory study of the de-escalation of commitment to failing courses of action', *Journal of Management Information Systems*, **15**(4), 63–87.

Alignment Fit between variables such as strategy, information systems, structure and culture.

Analysis and design The stage of analysing what users and business functions require of an information system, and designing the system to take account of them.

Application service provider A company providing business applications such as e-mail, workflow or groupware to other companies under a contract.

Autonomy Degree of freedom a person has in deciding how to do their work.

Back-office systems Administrative processes or systems that companies can often centralise in specialised processing centres or outsource to other companies.

Balanced Scorecard A framework for setting and monitoring business performance. Metrics are structured according to customers, internal efficiency, financial performance and innovation.

Big Bang approach The practice of installing all parts of a new system simultaneously at all operational sites.

Bottom-up approach The practice of developing the IS plan by concentrating on the current and expected problems as expressed by people at the operating level of the organisation.

Bricks-and-mortar model A traditional organisation with limited online presence.

Business alignment strategy The IS strategy is generated from the business strategy through techniques and models such as those suggested by Porter or Treacy and Wiersema.

Business information systems Information systems used to support the functional areas of business such as sales, marketing and human resource management.

Business model A summary of how a company will generate revenue by identifying its product offering, value added services, revenue sources and target customers.

Business process innovation Identifying new ways of carrying out business operations, often enabled by new information systems.

Business process view Sees satisfying customers' requirements as central to the process of developing a supply system that will operate without waste. The orientation is towards speed of response and two-way flow of information.

Business-to-business (B2B) Using the Internet to conduct commercial transactions between organisations.

Business-to-consumer (B2C) Using the Internet to conduct commercial transactions between organisations and consumers.

Centralisation This occurs when a relatively large number of decisions are taken by management at the top of the organisation.

Channel conflict The conflict between existing distribution channels and a new channel of selling directly to customers, often enabled by the Internet.

Clean sheet approach When people fundamentally rethink the way that the product or service is delivered and design new processes from scratch.

Clicks-and-mortar model A business combining an online and off-line presence.

Clicks-only model An organisation with principally an online presence.

Competitive advantage Arises from discovering and implementing ways of competing that are unique and distinctive from those of rivals, and that can be sustained.

Competitive forces model A business framework devised by Porter, depicting five forces in a market (e.g. bargaining power of customers).

Competitive strategy Describes a firm's position relative to its competitors in the markets in which it operates.

Configuration Redesigning a piece of software to suit the needs of a particular business.

Context – inner The immediate organisational setting of an IS – such as culture, structure, business processes, existing technology and people.

Context – outer External factors relevant to an IS – such as developing technologies, competition, legal and political factors and potential partners.

Contingency approaches Express the idea that performance depends on an organisation having a structure appropriate to its environment.

Convergence A trend in which different hardware devices such as television, computers and telephones merge and offer similar functions.

Corporate strategy Corporate strategy is concerned with the firm's choice of business, markets and activities, thus defining the overall scope and direction of the business.

Cost–benefit analysis A technique that helps in IS investment decisions by determining if the benefits (including intangible ones) exceed the costs.

Cost leadership The ability of a company to produce quality products at the lowest cost in its industry group.

Counter-implementation An attempt to block change without displaying overt opposition.

Culture The pattern of beliefs developed by a group about effective task performance and the values they share about themselves and others.

Customer acquisition Techniques to gain new customers.

Customer extension Techniques to encourage customers to increase their involvement with an organisation.

Customer relationship management (CRM) The process of maximising the value proposition to the customer through all interactions, both online and traditional. Effective CRM advocates developing one-to-one relationships with valuable customers.

Customer retention Techniques to maintain relationships with existing customers.

Customer selection Picking the ideal customers for acquisition, retention and extension.

Customisation Adding non-standard features to the software by adding or changing program code.

Data Raw facts, figures and events that have not been analysed.

Data mining Using software to look for unexpected patterns and relationships in large sets of data.

Database A collection of related information. The information held in a database is stored in an organised way that enables specific items to be selected and retrieved quickly.

Decentralisation When a relatively large number of decisions are taken lower down the organisation and in operating units.

Decision support system A computer-based system, almost interactive, designed to assist managers in making decisions.

Determinism The view that environmental factors determine the most suitable form of structure, technology and management style.

Differentiation A strategy of gaining competitive advantage by providing a product or service with feature(s) that make it unique and so of greater value to customers.

Disintermediation Removing intermediaries such as distributors or brokers that formerly linked a company to its customers.

Distributed computing Computing architecture that breaks centralised computing into many semi-autonomous computers that may not be (and usually are not) functionally equal.

Dot-coms Companies whose main trading presence is on the Internet.

Dynamic pricing Setting prices based on supply and demand relationships at any given time, such as in auctions or stock markets; results in constantly changing prices.

Effectiveness The degree to which an organisation meets its objectives and the expectations of stakeholders.

Efficiency A measure of the output produced with each unit of input.

Electronic business (e-business) When all information exchanges, both within an organisation and with external stakeholders, are conducted electronically.

Electronic commerce (e-commerce) When all information exchanges between an organisation and its customers are conducted electronically.

Electronic data interchange (EDI) A set of standards, hardware and software technology that permits computers in separate organisations to transfer documents electronically.

Electronic government Using the Internet to improve the internal operations of government as well as its communication with the general public and businesses.

Electronic mail (e-mail) A system whereby users send and receive messages electronically, permitting fast textual communication between people and groups of people.

Electronic procurement The electronic integration and management of all procurement activities including purchase request, authorisation, ordering, delivery and payment between a purchaser and a supplier.

Emergent model of change Recognises that some departure from a plan is inevitable, and that outcomes cannot be accurately predicted.

Emergent strategy The idea that the analysis, development and implementation of strategy are interrelated and take place iteratively rather than sequentially.

Enterprise resource planning (ERP) An integrated process of planning and managing of all resources and their use in the entire enterprise. It includes contacts with business partners.

Enterprise software An integrated software that supports enterprise computing and ERP. The most notable example is SAP R/3.

Enterprise-wide system An IS that encompasses the entire enterprise, implemented on a network.

Ergonomics A method for taking account of human physical characteristics when designing work.

Expert system (ES) A computer system that applies reasoning methodologies or knowledge in a specific domain to render advice or recommendations – much like a human expert.

Explicit knowledge Can be readily expressed and recorded within information systems.

Extranet Formed by extending an intranet beyond a company to designated customers, suppliers and other business partners.

Feedback Providing information to people about their performance.

Formal–rational evaluation Expresses the idea that costs of an investment need to be related to the tangible benefits brought by the investment.

Globalisation The process whereby organisations increase the integration of internationally dispersed economic activities.

Groupware Systems that provide electronic communication between members of geographically dispersed teams.

Hardware Physical components of a computer system, consisting of devices for input, memory, central processing, output, communication and storage.

Human resource management A business function aimed at establishing systems and processes for managing people in a way that enhances organisational performance.

Implementation Putting a system into use.

Influence The process by which one party attempts to modify the behaviour of others by mobilising power resources.

Information Useful knowledge derived from data.

Information architecture A conceptualisation of the manner in which information requirements are met by the information system.

Information centres Facilities that train and support computer users with end-user tools, testing, technical support information and standard certification.

Information economics An approach to cost–benefit analysis that incorporates organisational objectives in a scoring methodology to assess more accurately the value of intangible benefits.

Information infrastructure The physical arrangement of hardware, software, databases and networks.

Information intensity A measure of the actual, or planned, use of information.

Information resources management All activities related to planning, organising, acquiring, maintaining, securing and controlling IS resources.

Information system A set of people, procedures and resources that collects and transforms data into information and disseminates it.

Information systems management The planning, acquisition, development and use of information systems.

Information systems plan A document that describes how the company will realise the information vision by allocating time and resources to it.

Information vision An expression of the desired future for information use and management in the organisation.

Infomediary A business whose main source of revenue derives from capturing consumer information and developing detailed profiles of individual customers for use by third parties.

Innovation Incremental and/or step (breakthrough) changes in products and processes.

Integration Achieving unity of effort among the subsystems in accomplishing a task.

Interaction model The view that people interpret and respond to their context, and in doing so change that context.

Interdependence Indicates how the stages of a task are related. One typology distinguishes between pooled, sequential, reciprocal and team interdependence.

Interest groups Groups that have an interest in the outcome of a project or plan.

Intermediary An organisation or e-commerce site that brings buyers and sellers together.

Internet A self-regulated network of computer networks connecting millions of business, individuals, government agencies, schools and other organisations across the world.

Inter-organisational system Information system that links organisations electronically.

Intranet A private network within a single company using Internet standards to enable employees to share information.

Inventory Materials, components and finished goods held in anticipation of requirements.

Knowledge management Techniques and tools for disseminating knowledge within an organisation.

Learning organisation An organisation that is able to learn from its experience, implying an organisational memory and a means to save, represent and share experience among its members.

Legacy systems Older systems that are central to business operations and may still be able to meet business needs.

Life cycle model of change The belief that projects go through successive stages, and results depend on conducting the project through these in an orderly and controlled way.

Manager Someone who gets things done with the aid of other people.

Marketing information system System for collecting, analysing and distributing marketing information.

Mass customisation Delivering customised content to groups of users through web pages or e-mail.

Monitoring system A computer-based system that processes data to provide information about the performance of an activity or process.

Open source software Software that is developed collaboratively, independent of a vendor, by a community of software developers and users, e.g. Linux.

Open system A system that interacts with its environment.

Organisational structure The ways in which tasks are divided and coordinated.

Outsourcing Contracting tasks to another organisation.

Participative models of change Recommend change managers to consult widely and deeply with those affected and to secure their willing consent to the changes proposed.

Political models of change Emphasise that change is likely to affect the interests of stakeholders unevenly and that those who see themselves losing will resist the change despite the rationality of the arguments or invitations to participate.

Process Set of logically related tasks performed to achieve a defined business outcome.

Process modelling The activity of mapping business processes directed to description, analysis and design.

Programme of projects A coherent set of projects.

Project management Combining people and other resources to complete a distinct task.

Prototyping method Dividing development work into sub-tasks that IS staff can complete quickly and then test with users.

Quality The (often imprecise) perception of a customer that what has been provided is at least what was expected for the price paid.

Rational–linear models of change View change as an activity that follows a logical, orderly sequence of activities that can be planned in advance.

Reintermediation The creation of new intermediaries between customers and suppliers providing services such as supplier search and product evaluation.

Relationship marketing An approach that focuses on developing a series of transactions with consumers over the long term.

Remote working Doing work away from the conventional central office space.

Skill variety Extent to which a job makes use of a range of skills and experience

Social choice The view that people have free will and can influence the course of events, especially whether or not to use available technology. Technology is a dependent variable.

Socio-technical approach Aims to change both the social and the technical aspects of a system to improve performance and the quality of working life.

Socio-technical system One in which outcomes depend on the interaction of both the technical and social subsystems.

Software A series of detailed instructions that control the operation of a computer system. Software exists as programs that are developed by computer programmers.

Stakeholders People and groups with an interest in a project and who can affect the outcome.

Strategy Sets out the direction and actions of a company to achieve specified objectives.

System A set of interrelated parts designed to achieve a purpose.

System boundary A system boundary separates the system from its environment.

Systematic design The activity of identifying and analysing existing processes, evaluating them critically and planning major improvements.

Systems approach Looks at the different parts of an interacting set of activities as a whole and considers the best way for the whole to function.

Tacit knowledge Knowledge that is subjective, highly personal and hard to formalise.

Task identity Whether a job involves a relatively complete and whole operation.

Task significance How much a job matters to others, or to the wider society.

Technological determinism The view that technology itself will produce the results required. Technology is an independent variable.

Technology acceptance model (TAM) Predicts whether or not people accept and use an IS according to two variables: perceived usefulness (PU) and perceived ease of use (PEU).

Top-down approach A top-down approach develops the IS plan by identifying those applications that senior management believe would be most helpful to the organisation.

Value chain 'The value chain divides a firm into the discrete activities it performs in designing, producing, marketing and distributing its product. It is the basic tool for diagnosing competitive advantage and finding ways to enhance it' (M.E. Porter, *Competitive Advantage* (Free Press, 1985)).

Virtual organisations Virtual organisations deliver goods and services but have few, if any, of the physical features of conventional businesses.

Work design model A model that proposes that the intrinsic features of jobs can be designed in a way that promotes employee motivation and job satisfaction.

Workflow management system Automation of information flows and tools for processing the information according to a set of procedural rules.

INDEX